Praise for *Digitizing Government*

"A compelling guide that shows how public services can use new technology to create entirely new organizations, structures, systems, processes and business models that deliver services in better, easier, cheaper and faster ways."

– Steve Denning, former CTO, World Bank, author of *The Leader's Guide to Radical Management*

"This book gives practical insight and encouragement for everyone leading, building, operating and assuring the new digital future for UK government. But it is also an essential read for those who need to understand what digital means and how much more than just new technology it is going to take to make digital public services a reality."

– Sally Howes, Digital Director, National Audit Office, UK

"*Digitizing Government* provides real insight into the challenges of bringing large public sector institutions into the digital age. But don't be fooled into thinking that this is a book about technology – it is actually about how you bring about fundamental transformation in large organizations. Technology matters, but so does openness to new ideas and an emphasis on getting things done."

– Julian Birkinshaw, Professor of Strategy and Entrepreneurship, London Business School

"This is without doubt the most comprehensive and approachable account of the digital government movement, its recent developments and future potential. A fascinating insight for the general reader and a guidebook for policymakers wishing to understand why past public sector IT initiatives have so often failed and how smarter use of technology can genuinely transform government and public services. This book should be compulsory reading for those who seek radical reform in the way government works."

– Eddie Copeland, Head of Technology Policy Unit, Policy Exchange

"Few would disagree that digital technology is radically changing the relationships between people and institutions – both private and public. Government has a choice – to embrace digital change or risk entrenching costly, inefficient services that will increasingly frustrate citizens. As key influencers of the UK government's digital strategy, the authors understand the huge benefits and potential pitfalls that the digital revolution offers – their insights provide vital guidance for policymakers and practitioners alike on how technology can transform public services."

– Bryan Glick, Editor in Chief, *Computer Weekly*

"*Digitizing Government* is a must-read for all political leaders, public officials and the technology industry. Its insights challenge outdated industrial age approaches such as 'egovernment' – still being mistakenly pursued by governments around the world. Unlike many other commentators on governments and their relationship with technology, the authors' perspectives draw deeply on their experiences as industry practitioners, public servants, government advisors and academics. *Digitizing Government* is not about technology – that would be relatively easy. It is about the re-imagination and redesign of government and its relationships with citizens in the twenty-first century."

– Marie Johnson, Chief Digital O⸻ ⸻ ⸻ ⸻ ⸻ Business Australia; formerly Worldwide Di⸻ ⸻ ⸻ ⸻ ⸻ Microsoft

"*Digitizing Government* complements la⸻ ⸻ ⸻ ⸻ ⸻ Wilson and Mike Martin… It is the mix of so⸻ ⸻ ⸻ ⸻ with the practical learnings from the teams buil⸻ ⸻ ⸻ ⸻ hat gives delivery teams and policymakers useful⸻ ⸻ ⸻ ⸻ ment and helps form the evidence base for the future of digital go⸻ ⸻

– Chi Onwurah, MP for Newcastle upon Tyne Central and Shadow Cabinet Office Minister

"A great exposition of how and why UK government has so often failed to implement digital government in the past – and a roadmap for success in the future."

– Professor Helen Margetts, Director, the Oxford Internet Institute

"*Digitizing Government* is a 'must-read' for all senior management within local authorities, not just those who work in technology. Mark's exciting vision of the service of the future is a far cry from today's reality and the road to achievement will crumble if the willingness to change is not there. Authorities must be prepared to break down the traditional service delivery models and embrace advancing technologies if we are to deliver customer-centric services of the future."

– Richard Godfrey, ICT Strategy, Infrastructure and Programme Manager, Peterborough City Council

"The definitive field guide to digital government – an essential resource for any public leader who wants to stop deliberating and start doing."

– Chris Yiu, Director Digital Participation, Scottish Council for Voluntary Organisations

"This important book is a powerful and practical call for action for anyone in government or business who wants to make a difference to our long-term economic prosperity and our ability to provide high-quality public services. Developed for practitioners in the public and private sectors, and based on field experience, this book sets out clear, practical and at times challenging recommendations for how government and suppliers can change their approach, learn from the world's most successful disruptive digital companies and work together to redesign our public services so that we can meet the future needs of users at a cost that future generations of taxpayers can afford."

– Antony Walker, Deputy CEO, TechUK

"From policy to culture to technology, this book has the trifecta of solid research, groundbreaking ideas, and practical examples. Simply wonderful."

– Simon Wardley, Researcher, Leading Edge Forum, CSC

"*Digitizing Government* provides a manual for CIOs and Chief Digital Officers to take a case forward for the required paradigm shift for a new kind of public sector model that is best placed to work in the digital age. This is not about digitizing government per se; it is about reshaping the public sector in terms of people, process, organizational structures, new agile practices and approaches. It neatly fits into the new local public service context and provides part of the framework for a new whole place approach that spans traditional organizational and sectorial boundaries to resolve some of the greatest challenges ever to face the public sector."

– Dylan Roberts, CIO, Leeds City Council

"A highly readable and thought-provoking look at why digitizing government has never fully succeeded, with a blueprint for a more sustainable, outcome-focused approach building on existing principles but requiring a radical change in the workings of government itself."

– Rachel Neaman, CEO, Go ON UK

"The opportunities of the internet for government are becoming apparent. If we are to make the most of them, we need to understand the problems of the past, establish new models of thinking for the future and markedly change the way we handle change. *Digitizing Government* does an excellent job of exploring these critical areas. Hugely useful reading for anyone involved."

– Mark Foden, Independent Consultant, Foden Grealy Ltd

"Sets out a compelling case for the accelerated digital transformation of public services. Builds on a fascinating analysis of the challenges of the last two decades to identify the social and technological foundations needed for future success."

– Martin Bellamy, Director of Information Services, University of Cambridge

"Thank goodness for this. A clear view and reason why and how local government IT delivery should change."

– Martin Sadler, Head of IT and Shared Services, Walsall Council, Regional Chair, SOCITM (Society for Information Technology Management), UK

"This book shows government what it needs to do to be able to rapidly reshape and be a part of the networked public service delivery of the future. From pipeline transactions to networked collaboration, vertical line of business systems to horizontal platform capabilities, costly closed proprietary systems to open and interoperable components, *Digitizing Government* has got it all, showing us how to approach this change in our highly complex, 'brownfield' environments. It is essential reading for anyone serious about improving public services in our times."

– Paul Brewer, Director of Digital and Resources, Adur and Worthing Councils

"At a time when government is crying out for transformation and innovation, *Digitizing Government* challenges current practices and offers an insightful approach to delivering software and services."

– Andrew Webb, ICT Customer Services Manager, Chelmsford City Council

"This is an excellent and highly readable text on the opportunities for 'how we are governed' emerging from the digital economy. It is a must-read for policymakers, senior administrators, advisors and consultants and will be a major text for those teaching and learning in public administration."

– Professor Roger Maull, Lead Investigator, RCUK's New Economic Models of the Digital Economy

"Finally a publication which provides an honest insight into the challenges of delivering public services in the digital age and how you can navigate the inertia-infested Ethernet cables of public sector technology."

– James Findlay, CIO, HS2 Ltd; Tech Leader, UK Department for Transport

"If you think digital is just technology rebadged, think again. This book sets out the case for digital as more than just a bolt on. Rather, the authors argue that digital represents a fundamental shift in approach to the design, development and operation of public services that takes us away from the failed approaches of the past to one focused on outcomes and citizens. Above all, this book provides politicians and chief executives, as well as managers and operational practitioners, with a coherent guide to 'implanting' the many facets of digital needed to deliver on the promise of truly modernized, transformed and improved public services."

– Martin Ferguson, Director of Policy and Research, SOCITM (Society for Information Technology Management), UK

"This is a significant contribution to the debate on how change and innovation can be most effectively implemented across public sector organizations. Digitizing existing practices is pointless unless governments reinvent their business models for the digital economy, finding new ways to connect with citizens. *Digitizing Government* is required reading for public sector strategists, technologists and modernizers who want to make a lasting difference."

– Professor Sa'ad Medhat, CEO, NEF: The Innovation Institute

"This book provides a critical insight for politicians and the public – a digitally transformed government is a far more radical and empowering prospect than renewing your vehicle tax, claiming benefits or filing a tax return via your mobile phone. It is the means by which government itself could be incrementally transformed. In a surprisingly readable and accessible book, the authors present some of the key tools and techniques that could enable a Netflix-like transformation. They argue that a lean thinking mindset, a focus on citizen outcomes and an adherence to open standards could result in a flexible and efficient ecosystem of reusable government 'platforms', enabling improved outcomes and significant costsavings compared to the slow-moving brownfield silos of today."

– Richard Hopkins, IBM GBS Europe, Public Sector CTO

Digital technologies are revolutionizing the business world – challenging existing practices and enabling a new generation of business models.

Business in the Digital Economy is an accessible new series of books that tackles the business impacts of technology and the emerging digital economy. Aimed at non-technical, mid-senior executives and business managers, this series will help inform choices and guide decision-making on all major technological trends and their implications for business.

Series editors: Alan Brown and Mark Thompson

Available titles:
Predictive Analytics, Data Mining and Big Data
Steven Finlay
9781137379290

Forthcoming titles:
Building a Digital Enterprise
Mark Skilton
9781137477705

Series ISBN: 9781137395245

Understanding and Implementing New Digital Business Models

Digitizing Government

Alan Brown
Associate Dean and Professor of Entrepreneurship and Innovation, Surrey Business School, UK

Jerry Fishenden
Independent Technology Advisor, UK Government, and Senior Research Fellow, Bath Spa University, UK

Mark Thompson
Strategy Director for Methods Group and Senior Lecturer in Information Systems, Cambridge University Judge Business School, UK

palgrave
macmillan

Part 2: The Big Idea

Part 3: Service Providers and Digital Delivery

List of Figures

Acknowledgements

The collaborative effort involved in writing a co-authored book is both thrilling and challenging. The chance to learn from and build on the experiences of others has been enormously rewarding. However, it has left us with the problem that there are so many people that we need to acknowledge that we run the risk of forgetting some and causing offence. So we would like to thank *everyone* we have worked with or spoken to, debated or disagreed with, or otherwise communicated with at events, meetings, conferences, or in coffee shops for their help, either directly or indirectly, in pulling this book together and helping us distil our experiences into a more coherent and useful form.

Now, having tried to cover our backs with our universal gratitude, we would like to call out one or two specific people from a very long list. So many thanks in particular to Simon Wardley for his original research and contributions to mapping and in particular the creation of the Wardley Map, which is rapidly becoming an essential new tool in the modern organization's kitbag. Equally, Mark Foden's insight and growing cadre of short videos that somehow tirelessly capture in a few minutes the essence of what moving to a truly digitized government involves – no mean feat. Tireless work from practitioners such as James Herbert, Sacha Rook, David Biden, and David Carboni at Methods Digital and others at Methods Group, who have evolved many of these concepts – particularly in relation to local public services – has led the practical implementation into live public sector environments.

The research of Professor Patrick Dunleavy, Jane Tinkler and Simon Bastow (London School of Economics), and Professor Helen Margetts

(Oxford Internet Institute) and their work on Digital Era Governance has provided a bedrock of reflective insight and factual analysis that has helped identify problems and potential solutions to numerous aspects of governments' historic attempts to transform technology into something useful rather than merely an embarrassing headline on the evening news. Thanks also to Professor Douglas McWilliams of Gresham College for insight into the statistics and evidence behind the 'economic wakeup call' in our Introduction. There are also a host of inspirational people helping to develop the vision of just how our future governments might function better, spending their days tirelessly championing, mentoring and driving change – from Chris Chant (now semi-retired to a rural idyll in France, but formerly Executive Director of the Cabinet Office) who was an early pioneer of adopting cloud computing in the public sector, to Dr Sally Howes (Executive Leader of Digital and Innovation at the UK National Audit Office), Mike Bracken (Digital Director, UK Government), Liam Maxwell (Chief Technology Officer, UK Government) and James Findlay (CIO, High Speed 2).

We also owe Simon Wardley, Mark Foden, James Findlay and Alan Mather (formerly Director of the UK Government's e-Delivery Team) a debt of gratitude for acting as genuinely critical friends, and taking the time to review and dispassionately critique working drafts of this book. It is notably better than it would otherwise have been – its remaining faults and flaws are entirely the authors' original contribution.

Figures Acknowledgements

We gratefully acknowledge all copyrights. The sources of figures used in this book are as follows:

Figures 3.1, 4.1 and 4.2 are reproduced from GDS publications and licensed under the Open Government Licence v2.0.

Figure 3.2 is licensed under the Open Government Licence v2.0, see http://www.nationalarchives.gov.uk/doc/open-government-licence/version/2/. It was obtained via the National Archives online site.

Figures 6.2 and 6.3 are reproduced with kind permission of Mark Foden of Foden Grealy Ltd.

Figures 6.4, 6.5, 6.6 and 8.4 are reproduced with kind permission of Simon Wardley.

7.1 is reproduced with permission of *Harvard Business Review*.

Figures 8.1, 8.3 and 8.4 are reproduced with kind permission of James Herbert.

11.1 is licensed under the Open Parliament Licence v1.0, see http://www.parliament.uk/site-information/copyright/open-parliament-licence/. It was obtained via the Parliamentary Office of Science and Technology (POST).

All other figures have been developed by the authors.

Preface

This book sparked into life in a London café in 2013 as we relaxed late one afternoon over coffee and HobNob biscuits. We had just finished another engagement with a major customer when it suddenly struck us how frequently we were encountering organizations – and people – struggling to understand and take advantage of the riptide of digital innovations flowing around them.

We agreed, over our much-needed caffeine and sugar infusion, that there had to be a way of capturing and sharing experiences – both good and bad – more effectively than through endless one-to-one engagements. A practical 'why', 'what' and 'how' book seemed a good way of doing this, however old-fashioned a book might seem in the digital age.

Since that original conversation, this book's purpose has been improved by a wide variety of client engagements, discussions (and sometimes rather more heated 'debates'), public and private events, more meetings in cafés, coffee shops and pubs, and Twitter exchanges and blogs.

The result draws on lessons learned from across private and public sectors. We decided to make government our focus because the future of our public services matters to us all. At some point in our lives we all use public services, whether that's at the mundane administrative level (such as the renewal of a passport or driving licence), or for more essential, quality-of-life critical services (such as the timely receipt of social welfare or emergency healthcare).

There's also a surprisingly widespread concern that governments face a significant struggle in adapting to the digital age. In the private sector we've grown accustomed to almost constant digital change, simplifying and improving many aspects of our daily lives – from online banking to real-time travel information, and from on-demand films and music to free international video calls. Yet all too often the media seems to be full of screaming headlines about so-called government 'IT failures', with tales of vast amounts of money lost or squandered on programmes that are cancelled, or which run late and over budget.

As a result, governments in particular stand criticized of failing to harness technology well. Even where technology has been extensively deployed, often it has largely automated old manual procedures based on the paper-age world of forms. Far from helping make government more nimble, effective and efficient, the use of technology has often fossilized the past, 'freezing' inefficient processes, hierarchies, services and organisations. As a consequence, we share the concern that government has not generally benefitted from the major improvements in organizational practices that have become typical of the digital era.

The true opportunity of 'digital' lies in a fundamental reshaping and improvement of government and our public services. Industrial age organizational structures and processes (as the bellwethers of the private sector have long since shown) are a busted flush – and an increasingly expensive indulgence – in the digital era. The challenge now is to agree how government should be redesigned, and to stop merely throwing yet more technology and more money at fossilizing the way it worked yesterday.

This redesign is not about the simplistic polishing of government websites and the production of online copies of existing paper-based transactions – broken services delivered onto a computer screen – but about services clustered around the needs of citizens, businesses and public employees alike. 'Digital' means far more than a meaningless rebadging of 'technology'. For government, it's about a new, better approach to the design, operation and consumption of its services – an approach that focuses on citizens and outcomes.

We don't believe that responding to the opportunities of the digital era is something governments can casually choose or not choose to do: governments *have* to respond if our public services are to avoid a painful and debilitating existential crisis.

Understanding how to take advantage of these opportunities is what *Digitizing Government* is all about. Based on our experiences – and those shared with us by many other practitioners, organizations and academics with whom we have had the privilege to work – we've aimed to provide both insight and practical guidance about what being 'digital' truly means.

We don't pretend we can provide a simple, one-size-fits-all solution in a single volume. Our intention is for this book to inspire constructive debate and – most importantly – to help governments begin delivering well-designed, sustainable and better public services.

Alan Brown, Jerry Fishenden and Mark Thompson
London, 2014

Introduction

╱ Pressure for Change

Governments and public sector organizations across the world are trying to balance essential, and often conflicting, demands: to deliver better, more relevant public services centred on the needs of the citizens and businesses they serve; to reduce costs and improve the efficiency of their operations; and to reinvent supply chains to deliver services quickly, cheaply and effectively.

The UK well illustrates the challenges of this struggle: although the initial years of the government from 1997 to 2010 were associated with public expenditure restraint, sources from the Organisation for Co-operation and Development (OECD) show that public expenditure as a share of GDP rose from around 40% in 2000 to around 50% in the recession year of 2009. In parallel, the global shifts towards emerging markets have been increasing the role and influence of these rapidly emerging economies. Without exception, these economies have much lower public spending as a percentage of their GDP than the more mature economies of the UK, North America and Western Europe. Because these emerging economies are offering goods and services at 'super competitive' prices, and also improving their skills and hence productivity very rapidly, there is a considerable risk of other governments being caught in a trap where it becomes difficult to develop and sustain a higher cost public sector without losing competitiveness. This is an increasing problem in many EU economies, where it is simply not possible to afford a high ratio of public spending to gross domestic product (GDP) without doing considerable damage to much-needed growth that, in turn, puts upward pressure on the ratio of public spending to GDP.

Within the UK (the case example for many of the discussions in this book), global competitiveness is set to decline from just under 5% of world GDP around the turn of the twentieth century to 2.6% by 2028. Meanwhile, the East Asian economies are rising from about 20% of world GDP to 32.6%, or more than double the size of the Western European economy – which by 2028 will represent just 14.5% of world GDP. Within the UK, as within other Western economies, this picture has a stark implication: in order to maintain our existing standards of public services within this era of relative decline, we need to have a serious and open public debate about how we reorganize our public service delivery models or accept lower public service standards. We cannot continue to pretend that we can have both.

In fact, pressure is mounting not only to maintain but to *improve* service levels: for instance, Don Tapscott, author of *Grown Up Digital*, observes that younger, digitally native generations now *'demand better services, more convenient access to information and an on-going opportunity to personalize or customize the services they receive from government. They want the public sector organized in ways that maximize convenience to the citizen as opposed to the bureaucracy.'*

If governments are to relieve these growing internal and external pressures, they need to rethink, redesign and optimize their services, and place the user – citizens, businesses and the voluntary sector alike – at the centre of their operations, rather than the needs of government organizations and service providers. And they need to move rapidly and effectively away from outdated business models, management cultures, technology and processes inherited from earlier eras.

This transition will involve a disruptive and painful move away from closed, top-down, bureaucratic and paper-based transactional services towards online, integrated digital offerings that encourage a new kind of interaction between citizens and the state. The confluence of citizen demand for greater speed and more transparency in service delivery is being met with an increased appetite within the public sector to deliver services in more innovative ways – through the use of open technologies; more inclusive citizen engagement; the increased involvement of smaller, more innovative companies; and the adoption of agile delivery practices that are better able to meet ever-changing socio-economic demands.

Since the mid-1990s, much has already changed in our private and business lives. In the private sector entirely new business models have emerged, enabled by rapid advances in technology. Many old and once-treasured high-street brands have gone into decline, or even disappeared entirely, whilst new organizations – such as Twitter, Netflix, Whatsapp and Facebook – have appeared to come from nowhere, either to define entirely new opportunities, or to reimagine and reinvent old business models. They are delivering new models of innovation and services at a scale and speed previously unknown.

As a monopoly provider of many services, however, governments have remained largely shielded from the benefits, as well as the business challenges, of these revolutionary changes. This lateness to engage effectively is damaging to governments, as well as to the citizens and businesses they serve. With such a privileged, monopoly status comes great responsibility: governments need urgently to rethink their role, engagement approach and delivery model for the digital world. Perhaps partly because governments were often amongst the earliest adopters of information technology (IT) – doing much in the 1960s and 1970s to automate their basic internal operations in areas such as taxation – it has often become more difficult for them to change: and whereas they were once often amongst the largest users of computer technology, their size and scale is now dwarfed by the largest technology-driven corporations, such as Facebook, Google and Amazon. Where government technology and services were once seen as big and 'special', today – with a few notable exceptions, such as national defence systems – they now often appear relatively small-scale, unnecessarily complicated and increasingly outdated.

The Gap – Political Vision versus Operational Reality

Politicians have long recognized the opportunities offered by the internet and digital technology to bring significant benefits to the public sector. Indeed, fine sentiments have been expressed for decades about modernizing and improving public services, but such sentiments have remained relatively unmatched by meaningful delivery on the ground. Public services appear largely to have been bypassed by developments in the private sector, and have become increasingly unable to meet the needs of a tech-savvy population accustomed to responsive, tailored and personal services. In consequence, governments run the risk of becoming isolated and outdated – almost aloof – from the internet age, artificially separated from the world outside and citizens' expectations by their exclusive monopoly provider role, yet unable to deliver the quality and responsiveness expected from their uniquely privileged position. As a result, their relevance, and even legitimacy, is at stake.

Whilst governments have been preoccupied with their repeated efforts to move online, elsewhere we have seen the emergence of truly digital organizations. Modern technology is typically the enabler of change, but being digital is *not* principally about technology: their behaviours, actions and culture must also adapt to a digital world. So, for example, successful digital organizations usually have operating models clustered around speed and adaptability, exemplified by maxims such as 'show don't tell' and 'done is better than perfect'. The culture that enables organizations to work well in this way often contrasts strongly with accepted best practice. So digital transformation actually requires redesigning and re-engineering organizations on every level – people, process, technology and governance.

Yet just how do public service organizations successfully reinvent themselves as truly digital organizations, and ensure that investment in digital transformation delivers the intended outcomes in terms of service improvements? Nearly two decades of online government, e-government and transformational government initiatives have promised so much, spent so much, and yet delivered relatively little in terms of significant, sustainable benefits. One analysis suggests that an estimated US$3 trillion was spent during the first decade of the twenty-first century on government information systems, yet 60% to 80% of e-government projects failed in some way, resulting in massive wastage of financial, human and political resources, and an inability to deliver the potential benefits. We need to develop an improved understanding and consensus on what being a public sector organization means in the digital, twenty-first century.

Building Truly Digital Public Services

In this book, we focus on transforming public services and their relationship with citizens and businesses alike. We provide a perspective of digital change efforts, using the UK public sector as an illustration of the more ubiquitous challenges faced and improvements required to reimagine public services everywhere. We look at the mismatch between aspects of some public and private services, and the role of culture, leadership and technology in delivering truly digital organizations. We aim to provide both a vision for the future of public services in our digital world (revealing the close relationship between organizational improvement and digital culture), as well as mapping out a framework for how public services need to reform and modernize in order to play their rightful, and essential, role in the digital economy at local, national and international scale.

The context within which this digital public services reinvention needs to happen is the much broader transformation taking place in our personal lives and how we conduct business – driven by a constant stream of digital technology changes, optimized production practices and flexible global delivery models. There has been a sea change in the way users expect to use technology: it has become cheap, easy to use, consumable like a utility, always on, mobile, and open (working seamlessly with everything else – well, most of the time anyway). At home, we have become sophisticated users of such technologies, and of the flexibility and freedoms they enable. There is an increasing, and undeniable, demand to see these same benefits realized in public services as everywhere else.

One example of this digital transformation has been the use of technology platforms, whether these are proprietary (such as Apple's iOS, which powers iPods, iPhones and iPads alike) or more open (such as Google's Android, which powers the majority of today's mobile devices). These platforms have stimulated whole ecosystems of organizations to build products and services, attracted by the volume of demand that they generate. Such platforms can drive astonishing rates of innovation, investment, choice and competition. However, until recently very little of this platform-based thinking – and its associated benefits – have been emulated within our public services. Accordingly, the essential role of platforms forms a core theme of this book.

There is a stark contrast between these emerging business models based on digital platforms and interfaces in the best organizations in the private sector and the general state of public services: the latter are all too often underpinned by idiosyncratic processes, point solutions, top-down assumptions about users' needs, often exclusive contracts based on obsolete commercial models, and outdated systems. Whilst some of the worst organizations in the private sector also share similar structural and management failings, their existence in a competitive market means we are able to take our custom elsewhere. As a result, poorly performing companies ultimately decline and fail, whereas governments – isolated from such dynamics – need to take conscious and deliberate corrective action if they are to modernize and improve: as citizens, we have nowhere else to turn for our public services.

The Challenge is not Primarily Technology

Despite considerable media attention on public sector 'IT failures', the underlying challenge is not primarily one of technology (although this is certainly important), but a lack of the capabilities and leadership skills needed to manage and deliver meaningful reform. There continues to be a widespread lack of understanding of how digital models of public service design can deliver agile, easy-to-use, consumerized services at lower cost and in a way that emulates our daily experiences in the best of the private sector. This lack of understanding – and the missed opportunity for public services – crystallizes the urgent need to build a common view of what the transition to digital public service delivery actually involves. Digital thinking, and its associated technologies, need to impact and influence the design and operation of public services as they are being contemplated, developed and evolved, rather than being applied merely as a means of automating old processes from the world that has passed.

The misunderstanding of the gap between applying digital technology versus implementing a digital strategy is both pervasive and common to the public and private sectors. A recent Forrester 'State of Digital Business 2014' report, which polled almost two thousand senior business leaders in the UK and US early in 2014, highlighted this gap and called it a 'digital strategy execution crisis'. The data showed that only one in five business leaders had a meaningful vision for digital transformation, and that a majority of organizations had a 'bolt on' approach where existing practices were simply augmented with new digital technology delivery channels.

Killing the Myths

To be truly effective, digitizing government involves reimagining the way in which governments design and deliver services: a transition from traditionally organized state corporates (who have outsourced much of their work and expertise to large private corporates) to a new, diverse ecosystem of state, private and third sector activity, organized around the citizen in the form of services.

Such a de-corporatization of the state and its favoured suppliers requires an untangling of the black boxes of many siloed organizations, paper-oriented processes, proprietary technologies and opaque cost structures. Separating these out will enable easier cost comparison between commoditized components in a manner that resembles, for example, the domestic electricity market: despite electricity suppliers' attempts to build brand value, electricity remains fundamentally a price-sensitive commodity. The same applies to much of the infrastructure running our public services. We can ring-fence total government spending, and yet *increase* the amount spent on services, by becoming much more selective about whether we wish to spend our taxes on institutions, bureaucracy and supplier margins – or on people and services.

But before we get into the detail of this transition, it is important that we lay to rest two misconceptions that are sometimes raised in relation to these concepts.

The first is the fear that the transformation we propose will hand the soul of our public services to large companies. This is simply not the case. Indeed, this description actually better describes the operating model of public sector IT as it has been for the past 20 or so years, and represents a major part of what we are keen to get away from. Whilst we will show how many of the old distinctions between public sector and private sector do start to become redundant within a genuinely transformed, digital public sector, *this does not disrupt the political settlement*. The most accurate characterization of this transformation is that it is *anti-corporate*: it is both pro public services and pro market, *not* pro organization. It does not seek to protect the institutional or organizational self-interests of either sector: it seeks to protect those of the citizen.

The second misconception is that when we talk about digital we are discussing the wholesale replacement of face-to-face public services with so-called zero touch, or electronically mediated forms of self-service. Digital government is emphatically *not* about some flashy Internet of Things gadget dangling around a lonely, housebound patient's neck as a substitute for all-important face-to-face visits that may serve a host of other useful purposes (combatting loneliness, for instance). Quite the opposite. For us, digital public services will help drive a *larger* share of the public wallet to the front line – which will increase, not decrease, the resources available to spend on appropriate face-to-face services. It is about improving the funding for those activities – particularly caring, educating, policing – that (in our view) are best performed by public officials. This can only be achieved by spending less on all those unnecessary activities, layers of bureaucracy, or even suppliers that have inserted themselves in the way, as governments consume standard services directly from a plural, vibrant marketplace. Digital allows us to separate out important services from internal overheads: to move from multiple versions of the same thing, organized around the internal needs of the bureaucracy, to the same version of different things, organized around the citizen.

Aim and Structure of the Book

Importantly, however, we make no claims to have all the answers: instead, this book is intended to assist in opening up a broader dialogue about the future of public service delivery, by making the subject more accessible and relevant. Accordingly, instead of adopting an academic style, we offer instead a manifesto or call to arms, combined with a practitioner's field guide. Our purpose is to bring together a wide range of experiences and lessons learned in a variety of organizations inside and outside the public sector, to set out a vision for what a truly digitized government needs to achieve, and to offer insight and guidance on how to get started on that journey. In setting out an improved set of principles for organizing our public services, our aim is to introduce our experiences and thinking to a much broader audience of citizens and practitioners who, we hope, may also start to demand better public services from an informed standpoint of the art of the possible.

The future of public services – their design, relevance and quality – is an important topic. Our aim is to provide not only an analysis of the current situation and the opportunities on offer, but also a path through this complex maze. We believe that the most effective way of accelerating the evolution of digital public services is to raise levels of awareness amongst citizens, policymakers, public officials and their supplier community about the benefits of digital thinking, how these can be achieved, and ways in which their achievement will require us to alter some of our past patterns of behaviour.

In Part 1, 'Online Services – A Road Much Travelled', we first review and summarize some of the history of previous attempts to implement technology-based public service transformation, examining the opportunities and challenges. Part of truly understanding digital government lies in building a clear view of how it differs from those earlier attempts at using technology to drive the modernization of public services (the 'why' – the context and pressures that shape the current move to digital approaches).

In Part 2, 'The Big Idea', we develop these insights into a discussion of the objectives of digital culture and services, the digital business models that enable achievement of these objectives, and the balance that needs to be achieved between consuming services and building services: 'the yin and the yang' of digital (the 'what' – the principles we believe guide successful digital transformation).

In Part 3, 'Service Providers and Digital Delivery', we drill down into more detail about some of the primary tools and techniques being used as part of the move towards digital organizations. Whilst the move to digital government is not *primarily* about technology (and should certainly not be technology-led), the technology is an essential part of the process. Fundamental technology ideas are outlined as the basis for a discussion on digital delivery and the wider lessons to be drawn from approaches to software, the use of cloud computing, agile processes and practices, and the application programming interface (API) economy (the 'how' – the tools and approaches to help deliver successful digital transformation).

One of our key messages in this book is that digital transformation requires open, honest debate on the major principles and practices for the digital age. However, we recognize the need to bring these ideals to ground in practical steps that can be taken by practitioners to effect change in the projects and programmes in which they work. Consequently, we have grounded our analyses, observations and recommendations on in-depth experiences with the UK government's transformation efforts, where the authors have detailed insight over past decades: but we do so to draw out common problems and solutions that face almost all public agencies across the world. Indeed, these challenges are not exclusive to governments and the public sector, but are shared by any large enterprise struggling to adapt to the digital age – as the authors have witnessed at first hand.

We also believe that the UK is one of the most relevant case studies since it aims to become a bellwether itself of digital reinvention after many decades of disappointment. Technology thought-leader Tim O'Reilly has referred to the UK government's current digital strategy as:

> *the new bible for anyone working in open government ... [it] could be applied to every major corporation on the face of the planet. You guys are working in government and making a big difference there but I think you are potentially showing the way to a transformation of the IT sector in every organization and it's really inspiring. When you put that 'simple, beautiful and easy to use' interface on government, you're actually not just changing how government 'appears', you're changing how it 'works'. You're changing the relationship between government and citizens. Can you imagine if people started to feel good about government again? That's really part of what you are accomplishing. It's not just improving government websites, it's literally going to change the relationship between citizen and governments.*[1]

The lessons we highlight here, and the framework we set out, we hope will be of use to all of those interested in helping redesign and reimagine public services for the digital age – enabling a new era of digital public management. They relate to the major shift taking place in the digital economy, and provide relevant insight into what is needed to succeed – and how we might begin to make people *'feel good about government again'*.

---

[1] See http://www.eduserv.org.uk/blog/2013/04/18/pioneers-of-the-new-public-sector/.

Online Services – A Road Much Travelled

Moving public services online should be a classic win–win. For government, redesigning services and operating many of them digitally will make them cheaper and more efficient. For citizens and businesses, it will provide services designed around their needs, and the convenience of 24-hour access, seven days per week. But it's not about merely moving services on to a computer or iPhone screen: it's about ensuring that even front-line services such as meals on wheels, care in the home and mental health can all be improved if the processes and services behind them are redesigned and optimized around the needs of citizens and those directly involved in meeting their needs.

What government would not want both to save money and to improve the quality and efficiency of public services? And what citizen would not want them to do so? The resulting savings can then be redeployed as governments and electorates see fit according to their own political, economic and social beliefs: reinvested into improved front-line services for those who most need them, or into programmes that would otherwise need to be cut – or even redistributed directly to citizens and business through tax cuts. That is the political choice – and opportunity – that digital represents.

Political interest in the role of technology in improving public services and the efficiency of their administration and operations is nothing new. Governments have seen the potential for technology-enabled change – rather than merely the automation of existing services – since at least the early 1990s. A variety of modernization and improvement initiatives have been attempted by governments over the last few decades, spurred on in particular by the game-changer of the internet. This political interest has journeyed through several successive brands with mixed results – from online government to electronic government (e-government), through transformational government (t-government) to today's focus on digital government initiatives.

It would be easy to assume that current digital initiatives are merely the latest rebrand in this long journey. That would be a mistake: earlier online and e-government initiatives were often technology-led, focused particularly on the production of websites, and placing existing manual services online. The move to digital is about much more than this, and is not primarily about technology: it's about the reimagining and reinvention of the way public services are conceived, designed, operated and managed. This time, it's not simply about the window dressing – the websites and online forms – but about the complete design, from back end to front end, of public services and the organizations that deliver them: a rethinking of the very plumbing of government. Yet if the move to digital is going to succeed where previous programmes failed, it's important to understand why the long-standing gap between the political desire to improve public services, and the challenge of delivering this vision on the ground, exists – and how best it can be overcome.

An International Problem

Over the past 20 years many governments have promised (often repeatedly and at great length) to use technology to modernize public services. Yet most have also struggled to make long-term improvements on anything like the scale of reinvention and innovation seen in the best of the private sector.

Amongst these early efforts was the National Partnership for Reinventing Government (NPR) in the United States, announced in 1993 as part of the Clinton administration's attempt to reform and streamline the US federal government and its functions. Initially known as the National Performance Review, its aim was to improve government, producing one that *'works better, costs less, and gets results Americans care about'* and to *'invent government that puts people first, by: serving its customers, empowering its employees, and fostering excellence'*.

Part of this plan involved the creation of 'Electronic Government', which intended to help transform government in the same way that *'amazon. com transformed bookselling'*. In 1997 it committed to the principle that *'anyone who wants to transact business with the government electronically [will be able] to do so. By the end of FY 2000, nearly 40 million Americans will. Emerging forms of information technology will be vital tools in changing Americans' experience with their government. They will be able to access information to solve problems themselves through the Internet, via telephones, and through neighborhood kiosks.'*

More recently, President Obama announced his Technology Plan, saying at its launch in 2007: *'Let us be the generation that reshapes our economy to compete in the digital age.'* The plan recognized that the internet and information technology can be applied to make government more effective, transparent and accessible to all US citizens. With this in mind, one of Obama's first key actions was the appointment of Aneesh Chopra, a successful venture capital manager and technology visionary, as the nation's first Chief Technology Officer (CTO). Once installed, Chopra sought to build on his earlier successes as CTO for the state of Virginia by advocating similar practices across federal government. In particular, his primary goal was to challenge the closed, proprietary nature of many government IT systems and move them towards adoption of open practices based on open standards and technologies.

In Canada, the government recognized early on that the internet, and technology in general, promised a significant opportunity for both businesses and citizens alike, providing convenience and 24/7 access to services. Alongside the improvement of public services, the use of technology also held out the promise of significant operational efficiencies and cost savings. As a result, Canada invested heavily in online government services and was often amongst the most highly rated countries internationally in terms of the impact that e-government had upon its services and operations. By 2005, the government had been successful in shifting transactions to the internet, providing 130 of the most important government services electronically.

In 2003 the New Zealand government set out a vision for e-government that foresaw it as *'a way for governments to use the new technologies to provide people with more convenient access to government information and services, to improve the quality of the services and to provide greater opportunities to participate in our democratic institutions and processes. E-government presents New Zealand with some tremendous opportunities to move forward in the 21st century with higher quality, cost-effective, government services and a better relationship between New Zealanders and their government.'* In their progress report of 2007, the government recognized that: *'The e-government programme is long term and spans multiple decades. For this reason, this review needed to recognize the 2007 milestone not as an end in itself but a stepping stone towards future transformation of government.'*

In Australia, the 'Better Services, Better Government' strategy of 2002 set out the direction and priorities for the future of e-government, building on the earlier policy from 2000 of 'Government Online'. The strategy aimed to require public agencies to achieve improved efficiency in the provision of public services and foresaw that e-government would deliver tangible returns (such as cost reductions, increased efficiency and productivity, or improved services to businesses and the broader community).

Similarly, in the United Kingdom, the 'Government Direct' report of 1996 stated that: *'The Government is determined that the methods of direct service delivery which information technology is now making possible, should be harnessed in the UK in order to: provide better and more efficient services to businesses and to citizens; improve the efficiency and openness of government administration; and secure substantial cost savings for the taxpayer.'*

It's clear that many governments, for many years, have shared similar political aspirations for technology to help improve public services. And yet many of them have faced similar challenges in turning these worthy aspirations into meaningful and sustained improvements on the ground. Yes, there have been some successes here and there – but few, if any, of the same scale of organizational change, disruption and improvement that has been seen in other sectors.

An Australian National Audit Office report from 2004–5, for example, found that government organizations were *'generally unable to determine whether their investments in e-government were delivering tangible returns, such as cost reductions or increased efficiency and productivity.'* Not unusually, much of the focus of the agencies was on websites – a similar focus to other governments at that time – demonstrating a fundamental misalignment between the high-level aspiration (to redesign services) and its execution (using websites to serve up existing paper transactions online). Such criticisms provide evidence of a clear distinction between earlier e-government initiatives and what a truly digital enterprise means – where the entire management, design and operation of its services becomes digital, not merely the shop window (website) at the front.

The Canadian auditor general has recently commented on the lack of 'an overall service delivery strategy' and the lack of an 'overall strategy that focuses on service delivery or online services'. Such comments are not unique to Canada. They reflect what has been experienced elsewhere, such as in the UK, where early initial efforts to put services on to the internet later stalled. Many online services were little more than electronic versions of previous paper services, or, worse, merely an online PDF that could be downloaded, printed, filled-in and sent back in the post in the usual way. Described dismissively by some critics as merely 'lipstick on a pig', the rush to put things online often did little to address fundamental problems of poor service design and management that lay behind them. Few of these efforts turned their focus on to the internal design and operations of public services, limiting themselves instead to externally facing transactions that often merely sought to replicate online equivalents of previous paper-based forms and processes.

This long and sustained gap between what politicians have wanted to achieve with technology, and the lack of meaningful delivery on the ground, is important to understand and fix if governments are to realize the benefits enjoyed by the best of the private sector – where digital organizations have completely reimagined and reinvented their businesses.

Between Aspiration and Implementation Falls the Shadow

In spite of these aspirations, the history of government efforts to apply digital technology to solve its problems shows that they have not always had sufficient impact. The long, and often repetitive, track record of government initiatives and announcements since the mid-1990s or so illustrates that the long-standing political interest in using information technology (IT) to improve public services is nothing new. Table 1.1 illustrates just how long politicians in the UK, for example, have expressed – and continue to express – near identical aspirations to use technology to reform public services.

Similar aspirations are commonplace in many other countries over broadly similar timescales. Like the UK, they too have embarked on programmes to help use technology to reform public services, yet few appear to have delivered anything like the scale of change and value originally foreseen. This lethargic pace of improvement in public services compares poorly with the significant revolution in the private sector that has been enabled

TABLE 1.1   Recurrent political promises of better public services

Year	Policy	Source
1996	'[IT will] provide better and more efficient services to businesses and to citizens, improve the efficiency and openness of government administration, and secure substantial cost savings for the taxpayer.'	Government: Conservative. Source: Government Direct.
1999	'[IT will help us] make sure that public service users, not providers, are the focus, by matching services more closely to people's lives … [and] …deliver public services that are high quality and efficient.'	Government: Labour. Source: Modernizing Government.
2009	'[IT will] allow us to give citizens what they now demand: public services responsive to their needs and driven by them. It provides us with the means to deliver public services in a way that maintains their quality but brings down their cost.'	Government: Labour. Source: Putting the Frontline First: Smarter Government.
2011	'[IT will enable us to] deliver better public services for less cost. ICT can release savings by increasing public sector productivity and efficiency … [and] will enable the delivery of public services in very different ways to the past.'	Government: Coalition. Source: Government ICT Strategy.
2013	'technology can be a powerful tool and reshape how government and citizens interact with each other. We must see digital government as a way of empowering people – service users and public sector employees, citizens and consumers – and enabling cost reduction in the process.'	Labour Party announcement of a Digital Government review – 'Digital Britain 2015'.

by technology since the mid-1990s – everything from on-demand music, films and TV to iPhones and iPads, to ATMs and 24-hour online banking, to Twitter, Facebook, eBay, TripAdvisor and Patient Opinion. IT has disrupted and changed numerous industries and businesses beyond recognition, challenging once dominant brands such as HMV and Kodak and replacing them with organizations such as Netflix, Flickr and Amazon that are by-products of the digital age. The leisurely progress of the public sector has certainly not been caused by any lack of ambition or public funding – quite the opposite: eye-watering amounts of public funding have been thrown at IT over many decades, yet with remarkably little to showcase in terms of meaningful, widespread improvements in overall public services.

The experience of UK governments since the early 1990s provides valuable insight into why earlier efforts failed – and helps to identify how the current move towards digital public services will need to differ if governments' attempts to modernize public services are to succeed. We have selected the UK partly because of our familiarity with its initiatives over the last two decades, but also because the lessons of the UK's experience broadly mirror those of many other countries: they have wide applicability to the pressing problem of how to fix the long-standing schism between political and citizen aspirations for better public services – and the reality on the ground.

To help identify some of the historic approaches, and why these approaches failed to achieve what was intended of them, we explore the period since 1994. This was the year when the UK government unveiled its first online portal, intended to provide a 'one stop shop' for 24/7 online government services. Sounds familiar? It should: 20 years on, after multiple rebranding and relaunches, it still remains a work in progress.

2

The UK's Journey,
A Lesson for Us All

The apparent inability to exploit technology in a genuinely transformational way in the UK public sector sits particularly uneasily with the UK's
reputation as a pioneer in computing. After all, it was the UK that brought
the world figures such as Charles Babbage, Ada Lovelace, Alan Turing and
Tim Berners-Lee, and innovations from Colossus to the BBC Micro, Sinclair
ZX-80, ARM and most recently the Raspberry Pi. Add to this the fact that
the British civil service itself was an early pioneer in the use of computers –
and something appears to have gone seriously wrong.

As a single, monopoly supplier of essential services (some of them a matter
of life and death, and many of them arbiters of our quality of life), failures
in the public sector have an unavoidable impact on us all. The failure to
utilize IT well is also anomalous, given the fact that the UK government's
scale is relatively small, dwarfed by the daily digital operations of some
private sector organizations. In fact, this holds true of most governments,
with the obvious exception of those with populations that rival the reach
of international business. After all, corporations such as Facebook deal
with over 1 billion users, many of them on a *daily* basis. The UK banking
community alone typically transacts more in a few weeks than the entire
UK government transacts in a year across all of its services. So just why
does government struggle so much to reform its own internal operations?

The root cause of this failure to deliver meaningful reform lies not so much with IT, but with the outdated management culture, processes and capabilities of the public sector, and an idiosyncratic procurement model and supply chain that has discouraged innovation and impeded competition. To understand the causes of failure we therefore start by examining the wider culture of the UK public sector and, in particular, its experiences with 'new public management'.

The Wilderness Years: The Failed Allure of 'New Public Management'

From the 1980s onwards, and in common with many other governments, the UK civil service started to incorporate selective private sector practices into the public sector. The hypothesis was that efficiencies in the operations, costs and practices of the private sector would magically rub off and hence transform the quality, cost and timeliness of public services in the process. This so-called 'new public management', or NPM, was encouraged by a variety of organizations and fashionable 'management gurus' – even though the hierarchical, bureaucratic and multidivisional organizational theories that the public sector was busy ingesting were already becoming obsolete in the best of the private sector as it transformed itself in response to the digital age.

NPM is a creature of its time: a once-fashionable dogma that believed the public sector could be improved by simplistically importing ideas and values from the world of commercial business. Governments became preoccupied with the setting of performance targets and the measurement of inputs and outputs rather than the meaningful improvement of public services and their outcomes. Citizens found themselves rebranded as 'customers', ignoring the fact that the majority of the public sector's services are a state monopoly. For many public services it is impossible for citizens to take their 'custom' elsewhere, unless they have healthy wallets and can opt out of state-provided services entirely (almost impossible: as an example, try applying for a passport from anyone other than the government). Yet the idea that we were 'customers' with choice became the comforting myth on which the failures and lack of accountability of NPM were built.

The allure of NPM encouraged numerous public services to be moved away from direct political control and accountability. The result was a crazy-paving of fragmented agencies and quangos, one step removed from government, and locking in the configuration of government at an arbitrary moment in time, further complicating any attempts at modernization and reform. Pseudo-markets were introduced with the intention of creating internal competition. Too often, however, they generated bloated and self-serving internal bureaucracies and costly administrative overheads required to manage and account for the entirely artificial billing and transfer of public finance between the new agencies that had been created. As part of this agencification of the public sector, resources were redirected from the front line and focused instead on supporting the artificial administrative and bureaucratic edifices needed to support this inefficient model. Worse, this same bloat appeared in nearly every stovepipe and silo of the public sector, creating duplicate management overheads and administrative processes focused on internal needs rather than those of their users.

Whilst arguably done for the best of intentions – to take public service delivery out of the arms of policymakers and let organizations get closer to the front line and become more responsive to users' needs – this proliferation of agencies and other organizations under both Conservative and Labour governments in the UK during the 1980s and 1990s instead often created costly complexity and a high administration burden. The resulting problems and inefficiencies were implicitly acknowledged in Prime Minister Tony Blair's early e-government initiatives, which challenged the public sector's inwardly focused and top-heavy bureaucracy and hoped to modernize and improve the way the public sector functioned. The concept of e-government was seized upon as an almost magical elixir that would solve the growing problems in the public sector and help streamline and reorganize service provision around the citizen rather than departments and agencies. Top-down, centrally imposed IT became seen as the way that public sector modernization would be forced to happen – yet the result was that it largely fossilized at a moment in time the segmented nature of the organizations into which it was introduced. The IT itself was provided by a small number of large suppliers, who secured long-term, exclusive contracts that removed any sense of commercial competition or innovation from government's supply chain. These contracts rarely, if ever, incorporated provisions or incentives to simplify, modernize and re-engineer public services: instead, they froze the arcane, paper-based processes of the pre-internet era and applied IT to automate them, complete with all their flaws, duplications, costs and idiosyncrasies.

Labour's 'Transformational Government' strategy of 2005 was to become the nadir of this trend. It foresaw intrusive, centralized IT enabling government to acquire 'deep insight' into detailed aspects of the lives of every citizen in order to provide them with a joined-up experience – like a form of precognition from the 2002 film *Minority Report* – applied to public services. In this sense, it remained 180 degrees out of step with what was actually happening in the world around it, imposing a command-and-control approach towards anticipating citizens' needs and missing the essential dynamic of the internet age, with its user-driven, ground-up, open, collaborative and responsive focus. In part it was a reflection of how detached the centralized public sector administration had become from the front line of public services. Without insight into and a connection with the front line, in terms of both employees and users of public services, NPM administrators saw IT as a way of filling the vacuum in their knowledge. It also entirely reversed Labour's earlier vision of the late 1990s, which had aimed to place the citizen and their needs at the centre of public service design. Instead, it reasserted the pre-eminence of the state and its increasingly outdated institutions over the needs of public service employees and users alike.

'Transformational Government' and related e-government initiatives have been extensively analysed by Professor Patrick Dunleavy from the London School of Economics and Professor Helen Margetts from the Oxford Internet Institute. These authors identify a subsequent attempt to move away from the failures of NPM and towards a number of IT-enabled improvements for which they create the term 'digital-era governance' (DEG). They explain DEG in terms of three themes promoted by the Labour government during the early 2000s – reintegration, holism and digitization:

- **reintegration** is about joined-up governance, rolling back the agencification of public services, centralizing procurement activity, better integrating the use of outsourcing, encouraging the increased use of shared services, and simplifying service delivery chains;
- **holism** is about reorganizing services around the citizen, and includes one-stop service provision supported by data warehousing, simplified and integrated social insurance processes, and citizen audits and evaluation of services, based on notions of the social web;
- **digitization** is about the idea of 100% online channel strategies in which services are assumed to be digitally delivered by default, combined with automated processes, open information and data, the use of government cloud and web-based utility computing, isocratic ('do it yourself') administration, and social web behaviours (open-book government, mash-ups, co-production of services).

DEG's significance is that it relies on the emergence not only of new technologies, but also of new business models and supporting commercial incentives. Table 2.1 highlights some of the innovative features of DEG, taken from Dunleavy and Margetts's work. Very few of these features can be delivered via a traditional, centralized, command-and-control or top-down approach. This is because the majority of DEG features involve new technologies, incentivization mechanisms and organizational behaviours that do not currently exist – either within public services, or within traditional outsourcing arrangements.

Dunleavy and Margetts speculate about how DEG will fare in the current age of budget deficit, growing national debt and economic austerity, and consider three scenarios: first, the revival of NPM; second, a lengthy 'investment pause' in public sector transformation involving a mothballing

TABLE 2.1   Innovative features of DEG

DEG Theme	Innovative Feature
Reintegration	Network simplification. Single tax and benefit systems using real-time data. Decentralized delivery. Radical disintermediation in public service chains. Delivery-level joined-up governance.
Holism	Interactive and ask-once information seeking and provision. Agile processes (for example, exceptions handling, real-time forecasting and preparedness). Joined-up delivery of local public services. Co-production of services. Online reputational evaluations in public services, including citizens' testimonials and open-book government. Development of social web processes and field services. Single benefits integration in welfare states. Single citizen account. Integrated service shops at central/federal level. New service delivery models linked to austerity and central disengagement.
Digitization	Active channel streaming, citizen segmentation. 100% online channel strategies and mandated channel reductions (potential removal in part or whole of government agencies and departments). Government cloud and apps. Free storage and data retention. Web-based utility computing. New forms of automated processes (for example, zero touch). Isocratic administration (for example, co-production of services). Rich technology driven by social web. Freeing public information for reuse, mash-ups and so on.

Source: adapted from Dunleavy and Margetts 2013

of capital expenditure intensive initiatives; and third, a continuing expansion of DEG as a response to *'the unrelenting waves of technological and social changes that show no signs of easing off'*.

The answer to Dunleavy and Margetts's important question about how DEG will fare lies in governments' ability to understand their role in transitioning to an era of digital public management. But just how should governments best locate themselves within the emerging digital economy to deliver successful DEG-style services and to move on from the failed dogma of the past?

A Serious Misalignment: Implementation of DEG Using Stone-Age NPM Tools

The desire for better, more efficient public services suggests that the failed dogma and practices of NPM are unlikely to be resurrected as the way forward. However, the UK public sector has yet to develop and sustain the necessary post-NPM organizational culture, maturity and management capability to build and deliver the innovation required for DEG at scale. Early attempts to build DEG were undermined by their foundation on an outdated NPM chassis, elements of which remain strongly rooted today.

Significant public investment in the centralized 'Transformational Government' agenda and other digital initiatives resulted in a profoundly counter-innovative public sector IT marketplace in the UK. Although government outsourcing of IT was theoretically based on the principle of achieving economies of scale from the aggregation of demand, the reality of UK government procurement practice led to the opposite: an aggregation of supply, producing a privileged elite of 'super-suppliers' in the marketplace. In 2004, just 11 IT companies handled 80% of the UK's annual IT public sector expenditure. By 2011, this was slightly improved, but still only 18 IT companies handled 80% of the UK's estimated £17 billion annual IT public sector business.

Such a narrow market concentration was peculiar to the UK. These high-level statistics also mask a more significant underlying market distortion: namely that a small number of suppliers artificially dominated and effectively controlled the supply chain – something the UK government and House of Commons Public Administration Select Committee have both referred to as an oligopoly, with the committee going further to refer to the domination and behaviour of the large suppliers as 'cartel-like'.

By comparison, one study found that in the Netherlands the top five IT suppliers claimed just 20% of the government market. In the US, it was 48%. In the UK, the lack of competition was notable: 2008 estimated public sector revenues for the top five IT suppliers alone totalled £7.09 billion out of a total IT expenditure of £13.65 billion, representing 52% market share.

TABLE 2.2   Estimated UK public sector IT supplier revenues in 2008

IT Supplier	Estimated Public Sector Revenues, 2008
HP/EDS	£2,235m
BT	£2,100m
Fujitsu Services	£1,200m
Capgemini	£900m
IBM	£650m

Source: Kable 2009

Table 2.2 paints an ironic picture of the results of the supposedly free-market doctrine of NPM: a closed market comprising a small number of large suppliers. In comparison with the Netherlands and the US, the top five IT suppliers held an artificial majority influence within the market. The aggregation of public sector needs, let through monolithic, long-term, high-value and high-risk contracts, severely restricted any form of genuinely open competition and precluded meaningful service innovation. It resulted in a disincentive to adopt disruptive new processes and technologies that could have reduced the complexity, and thus the cost, of public services. For suppliers, this disincentive towards innovation was commercial. For senior civil servants, it was a by-product of perceived risk avoidance (ironic, given the reality of the high failure rate of IT-enabled projects), and of a general deskilling of the in-house IT profession.

The result was an unfortunate combination: the expensive outsourcing of poor services, systems and processes with no clear model for their modernization and improvement; the creation of supplier lock-in, with a damaging dependency on IT systems that rarely met the needs of their users, either inside or outside government; and an internal administrative model that was costly, inefficient and bureaucratic, focused on internal metrics and measurements rather than the improvement of public services.

These problems undermined numerous political efforts at public sector reform. Often the systems involved merely succeeded, at best, in automating existing manual processes, including their inefficiencies, rather than using IT as part of a process to redesign and improve services from the ground up. This widespread use of IT to automate existing public administration processes and systems – rather than to innovate with new delivery models – was a calling card of the NPM-era, with even one senior industry executive observing that: *'Government expects its outsourcing service provider to maintain the complexity rather than to simplify and standardize the work processes.'*

The widespread failure to reform resulted in part from the development of a culture of IT-centric service delivery. Historically, there were few incentives to innovate and redesign processes and to adopt newer, standardized technologies that would produce greater competition and value for money. Instead, NPM-style outsourcing rewarded complexity, where external providers built and supported bespoke, complicated and siloed processes and technologies that only they understood and could maintain, and upon which government grew increasingly dependent.

It is useful to understand some of the historic approaches to the use of technology in public service reform in order to help identify what lessons need to be learned if today's digital initiatives are to succeed where their predecessors failed. To do that, we need to step back several decades in time. The successive waves of political attempts to use IT to modernize the UK's public services have their roots in the early 1990s, with the 1994 launch of the single government portal, the Government Information Service (GIS), a predecessor of today's GOV.UK. In 1996, Roger Freeman MP, Chancellor of the Duchy of Lancaster and Cabinet Minister for Public Service, launched Government Direct:

> *[This initiative] will be founded on the new possibilities offered by information technology, and it will learn from the way that these are starting to be harnessed by other governments and the private sector. It will change fundamentally and for the better the way that government provides services to citizens and businesses. Services will be more accessible, more convenient, easier to use, quicker in response and less costly to the taxpayer. And they will be delivered electronically.*

This initiated nearly two decades of political attempts to modernize and improve the design, operation and delivery of public services through the use of technology. However, turning such well-meaning political aspirations into effective operational delivery has proved a time-consuming, expensive and immense struggle, with few of the original benefits yet realized. To understand why, and what needs to be done to successfully transition public services into the digital age, in the next few chapters we set out a brief review and analysis of selected initiatives.

3

Decades of Hope

In the previous chapter we set out the wider context within which the UK hoped to redevelop its public services – and highlighted some of the problems of organizational culture. This chapter reviews some of the modernization and technology-led initiatives of the major political parties.

Our main focus is the general political consensus on policy and outcomes that were to be enabled by technology. So we start with a selective review of the last 20 years in order to provide a flavour of the thinking and activities over this period. We follow this by highlighting several specific areas of policy to examine how they developed over time – including the desire for a single, online government portal or website, and the idea of 'open' – a broad term that at times spans everything from open data to open standards.

Accessibility/Social Inclusion

One of the obvious distinctions often made between the public and private sectors is that the private sector can decide on its target audience and be selective (if it wishes) about whom it interacts with. It may, for example, choose to target only a specific segment of a market. The public sector, however, must provide universal services, potentially available to all. Equally, with that exclusive monopoly provider status comes great responsibility, since it is not possible for citizens to obtain most public services elsewhere.

Partly in consequence, there has been long-standing political concern with the concept of a digital divide. Public services need to be available to all, and yet with the increasing adoption of technology in all aspects of our daily lives, the understandable concern is that less technology-literate citizens are becoming disadvantaged. There are numerous causes of this divide between those with access to technology and those without, including more obvious aspects such as low income and the entry cost of many digital devices, as well as a variety of more complex reasons, including lack of interest in the internet or modern communications devices, disability or impairment that may render digital a less viable option, and a lack of confidence or skills, as well as the variable quality and user experience of many online services, which can often be frustrating and off-putting.

This divide was initially cast in simplistic terms of whether people had access to a PC and connectivity services such as broadband, but the widespread proliferation of other devices – such as smartphones and tablets – has produced an increased diversity of access and mechanisms by which people can interact with services in both the private and public sectors. An early policy paper from 1998, the 'View from the Queue', found that there are also some in society who simply do not wish to use technology – effectively producing a self-imposed digital divide. More recently, in 2014, the UK government published a survey looking at the extent of use of online services, proposing to use it as a benchmark to monitor progress against digital services reach (see Figure 3.1).

Confusion often seems to surround the important topic of social inclusion, partly from a simplistic, and mistaken, association of digital purely with the move to put transactional services online and hence deliver them on to a screen – triggering a concern that those not online, and in need of relationship-based services, will be disadvantaged.

UK population
Recent BBC/Go On UK Survey

14%   7%   79%

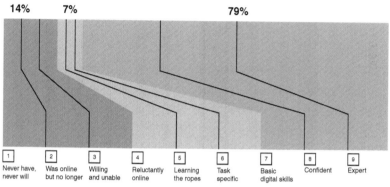

1	2	3	4	5	6	7	8	9
Never have, never will	Was online but no longer	Willing and unable	Reluctantly online	Learning the ropes	Task specific	Basic digital skills	Confident	Expert

Digital inclusion scale

FIG 3.1 / UK digital inclusion

Source: GDS

It seems slightly odd that talk of social inclusion/exclusion only seems to have become particularly prevalent as the option of digitally re-engineering public services has arisen. After all, it is not as if existing channels such as relationship-based front-line services and paper-based forms are always shining examples of socially inclusive service provision. Indeed, that same 1998 government paper found that existing (non-digital) government services could be incredibly frustrating – unhappy respondents complained that staff were unhelpful, lacked knowledge and were slow in handling claims. Citizens' experiences with paper-based services fared little better, with over half of benefits claimants finding it difficult to fill in the lengthy forms and needing help to do so. Yet little seems to have been done to tackle this paper-centric form of social exclusion – even today many services involve 50+ dense pages whether served online or offline.

These long-standing problems of social inclusion will only be fixed when the focus is not simplistically on one arbitrary delivery channel (e.g. screen, in-person, phone, paper-based) but moves instead to a holistic re-engineering and redesign of the organizations, processes and technologies that underpin them. The focus must shift to addressing the underlying complaint, well expressed in 1998, that *'existing transactions with govern-ment were seen as being complicated and time consuming ... respondents described feelings of humiliation and irritation with regard to ... dealings with government.'*

Tackling social inclusion requires comprehensive re-engineering of the entire life cycle of public services, redesigning them around citizens' needs. Digital should not be sidetracked into a meaningless focus on screen-based service delivery – but should be used to deliver meaningful and long over-due improvements to the design and operation of public services across all of the delivery channels that citizens and businesses use. Whilst digital is of course in part about online service delivery, its most important role is in improving the internal operations and processes of public service organiza-tions too – reducing the costs and inefficiencies of current transactional services from which everyone benefits: online and offline alike.

The resulting savings from properly designed digital government services can in turn be used to enhance service provision to those who require more traditional, and labour intensive, services such as the provision of face-to-face services in a local office, day-care centre or in their home. Citizens themselves have long recognized this potential, with one respond-ent to the 1998 government study commenting that such technology-enabled improvements to government services could *'"free-up" staff time to deal with queries of a more complicated and sensitive nature'*. Everyone will benefit from the modernization of internal processes of administra-tion, regardless of whether the final channel used is online or personal and relationship-based. Digital public services are public services: over time, hopefully the 'digital' label can be dropped because we will all come to understand that public services are inherently digital.

Privacy, Security and Identity

Since the earliest days of moving services online, concerns have been expressed about the privacy and security of citizens' information. Closely associated with these important issues is the issue of identity – which covers a whole range of related concerns, including government knowing who it is dealing with online, through to citizens being able to pinpoint public officials who have accessed and misused their personal data in order for them to be held to account.

These themes have been subject to many years of discussion and debate. A good example is seen in the 1998 UK government research paper 'View from the Queue', which reflected citizens' concerns about government access to, and use of, citizens' personal data. It noted that:

> It is essential to allay concerns of potential users about technology and how it will be used by government by:
>
> • ensuring 'confidentiality' or privacy in interacting with government
> • providing safeguards against fraud or computer hacking
> • providing guarantees about government's use of information
> • providing assistance and support to users.

Its qualitative research identified three aspects relating to confidentiality – namely the privacy of the facility or medium (as in the need to have an enclosed space or private PC or kiosk when using a device in a public space); fraud or computer hacking by other members of the public; and mistrust of government's use of information. Other respondents raised concerns over data protection, how to obtain proof of whether transactions had happened, and computer errors. There were also concerns relating to the security of data and the maintenance of confidentiality, together with the issue of trust (in both technology and in government).

These concerns are reflected in a range of policy and strategy documents through the online, e-government and t-government eras. The 2009 policy paper 'Putting the Front Line First: Smarter Government', for example, included the recognition that:

> It is a fundamental duty of government to provide security for citizens, and that security has to extend to the online environment. Information assurance and identity security are and will be at the heart of any thriving digital economy.

More recently, the US government's 'Digital Government: Building a 21st Century Platform to Better Serve the American People' recognizes the need to adopt a co-ordinated approach to ensure privacy and security in a digital age, to ensure the safe and secure delivery and use of digital services to protect information and privacy:

> *To support information sharing and collaboration, we must build in security, privacy, and data protection throughout the entire technology life cycle. To promote a common approach to security and privacy, we must streamline assessment and authorization processes, and support the principle of 'do once, use many times'. We must also adopt new solutions in areas such as continuous monitoring, identity, authentication, and credential management, and cryptography that support the shift from securing devices to securing the data itself and ensure that data is only shared with authorized users.*

Part of ensuring effective privacy and security requires a good system of identity – knowing who is trying to access (or provide) personal data, whether they are the right person or organization to do so, and that they can be trusted. As early as 1998, the UK's Parliamentary Office of Science and Technology (POST) described two approaches to identity that have often defined the boundaries of the debate ever since:

> *The first holds that it is the responsibility of government to provide an official 'citizens card' once it expects people to use it to access and validate official transactions – just as it provides other documents such as passports and driving licences. The alternative view is that if there is a 'market' for 'identity', then it can be met by any number of private means and does not need a single official mechanism which could be portrayed by some as the equivalent of a national identification card.*

The e-Government Authentication Framework from 2000 defined the core characteristics required of identity for online public services:

- a given identity actually exists;
- a person or official of an organization is the true holder of that identity;
- identity holders are able to identify themselves for the purpose of carrying out a transaction via an electronic medium.

However, a great deal of mistrust and misunderstanding surrounds attempts to impose schemes aimed at monitoring citizens. In some countries, such as the UK and the USA, there has been an historic suspicion of state-imposed national identity systems, leading to the cancellation of a national identity card scheme in the UK. Elsewhere, such as Estonia, single national identity systems encounter far less cultural resistance, and have established themselves as an important part of the overall move to a modern, digital state.

The UK has mainly focused on a federated identity system (effectively reflecting the second option in the description set out in the POST quote above), with the notable exception of the short-lived attempt to introduce a national identity card. Since the general election in 2010, there has been a renewed focus on returning to the earlier desire for a federated identity system. The Government Digital Service (GDS) is running an identity assurance programme, developing the technical standards needed to implement a federated identity model and putting into place the ecosystem of third-party identity providers required to make it happen:

> *Identity providers are organizations paid by the government to verify people's identity so they can sign in securely to government services. Identity providers will have to meet industry security standards and identity assurance standards published by the Cabinet Office and CESG (the UK's national technical authority). There are currently 5 identity providers—Digidentity, Experian, Mydex, the Post Office and Verizon— eventually there will be more. You can choose to register with more than one of them, and you can stop using an identity provider at any time.*

GDS has also recently announced a further initiative to encourage a growing marketplace of identity providers, to further expand the choice open to citizens and businesses in the future. They have set out five reasons for using third-party identity service providers rather than government imposing its own mandatory central solution:

1. *User choice – you will be able to choose your identity provider(s) and stop using a provider if you want.*
2. *No centralized identity database – instead, to protect users' privacy, each identity provider will be responsible for securely and separately holding data about the users that have registered with them. Each government department service will only have access to the data it needs.*

3. *Security – using several identity providers is more secure and less vulnerable; there is no single point of failure and no single service that holds all the data in one place.*
4. *Developing a market – we're giving identity providers freedom to design services to meet the standards. This will allow them to develop services that can be used by the wider public and private sector, which will help to reduce costs.*
5. *Making the most of available technology – the technology and methods for identity verification are constantly evolving; specialist private sector organizations are better placed than government to keep up with these developments.*

Governments have often appeared to struggle with the privacy, security and identity implications of moving to digital services. There has historically been a series of large-scale leaks of data from government departments, and continued abuse of sensitive systems (such as the UK's national police computer system), highlighting the risk of insider errors and intentional abuse as much as malevolent external attack. So too there appears to be little focus on the cross-departmental aspects of personal data sharing and release in the era of 'big data' – each data release in itself might be relatively innocuous, but when combined with other data sources (both from the public and private domains) far more can be revealed than many citizens might wish. Government needs to be careful not to undermine the lifeblood of the digital age – information – as a result of an inadequately designed and implemented approach to these important topics. It also needs to distinguish between public and private (personal) data and to understand the potentially toxic ways in which these can be linked, aggregated and analysed quickly and effectively – even when apparently anonymized or pseudonymized – in the era of big data and massive, low-cost computational capability.

In the light of the Edward Snowden revelations in 2013, it appears governments have been involved in intercepting and acquiring significant amounts of citizens' personal and private data relating to their lawful daily activities. As a consequence, government may find it difficult to re-establish and maintain the trust necessary to move to fully digitized services and operations.

Policy – or How Technology will Miraculously Improve Public Services and Cost Us Less

By the mid-1990s there was already a well-established political interest in how technology might help improve UK public services – reflecting an increasing awareness that the public sector was falling behind, contrasting poorly with the increasingly automated processes of service delivery being adopted in the private sector:

> *Information technology now makes it possible for citizens and businesses to deal directly with government ... this will give them access to services with quicker – sometimes immediate – responses, which are available in more convenient places and at more convenient times. To draw a parallel with the private sector: in order to withdraw money from a bank or building society it was once necessary to fill in a cheque or a withdrawal slip, and take it to the counter when the bank or building society was open. Now ... money can be withdrawn from a cash machine without form-filling, at any time of the day or night, seven days a week. The Government wants to bring the same or better levels of convenience to the services that it delivers directly to individual citizens and to businesses in the UK.* (Government Direct, 1996)

Within a year of the publication of 'Government Direct', the general election of 1997 saw a Labour government returned to power. As the new prime minister, Tony Blair, brought a renewed wave of political optimism about the role that IT could play in the modernization and improvement of the UK's public services, and sought to build on the work of the previous Conservative administration. Labour's critical analysis on coming to power was that a largely decentralized approach to IT had allowed departments and agencies to modernize their systems in ways that met their own narrow needs, but which had neglected the potential benefits of IT for government as a whole, observing that: *'As a result, we have incompatible systems and services which are not integrated.'*

Whilst this description of government IT was certainly true (and remains largely true today), it was a mistake to see this lack of integration as exclusively an IT issue. The state of IT was essentially a by-product of the fragmented nature of government departments and agencies and the services they provided – which were not focused on the users of those services, but on the needs and perceptions of their owners and their many separate administrative functions. The fragmented nature of IT was in effect a mirror that reflected the more fundamental problems of the increasingly outdated structure, management and organizational culture of the public sector. However, to fix its perception that it was the management of IT that was to blame, the government set about establishing a centralized corporate IT strategy, reflected in a series of papers and reports intended to direct the civil service on a journey of reform.

To push forward these plans for corporate IT, during the Labour government's time in office it released an ever-growing library of papers, reports and strategies that aimed to reforge the UK's public sector. Many of these were justifiably aspirational and insightful in their intent, and inherently understood the opportunities that technology presented – yet, time after time these political aspirations foundered. If current and future attempts to use technology to help modernize public services are to succeed where these earlier efforts in the UK and elsewhere failed, it is important to understand why – and how to fix these recurrent issues: a discussion we focus on specifically in Part 2.

In the following sections in this chapter, we draw upon a selective handful of initiatives to help provide a quick taste of how the proposed use of IT in the UK government developed during the Labour government of 1997 to 2010: it mirrors similar models in many other countries and demonstrates the frustrating gap between aspiration and practical improvements in the overall design of public services.

The Magic of 'e': Electronic Government

The 1990s and early 2000s became the era of 'e'. One of the earliest papers of this era was 'Electronic Government: The View from the Queue', published in October 1998. It included comprehensive research into potential take-up of online government services. This emphasis on citizen research is surprisingly unusual: many other papers published during this period rightfully highlighted the need to place citizens at the centre of public services, yet mention no research data or evidence of any engagement with citizens or businesses. Whilst politicians had clearly understood the opportunities offered by technology since at least the early 1990s, the papers drafted in their name over subsequent decades often demonstrate little evidence of any interaction with either front-line employees or the users of public services – a somewhat ironic reality gap given political aspirations to deliver 'citizen-centric services'. Such a significant omission appears even stranger when compared with what was happening in the private sector to understand consumers better – it was, after all, the mid-1990s when the supermarket chain Tesco first launched its shoppers' Clubcard and started to better understand the behaviour of its customers and how it might better meet their needs.

As one of the rare, evidence-based contributions, the 1998 paper recognized that it was essential to offer extra benefit by improving or enhancing existing services: citizens would not accept changes that succeeded only in *'moving the queue from the counter to a kiosk'*. That is, citizens did not want merely to be deflected from a face-to-face interaction to an electronic one that was no better. (It's useful to remember that touch-screen kiosks in public places were seen as an important means of access and social inclusion for online public services in the era that predated the widespread use of PCs, smartphones and tablets, amongst many other devices.) It also stated that:

> *Change must be based on evaluating the benefits to users and solutions found which are cost-effective for users as well as for government.*

The move to e-government was seen as an important way of improving public service provision in terms of the speed of carrying out transactions, convenience and access, flexibility (in options and hours of service) and empowerment (bringing services closer to the public and allowing them to choose how/when to carry out transactions).

These generic themes about the benefits that could result from the use of IT have largely persisted ever since: they would not appear out of place in a new government paper published today. Indeed, it would be possible to take many of these earlier policy papers, Photoshop into place an image of a current prime minister or president, and republish them largely as they are: they remain aspirational and often inspiring visions for the use of technology – and ultimately a damning indictment on the inability to deliver.

Modernizing, Information Age Government

In 1999, several initiatives set out a vision for making life *'better for people and businesses'* as part of a long-term programme of improvement. Prime minister Tony Blair emphasized that:

> Modernizing Government is a vital part of our programme of renewal for Britain. The old arguments about Government are now outdated – big Government against small Government, interventionism against laissez-faire. The new issues are the right issues: modernizing Government, better Government, getting Government right.

There was a commitment to move public services to 24/7 availability, although this commitment was sensibly caveated with the phrase *'where there is a demand'*. The target was also set for all dealings with government being electronic by 2008. That target was later reset to 2005, although the target was never delivered in either 2005 or 2008 and still has not been achieved in 2014. It was also undermined by including the use of telephones (and hence call centres) as part of the definition of 'electronic' delivery.

Such top-down attempts to change the culture of any organization are notoriously difficult to achieve and it is perhaps not surprising that these ambitious efforts failed. Technology remained notoriously distant from senior government officials, with little if any technology expertise evident in its top management boards. It became culturally acceptable for senior management to state: *'We don't need to understand technology to manage it'* – yet it would rightly be hard to imagine the word technology replaced with 'finance' or 'people' or 'public services' without such a complacent, outdated statement provoking understandable uproar. Technology is as integral to designing and delivering public services as any of these other factors – something that has historically been little understood.

Whilst outside government technology was reinventing the very nature of many organizations and the way they delivered services, inside government, technology had become seen as someone else's problem – and nothing to do with the way that public services could be completely reimagined. There was perhaps a degree of mutual self-interest in outsourcing IT to expensive suppliers on exclusive contracts – whenever problems arose, officials and suppliers could point accusatory fingers at each other without anyone taking either responsibility or accountability, leaving governments, front-line employees and citizens alike increasingly frustrated with the extent to which public services were falling ever further behind where they deserved and needed to be.

The 'Modernizing Government' initiative's three main aspirations remain familiar today: to ensure that policymaking was more joined up and strategic; to make sure that public service users, not providers, were the focus, by matching services more closely to people's lives; and to deliver high-quality and efficient public services. These aspirations were underpinned by five associated commitments, with one in particular that emphasized what it called 'Information Age Government':

> we will use new technology to meet the needs of citizens and business, and not trail behind technological developments ... Information technology is revolutionizing our lives, including the way we work, the way we communicate and the way we learn. The information age offers huge scope for organizing Government activities in new, innovative and better ways and for making life easier for the public by providing public services in integrated, imaginative and more convenient forms like single gateways, the Internet and digital TV.

Yet the reality was that the era of NPM had removed the very means by which government might realize its worthy ambitions – leaving the choice of technologies with a handful of dominant IT suppliers, and the civil service detached from the way in which processes, services and systems could be designed as an integrated whole built around the needs of users.

It's hard to understand how public services were ever going to be improved and redesigned when the one major new way of making that happen, and the one that was causing major disruption in the private sector – the use of technology – was kept at arm's length. Whilst the paper committed to *'a fundamental change in the way we use IT'*, it failed to address how this could be achieved within the constraints of NPM – other than by setting out a series of steps to aid delivery, including:

- *designating a senior official at board level within each Department to champion the information age Government agenda within the Department and its agencies;*
- *benchmarking progress against targets for electronic service delivery, and against the best performance in the private sector and in other countries;*
- *setting a target that by the end of the year all Departments should be participating in the Government Secure Intranet.*

It is interesting to note that as well as being metric-driven, many of the metrics themselves are opaque or meaningless: what, after all, is meant by 'all Departments should be *participating* in the Government Secure Intranet'? *'Participating'* leaves generous space for ambiguity. Others seem more concerned with measuring progress against *targets* rather than progress against *implementation*: for example, *'benchmarking progress against targets for electronic service delivery'* is all about being responsible for monitoring *benchmarks*, not about making *progress* itself. Rarely have the phrases *'be careful what you ask for'* and *'be careful what you measure'* seemed more apposite.

... and Yet more Strategies

The e-government strategy (subtitled 'A strategic framework for public services in the information age') was published in April 2000 as a major element of the 'Modernizing Government' initiative. It contained four guiding principles:

- building services around citizens' choices;
- making government and its services more accessible;

- social inclusion;
- using information better.

Later in 2000 another paper conveyed a sense of frustration with slow progress: 'Successful IT: Modernizing Government in Action' was a review of major government IT projects aimed at 'improv[ing] performance and avoid[ing] the mistakes of the past'.

The Minister of State for the Cabinet Office wrote in his introduction:

> It sets out a package of measures to help us deliver effective modernization through IT. Putting them into practice will require commitment across Government, as well as from our private sector partners ... The recommendations in this report will enable us to put our modernizing vision into practice. They are a vital part of turning our strategy into real improvements in public services.

In the body of the report, a familiar problem was set out:

> In the past, Government IT projects have too often missed delivery dates, run over budget or failed to fulfil requirements. This review was set up to improve the way Government handles IT projects.

It identified a key objective:

> A change of approach is needed. Rather than think of IT projects, the public sector needs to think in terms of projects to change the way government works, of which new IT is an important part. Our recommendations aim to achieve this change.

This was an important shift from Labour's position on taking power, which had largely seen the lack of a corporate approach to IT as the principal problem to be tackled. The paper seems to reflect a growing political awareness of a wider, systemic and much more fundamental problem – namely the public sector's often dysfunctional organizational structures, processes and operations. In prescient observations still as relevant today as they were then, the report noted:

> The change in approach ... is about bringing in a focus on business change. This means that, when organizations are managing programmes and projects, it is vital they concentrate on how to deliver improvements

to the way they do business. Too often we have seen an approach that looks only at part of the change programme (for example, bringing in new technology) and does not integrate this with other elements (such as culture change) or take an overall view of the whole change process. Achieving and maintaining this integration is a vital, and ongoing, managementt ask.

Other points appear to reflect upon possible reasons why the government had encountered repeated obstacles in delivering its policy objectives:

Achieving integration of all the aspects of change requires effective leadership and that is only possible where responsibility for the delivery of a project or programme falls to an individual. If it is not clear who is taking charge, then it is almost impossible for an initiative to succeed.

As well as the more barbed comment:

There must be people in place who have the ability to deliver.

Inadequate risk management was also highlighted, with the report setting out an approach to government programmes that almost predicts the more agile and incremental approach espoused by today's Government Digital Service:

Managing risk is easier if ambitious and complex programmes are broken up into sections that can be delivered independently. The recommendations ... address modular and incremental approaches to implementing IT-related change. They include introducing a presumption in favour of such approaches and supporting guidance.

Long-standing problems on the supplier side, together with procurement-related issues, were also flagged as in need of a fix if policy objectives were to be achieved:

The Government's radical change agenda cannot be delivered by the public sector alone. Suppliers have a major role to play, and implementing an improved approach will be impossible if relationships with suppliers are poor or procurement is badly done. The recommendations ... aim to establish improved interactions between Government and its suppliers. They include taking a more strategic approach to suppliers, addressing problems with current guidance and setting out actions suppliers need to take.

It recognized that implementing change effectively is problematic and sought to address this issue with clear responsibilities and timelines:

> Many of the reasons why IT-related change has frequently failed have been known for some time. However, translating that knowledge into practice is not easy. What this report does is to make specific recommendations for how Government will achieve improvement and states how those recommendations will be put into practice. Section 11, implementation, sets out all the recommendations. It also sets out who has to take action, and by what date, to implement them. The recommendations are prioritized, so that those that will make the biggest difference on their own are put into practice first.

It also hoped once again that clear ownership and accountability would make the recommendations stick.

TransformationalG overnment

The 2005 'Transformational Government' agenda aspired to be a major updating of the vision for the use and application of IT to the UK's public services. The prime minister's introduction included the following aspiration:

> The future of public services has to use technology to give citizens choice, with personalized services designed around their needs not the needs of the provider.

It's telling that this political vision was largely unaltered since Tony Blair had taken office in 1997, although the detail of the strategy that appeared often seemed at odds with the prime minister's vision. It foresaw technology as a tool that could be used by governments to glue together and share existing services (putting 'more lipstick on the pig') rather than recognizing the political and technical reality of a new model of engagement that could mirror what was happening elsewhere in the best of the private sector: a model that would enable citizens themselves to be active players in the way in which public services were redesigned and improved. As a technical-led approach to the much broader and more complex issues of public sector reform, the era of t-government proved to be shorter-lived than the e-government initiatives it had aimed to displace.

Putting the Front Line First: Smarter Government and Digital Britain

In 2009, under Gordon Brown's premiership following his succession to the role of prime minster on Tony Blair's departure, Labour released a report setting out its vision for modern public services, 'Putting the Frontline First: Smarter Government'. In his foreword, in words that could have been plagiarized from those written over a decade earlier by his predecessor, the new prime minister wrote:

> rapid technological advances are transforming the world at a speed and scale not witnessed since the industrial revolution. This allows us to give citizens what they now demand: public services responsive to their needs and driven by them. At the same time it provides us with the means to deliver public services in a way that maintains their quality but brings down their cost. This will be essential to help meet our commitment to halve the public deficit within four years ... This plan for reforming government sets out how we will meet these new challenges by strengthening the role of citizens and civic society; recasting the relationships between the centre and the frontline and between the citizen and the State; and streamlining government.

Once again, the aspirations and vision continue to echo those expressed when Labour took office in 1997. It talks of the:

> diffusion of power [as] the next stage of public service reform. We will embrace new technology to better inform the public; give citizens new rights to information; create a new dialogue between people and public service professionals; and reduce bureaucratic burdens. Public services will improve as they become more personal and more cost-effective, and at the same time they will strengthen democratic deliberation and control in local communities.

And goes on to assert:

> This redirection of power from Whitehall to citizens and public servants allows for a leaner central government. So we will merge back office functions; relocate staff and reduce Civil Service overhead costs; and sell off or mutualize assets that the Government does not need to own.

It recognized that: '*Digitalizing public services needs to keep pace with consumer demand.*' Perhaps reflecting frustration with the top-down models of the past, it also stated that: '*Service users will be directly involved in the design of online services in order to ensure that they are usable and meet their needs.*'

The same year also saw 'Digital Britain' published, a joint report from the Department for Media, Culture and Sport (DCMS) and the Department for Business, Innovation and Skills (BIS). In its introduction, it commented that: '*The move from analogue to digital technology ... will define the competitiveness of our economy and change dramatically the way we live our lives.*' One of its four objectives was '*for government to continue to modernize and improve its service to the taxpayer through digital procurement and the digital delivery of public services*'.

It covered ground that had long been familiar since the 1990s, stating that:

> *An ambitious and clear programme of the Digital Switchover of Public Services, to primarily electronic and online delivery, will unlock significant cost savings, whilst at the same time serving to increase levels of satisfaction.*

Its ambition was to ensure that the delivery of public services in the UK kept pace with users' expectations of new technology and that the public sector became efficient and smart in procuring and using IT. Despite OECD and EU reports indicating that the UK was reasonably mature in its delivery of online public services, in comparison with the private sector (which was not only increasingly online but also engineering entirely new models of business organization and operations), it was in reality lagging well behind. It is not clear whether it was a flawed method of assessment to blame for the UK's apparent good progress in moving public services online, or whether it was merely being measured against a particularly low bar. Apart from a few well-worn poster child online projects – HMRC's self-assessment tax and DVLA's vehicle excise duty were regularly trotted out to a weary fanfare for many years – the majority of the UK's services were not only not online, but also had not even begun the process of redesign and re-engineering for the digital age.

'Digital Britain' also took a look back at efforts since 1997 to develop online services and readiness, both in terms of the UK as a whole and in the specifics of public services. It described the first phase *'from the later 1990s to around 2004/05 [as] about driving Britain, private sector and public sector, from being a laggard, as we were in the mid-1990s, to a leading economy in terms of e-readiness'*; and *'The second phase, since 2004–05 can best be described as "Government on the web", characterized by the creation of the office of Chief Information Officer and the CIO Council across Whitehall and the institutional support for the Transformational Government programme in the Cabinet Office.'* Its perspective is a mix of talking-up some achievements, whilst being admirably honest about others:

> *The proportion of public services online went from less than 30% of the total available (and that mostly alternative access to paper-based brochures) to 75% plus by 2005; though still in many cases they were an online replica of the offline service, based around the silos of providing departments rather than the actual public service needs of the citizen.*

After 12 years in office, this was the most honest and frank admission that the original ambitions of the government – to reforge the UK's public services through the use of technology – had not been achieved. 'Online services' largely meant the availability of paper forms on a website. It also repeated the long-standing desire to bring information and services together in a more streamlined way through continuing *'cross-Government work in improving the offer to customers by streamlining the sheer number of Government websites and brigading them either through the Directgov portal (for citizens) or the Businesslink portal [for business]'*.

Perhaps most telling is its observation that:

> *Government will need to become genuinely 'of the web', not simply 'on the web'. That means designing new services and transactions around the web platform, rather than simply adapting paper based, analogue, processes ... Bringing about this scale of change will require significant leadership and focus and a willingness to put this reform at the heart of Government activity as opposed to tacking it onto the side of existing ways of working.*

Here is finally a belated and welcome public recognition that it was not the fragmented nature of IT that was the root cause of the problem – but reform of the very nature of public services, and the way they were managed, designed and operated.

We now take a quick look at two themes that have developed and persisted through various changes of policy, strategy and emphasis: portals (or the idea of a single website for all government services), and 'open' (which has ranged from open source software to open standards to open data).

Portals, Portals, Portals

The idea of a single government portal or website, where all government services can be simply and conveniently accessed and used, has been one of the longest-standing elements of the vision for better integrated and more citizen-centric services. The Conservative government started to publish information online through the Government Information Service (GIS) site at 'open.gov.uk' in late 1994, the first attempt to provide a 'one stop shop' for all government services.

'Portals' during the 1990s were highly prominent in the private sector, with gatekeeper service providers such as Compuserve, AOL and MSN influencing the way government thought that its own services should develop. The GIS was intended to enable the public sector to emulate such private sector portal operators by providing *'access to information about more than 300 public sector organizations'* all in one place.

In 1999, the Cabinet published its 'Portal Feasibility Study', the start of a long, and expensive, journey leading towards improving the implementation of a single universal website for UK government services. Its rationale was to emulate the private sector portals of that era and to provide:

> *single, integrated means of access to Government information and services. This will allow information from different sources within Government to be brought together at one point, allowing the creation of new 'joined-up' services with a standardized presentation.*

The study set out a three-tier architectural model that was to influence the design both of initial work on websites, but also the Government Gateway – the systems that provided transaction handling and orchestration, payments, and the identification and authentication of users, for online government services. The outline of this model is shown in Figure 3.2.

Once again, the approach was to use IT as a type of sticking plaster that would magically make public services appear to be joined up, when in reality they remained fragmented across multiple administrative and operational departments and agencies. This focus on the 'quick' technology fix, rather than on reform of the often poorly performing organizational structures and processes behind them, has remained one of several reasons for the repeated failure to deliver any meaningful improvement to public services.

The paper set out a familiar list of potential benefits in delivering services that were:

- more accessible;
- more resistant to fraud;
- more convenient;
- easier to use to access information and services;
- quicker in response;
- less costly to the taxpayer, promoting efficiency between government departments.

The initial target service – enabling citizens to notify government *once* of a change of address – has never been delivered. (One persistent rumour from government insiders is that a cross-departmental working group spent over five years trying to define what an 'address' was, and was eventually disbanded having failed to reach agreement.)

Over the years, this idea of producing a single government portal has remained a dominant theme – with its emphasis on trying to focus services on the users perhaps best reflected in its early nickname of 'me.gov'. From the initial Government Information Service through the years of the UKOnline branding, through Direct.gov and Businesslink.gov to the present-day GOV.UK, government has spent 20 years working towards the

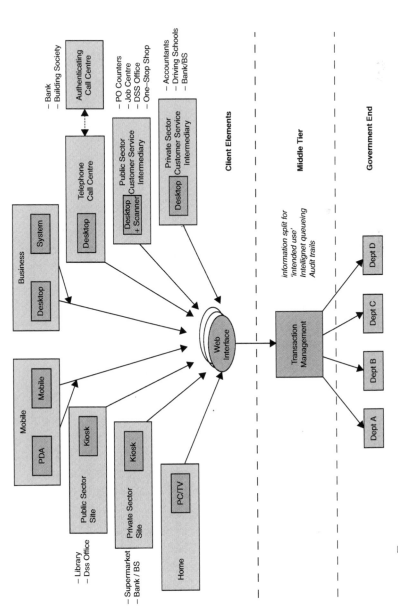

FIG 3.2 The three-tier portal architecture, 1999

idea of delivering online public services through a single, integrated web presence. The reason for this long journey is not so much a by-product of problems with technology, but one of trying to use technology as a top-down fix to problems that run much deeper and much broader – problems that relate to the way public services are designed, managed, structured, developed and operated, and which need to be tackled from a ground-up as much as from a top-down approach.

'Open'E verything

In 2002, the government published guidance on open source software use within the UK public sector. In a commendably brief four pages, this was the UK government's first significant attempt to assess how open source software (OSS) would fit within its wider IT vision. It followed on from the European Commission's initiative 'eEurope – An Information Society For All' which had stated that: *'during 2001 the European Commission and Member States will promote the use of open source software in the public sector and e-Government best practice through exchange of experiences across the Union'.*

The policy set out five objectives in the application of 'open' (Table 3.1).

There is little evidence that this policy was observed in either the spirit or letter of how it was intended. Given that government had already largely outsourced its technology to a select group of large suppliers, it is unclear that it possessed any meaningful mechanism by which it could dictate to those suppliers how to build their solutions. It was, after all, contracting them to provide a service: a major principle of such outsourcing was that the suppliers would choose the technologies that they felt best met the client's needs. Many of those suppliers had close commercial interests in proprietary software and related intellectual property, and were unlikely to see much advantage in promoting open source. So it is perhaps no surprise that, some seven years later, the Actuate 2009 Survey (covering both private and public sector activities globally), concluded with respect to the UK that: *'Significantly the UK continues to demonstrate a degree*

TABLE 3.1   Objectives of open source, 2002

UK Government will consider OSS solutions alongside proprietary ones in IT procurements. Contracts will be awarded on a value for money basis.
UK Government will only use products for interoperability that support open standards and specifications in all future IT developments.
UK Government will seek to avoid lock-in to proprietary IT products and services.
UK Government will consider obtaining full rights to bespoke software code or customizations of COTS (Commercial Off The Shelf) software it procures wherever this achieves best value for money.
UK Government will explore further the possibilities of using OSS as the default exploitation route for Government funded R&D software.

of reticence towards open source adoption with almost a quarter (22.4%) still monitoring developments but not yet evaluating.'

In 2009 there was an update to the government's open source strategy, which had previously been updated just once, in 2004. Its purpose was to establish a mindset of defaulting to open source software in procurements, all other things being equal, and to avoid lock-in to proprietary software. Like earlier policies in this area, it remained inconclusive about how the policy would be delivered in practice, and was to have little impact despite the strong political drive behind it.

Alongside the recurrent attempts to inject and exploit more open source software inside government, there was also increasing interest in how public data might be better used if it were to become more open and accessible. The 'Power of Information Taskforce' was established in March 2008 in response to the 2007 'The Power of Information Review', and sought to develop a plan to deliver social and economic gains from the better use of government-held public data. It delivered its report in early 2009, making 25 recommendations to improve the use of government information.

Drawing upon this work, in March 2009 the government published 'Working Together – Public Services On Your Side', which restated many of the objectives Labour had published since attaining office in 1997, but which now also included references to the new work on open data and sought to deliver the objectives set out in Table 3.2.

TABLE 3.2   Objectives for 'open', 2009

Open information	To have an effective voice, people need to be able to understand what is going on in their public services. Government will publish information about public services in ways that are easy to find, easy to use, and easy to re-use, and will unlock data, where appropriate, through the work of the Office of Public Sector Information.
Open innovation	We will promote innovation in online public services to respond to changing expectations. The Government will seek to build on the early success of innovate.direct.gov.uk by building such innovation into the culture of public services and public sector websites.
Open discussion	We will promote greater engagement with the public through more interactive online consultation and collaboration. We will also empower professionals to be active on online peer-support networks in their area of work.
Open feedback	Most importantly, the public should be able to have a fair say about their services. The Government will publish best practice in engaging with the public in large numbers online.

The use of open data is one area where tangible progress has been made, continuing through the move to the Coalition government in 2010 and the creation of the independent Open Data Institute (ODI) in 2012, assisted by government investment. It has seen a variety of initiatives delivered, including the publication of local crime maps and the Combined Online Information System (COINS), the database for all UK government expenditure, made available on data.gov.uk. By mid-2014 the site has made over 9,000 datasets available, from both central government and a variety of other public sector bodies, including local authorities.

Outcomes and Benefits

So what did these various initiatives ultimately achieve? In 2003, the UK Treasury released a document entitled 'Measuring the Expected Benefits of e-Government', in which it reiterated familiar potential outcomes:

> e-Government has the potential to improve greatly the delivery of public services, making them easier to access, more convenient to use,

more responsive, more transparent and so on. It also has the potential to free up resources in the public sector by delivering services more efficiently.

However, the Treasury also flagged some of the problems being encountered by the government in turning its vision into reality, commenting: *'the Government's record on IT projects is not good and the drive towards e-Government also comes with risks'.* It appeared to recognize the danger of using simplistic NPM metrics as any form of justification, stating that: *'It is important to develop a thorough business case for any major investment decision; it is not sufficient to justify action solely on the basis that it is needed to meet a target.'* Yet much of government's approach in practice was to remain unchanged, specifying technology and procurement objectives first and considering actual user needs only much later – if at all.

The UK government Treasury, however, hoped to improve the way that IT was specified and procured. It set out several steps to be evaluated in the context of public services:

- Identifying the options that are likely to result in the greatest external and internal benefits.
- Estimating customer take-up of e-Government services.
- Estimating customer costs and benefits of using an e-Government service.
- Estimating internal departmental costs and benefits of e-enabling services.
- Evaluating options.

In 2004, a further report – 'Improving IT Procurement' – was published by the National Audit Office (NAO). It highlighted that: *'The history of [IT] procurements has not been good, with repeated incidences of overspends, delays, performance shortfalls and abandonment at major cost.'* It identified three principles to help ensure a more successful approach: the rigorous challenge and scrutiny of projects and programmes at each key stage in their life cycle; the need for highly skilled and capable programme and project managers; and better and more effective engagement with suppliers.

TABLE 3.3   Common causes of failure

Lack of clear link between the project and the organization's key strategic priorities including agreed measures of success.
Lack of clear senior management and Ministerial ownership and leadership.
Lack of effective engagement with stakeholders.
Lack of skills and proven approach to project management and risk management.
Lack of understanding of and contact with the supply industry at senior levels in the organization.
Evaluation of proposals driven by initial price rather than long-term value for money (especially securing delivery of business benefits).
Too little attention to breaking development and implementation into manageable steps.
Inadequate resources and skills to deliver the total delivery portfolio.

Source: NAO 2004

Notably absent from the above is any obvious focus on user needs and how well they were being met. This partly reflects a wider audit approach prevalent at the time: it focused on checking whether projects had management boards in place to run them, and whether project timescales and milestones, and credible accounting practices, were in place. However, less attention was paid to whether the project was actually delivering anything of real value to its users – or indeed whether it would deliver the original policy intent. Reviews mainly focused on process not outcomes – something the NAO has recognized and has subsequently been working to fix by engaging earlier on programmes, and also by considering technical as well as financial and procedural assurance. The NAO report also highlighted '*a lack of skills and experience necessary to deliver major IT-enabled projects*'. The common causes of failure identified are shown in Table 3.3.

Many of the findings and recommendations of these earlier reports remain valid a decade later. It is only relatively recently that the focus has moved to centre again on users' needs – as Labour itself had once intended after taking office in 1997. Most recently, the Government Digital Service and the Treasury have published new clarification on business case guidance, with government organizations now able to spend up to £750,000 on early discovery of user needs and development work – part of a new approach designed to enable departments and agencies to begin focusing on user needs upfront and to iterate potential service designs around those needs before moving into full programme mode.

Undercurrents of Change: Prelude to the 2010 General Election

Whilst the Labour government continued to struggle to turn its long-standing policy objectives into meaningful delivery, towards the end of its administration the opposition parties began to develop, refine and update their own thinking around the role of technology in potential future administrations.

In 2009, and building on earlier speeches about the role of open source software, one of the authors produced an independent report for the Conservative Party, entitled 'Open Source, Open Standards: Reforming IT Procurement in Government'. It identified how the use of open procurement processes, open data standards, and effective technology and commercial leadership within UK government could lead to major operational savings and performance improvements across government whilst reducing risk and avoiding government's historic tendency to overspend. It found that:

> the government has been paying twice as much per computer 'seat' as it could have been – this alone is an overspend of the order of £600m per year, every year ... On the basis of the changes to procurement, sourcing, licensing and staffing proposed in this document, a saving of 10% of Government IT expenditure would not be an unreasonable goal. According to the estimates provided to us by UK Government this would indicate a savings figure of approximately £1.2 bn. The savings would come not just from reduced licensing costs and buying equipment at the market rate, but importantly by freeing government bodies (and citizens) from costly long-term, monopoly supply situations.

One of the other publications that was to have most impact on the Coalition government after it came to power in 2010 was the paper 'Better for Less', written by Liam Maxwell (who in 2012 was appointed as the

TABLE 3.4   The five principles from 'Better for Less', 2010

Openness	Open data – government data must be transparent.
	Open source works – its concepts should be applied to processes as much as to IT.
	Open standards will drive interoperability, save money and prevent vendor lock-in.
	Open markets – competition creates efficient market-based solutions.
Localism	The centre may set the standards, but local deployment is best.
Ownership and privacy	It is our data, government can have access but not control over personal data.
	Government should be accountable for data protection and proper use
Outcomes matter more than targets	
Government must be in control of its programmes, not led by them	

government's Chief Technology Officer), in conjunction with several other authors. It analysed the series of historic problems that had led to expensive IT being delivered by a limited number of large companies, often late and over budget and rarely meeting the original ministerial or policy intent. It set out five principles to improve the use of IT in government, as listed in Table 3.4.

'Better for Less' also set out a range of measures to help deliver the change – to close the long-standing chasm between policy aspiration and its execution:

- Audit – get and understand the numbers.
- Identity – the prerequisite for online delivery.
- Capability – build in the skills we will need for the long term.
- Delivering change through open markets.

The Conservatives ran a collaborative site called 'Make IT Better', which gathered various crowd-sourced ideas about fixing 'the problems of IT', whilst another group of enthusiasts developed an 'Ideal Government IT

Strategy',[1] in a similar crowd-sourced way using a public wiki and a series of events, the outputs of which were subsequently shared with all three of the main UK political parties.

Prior to the election, the Liberal Democrats' main focus was on their activities opposing the proposed national identity card, and related civil liberty concerns about how other types of IT might be misused. Their 2010 general election manifesto was fairly light on specific elements related to IT, but did include a commitment to 'Better government IT procurement, investigating the potential of different approaches such as cloud computing and open-source software.' The LibDem interest in open source was a genuine and long-standing one, and reflected the party's frustration with the slow rate of progress in its adoption, combined with a liberal suspicion of large, dominant corporate IT suppliers.

In May 2010, the general election was to see the Labour government that had been in power since 1997 removed from office – yet no single political party enjoyed an outright majority. After much media speculation, a coalition government was formed between the Conservative Party and the Liberal Democrats.

[1] See http://comment.idealgovernment.com/.

4

2010 and Beyond

The Coalition Agreement

As the first formal coalition government in the UK since the Second World War, some way of fusing and reconciling aspects of both parties' manifestos and policy commitments needed to be found. This was achieved through the 'Coalition Agreement'. The influence of Conservative Party and Liberal Democratic Party thinking whilst in opposition, together with some of the independent contributions discussed in Chapter 3, make their presence felt throughout this joint document issued after the two parties formed their Coalition government. Specific IT-related commitments include:

- *We will take steps to open up government procurement and reduce costs; and we will publish government ICT [information and communications technology] contracts online.*
- *We will create a level playing field for open-source software and will enable large ICT projects to be split into smaller components.*
- *We will require full, online disclosure of all central government spending and contracts over £25,000.*
- *We will create a new 'right to data' so that government-held datasets can be requested and used by the public, and then published on a regularb asis.*

These echo earlier policy ideas that provide a common strand across all the major UK political parties – notably the efforts to open up the IT marketplace to better, more effective competition and to drive a level playing field for open source software.

Viva la Revolución

In November 2010, Martha Lane Fox, who had earlier been involved in a report for the Labour government, issued 'Directgov 2010 and Beyond: Revolution not Evolution'. It restated the long-standing aspiration that public services should be delivered online or by other digital means – once again setting out the vision and commitment that governments had been stating since the 1990s. Its proposals bear an eerily familiar stamp to previous reports, publications and policies, including:

- Simplifying the user experience of digital public services by making all of government's transactional services available through Directgov [the single government site for online services].
- Ensuring online government information and services are available wherever people are on the web by opening up applications and services to other organizations.

What the report highlighted, by forcibly repeating the same vision and aspirations that had long been common currency, was the enduring problem of delivery and implementation – or rather, the lack of meaningful delivery and implementation of genuine public service reform. If any meaningful progress was to be made, it was in its implementation and execution, not the development of yet more shelfware strategies and grand plans disconnected from reality at the front line of public services. The report's recommendations were accepted and actioned by the Coalition government, which also asked its author to take on a continuing advisory role in its practical implementation.

'A Recipe for Rip-offs'

It was not only the Coalition government that was considering how best to improve the way in which technology was being used as part of a more systematic programme of civil service reform. Parliament too was taking an interest. In July 2011, the cross-party House of Commons Public Administration Select Committee (PASC) published the results of their detailed investigation into the state of the use of information technology in government, for which one of the authors was their specialist adviser. Their report was highly critical, reflected in its subtitle 'A Recipe for Rip-offs' – itself a direct quote from one of the many witnesses to their inquiry.

It found that:

> despite a number of successful initiatives, government's overall record in developing and implementing new IT systems is appalling. The lack of IT skills in government and over-reliance on contracting out is a fundamental problem which has been described as a 'recipe for rip-offs' ... government is currently over-reliant on a small 'oligopoly' of large suppliers, which some witnesses referred to as a 'cartel'. Whether or not this constitutes a cartel in legal terms, current arrangements have led to a perverse situation ... benchmarking studies have demonstrated that government pays substantially more for IT when compared to commercial rates. The Government needs to break out of this relationship.

It set out four steps for government to address these issues: improving its own information, publishing more information, widening the supplier base and working in an agile manner. It also recommended that government:

> needs to possess the necessary skills and knowledge in-house, to manage suppliers and understand the potential IT has to transform the services it delivers. Currently the outsourcing of the government's IT service means that many civil service staff, along with their knowledge, skills, networks and infrastructure has been transferred to suppliers. The Government needs to rebuild this capacity urgently.

As well as highlighting the need to fix government's most pressing capability issues, the report also set out the committee's vision for how online public services could be reformed. This relied on a mix of public data release, letting individual citizens control their own personal records, engaging users in the design and continuous improvement of services, and opening up the delivery of online services to a greater range of organizations.

Government ICT Strategy 2011

The government IT strategy published in 2011 was something of a curate's egg, reflecting various mid-flight ideas that were already at an advanced stage under the previous Labour administration together with a blend of Coalition government thinking. Amongst its strategic objectives were:

- Making government ICT more open to the people and organizations that use our services, and open to any provider – regardless of size.
- Reducing the size and complexity of projects, and better managing risks.
- Enabling reuse of existing ICT systems and 'off the shelf' components, reducing duplication, overcapacity and saving money.
- Moving towards a common infrastructure in government, increasing efficiency and interoperability.
- Reducing procurement timescales and making it easier and simpler for small and medium enterprises (SMEs) to compete for government business, supporting the aspiration that 25% of central government procurement spend should go to SMEs by the end of this parliament (2015).
- Improving the implementation of big ICT projects and programmes, and supporting the IT profession in government and the public sector.

As a hybrid document, some elements were in transition, showing clear fingerprints of earlier thinking, including overly complex and inwardly looking governance structures in the shape of multiple boards (character- ized by insiders as time-consuming, internally focused 'talking shops') tasked with producing yet more NPM-era paper strategies, metrics and outputs.

Later, a series of changes to governance and personnel (with a new leader- ship team installed, aimed at addressing the lack of experienced in-house resources) saw the focus move towards delivery and implementation in place of the endless cycle of producing yet more strategy documents. These changes have swept away layers of bureaucracy (abolishing 24 out of 26 committees) and aims to move government's IT model towards one of collective delivery in place of contemplation.

Digital Services and the Growth of the Government Digital Service

One of the most high-profile changes under the Coalition government has been the establishment of the Government Digital Service (GDS) under Mike Bracken's leadership, a move to bring back highly skilled IT and digital skills inside government, as the Parliamentary Public Administration Select Committee (PASC) and 'revolution not evolution' had recommended. GDS has grown from a handful of resources to in excess of 400 within a few years and has laid down ways of working that are new for most of government, but which merely reflect long-standing best practice elsewhere.

GDS has set out guidance for how programmes must be developed in future, with a focus on user needs reminiscent of the original Labour vision of 1997. The strategy has committed the government to ensuring all new or redesigned public services meet the digital design standard, which is mandatory from April 2014. Departments and agencies must demonstrate that they have met the criteria set out, and must be able to do so for the full life of their service. Liam Maxwell, the chief technology officer (CTO) for the UK government, has sent out clear signals that existing technology contracts developed under the old-school NPM-era model are finished. The current policy intent is that what will come afterwards will be very different from the old NPM-era outsourcing model that saw IT thrown at a large external supplier using long-term exclusive contracts. Instead, user needs are being broken down into smaller, more manageable packages rather than a single contract, and will need to comply with the digital design standard.

GDS illustrates this change by showing the old-school model, which is characterized by a focus on technology and commercial issues, and which addresses user need only much further downstream (Figure 4.1).

This is compared with the digital by default service design standard, which reverses the model (by putting the users' needs first) as well as developing the programme in a series of incremental, well-managed steps – rather than the 'big bang' waterfall approach of the past (Figure 4.2).

The digital by default design reflects the approach that has been taken for a long time outside government, and aims to improve the chance

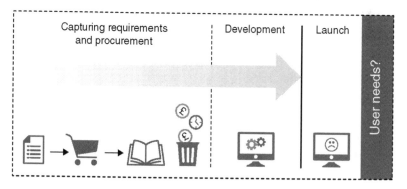

FIG 4.1 ╱ The 'old school' of government IT

Source: GDS

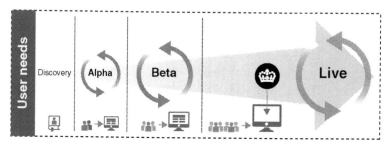

FIG 4.2 ╱ The digital by default design approach

Source: GDS

of success – from better meeting user needs, to delivery in a more timely way, to better control of finance and risk management.

Current State

The political vision, aspirations and rhetoric about the potential for IT to help improve the public sector have remained broadly consistent over the last 20 or so years. It is in its execution that significant problems have arisen. The Coalition government is making changes to the direction established over those decades – to attempt to regain control of government IT and the wider design, operation and management of public services. So just how effective are these current changes proving so far? Or will we merely see history repeat itself yet again?

A recent report by the National Audit Office (NAO) finds some early signs of progress. As part of the wider programme of cost controls and efficiencies being driven by the Cabinet Office's Efficiency and Reform Group (ERG), the NAO 'had confidence' in £5.5 billion of savings being delivered during the period 2011–12, although it is too early to comment on the longer-term sustainability of savings. One reason for this high level of savings is explicitly acknowledged in the report as being attributable to the 'central control over procurement of common goods and services and review of major ICT and other projects'.

Another NAO report, which looked specifically at the impact of the government's ICT savings initiatives, found that in 2011–12 central government spent an estimated £316 million less on IT-related goods and services than it would otherwise have done. It stated that the impact of the concerted policy attempt to reduce the dominance of large IT suppliers and increase the role of SMEs was in part unknown, itself ironically a victim of the long-term nature of the exclusive contracts with the old guard of IT suppliers that makes early intervention and improvement difficult. In many areas, government will only be able to make changes when these existing exclusive contracts expire. The NAO also found some frustration with 'the slow pace of change and the focus on cost-cutting, *rather than on exploring innovative opportunities to redesign digital public services'.*

The NAO identified several enablers of progress and several challenges to the programme of reform:

* Leadership from the Cabinet Office along with cross-government and cross-profession collaboration has been important for delivering IT savings that exceed targets so far.
* The introduction of IT spend controls by the Cabinet Office has been a powerful lever in driving departments to make IT savings and to comply with the IT strategy. Despite tensions, this new process is encouraging departments to become more disciplined in planning future IT spend and preparing more feasible proposals for scrutiny.
* Government has made a good start in reducing IT spend and reforming supplier relationships. The Cabinet Office is now facing the challenge of shifting its focus from saving money in buying 'big IT' to IT solutions that reform public services and the way that government works. We have identified two ways in which the Cabinet Office is facing this challenge:
  * Until recently, there has been insufficient resource for the IT spend control process, leading to delays. The IT Reform Group is now at its full complement and is able to increase the expert assistance it gives to departments, allowing them to save money and making deeper IT reforms that put users at the heart of public services.
  * Complex governance arrangements have existed for the five initiatives. The Cabinet Office is currently considering how to reform these arrangements so as to streamline governance and clarify roles and responsibilities.
* Relevant skills remain a challenge across government. There is progress in developing the ICT, digital and commercial professions in government. However, the pace, breadth and depth of the change required by the Cabinet Office's IT reform initiatives is opening up capacity and capability gaps across central government.

The current programme is effectively a pincer movement that relies on two complementary initiatives to work in support of one another. On one side are the changes the NAO has examined – the efficiency savings removing waste, duplication and bad practices, including breaking up major contracts and making them into more competitive lots that more companies, including SMEs, will be able to bid for. The intent is to move the UK away from its dependency on an 'oligopoly' of IT suppliers, and to introduce genuinely open competition and innovation into the marketplace.

On the other side is the equally important focus on improving the design, operation and delivery of public services, spearheaded by GDS. If the spend controls are the stick, the digital by default initiative is the carrot – encouraging a renaissance of skills and expertise within the public sector and enabling government to retake control of its own destiny. Although notionally about introducing best practices in user-driven needs and the iterative development of solutions, this initiative also carries with it equally important aspirations to improve capabilities across government – including ensuring that permanent secretaries and their direct reports do not see technology as something merely to be thrown at a project later downstream as in the past, but as part of the very nature of how modern, twenty-first century services can be entirely redesigned from the ground up. Digital aims to become an integral, pivotal part of both public service and civil service reform.

Outside of NAO and similar external reports, there are other ways to assess whether the changes are having an impact – including wider reaction from the IT supply base. It is presumably no coincidence that while many small- to medium-sized suppliers have welcomed the changes, some of the larger incumbent suppliers appear unhappy, with some complaining that they will lose business as a result – one even reportedly slamming the UK government 'for implementing reforms that have made it difficult for big suppliers to do business with the public sector'. This is in part a reflection of the important business at stake – with government hoping that replacing inefficient legacy systems, organizations and bureaucracy with new online, digital services based around the needs of users will save around £1.7 billion a year after 2015. That is a big chunk to be sliced out of the traditional IT market. For incumbent suppliers, the challenge will be to adjust and modernize their offerings around their undoubted strengths, or they will see other, newer and more nimble suppliers gain market share.

The Schism between Aspiration and Implementation: Turning a Corner?

What becomes clear from this brief review of attempts to use IT to improve the UK's public services is that this has been a failure not of high-level political vision and aspiration, but one of execution and implementation – combined with well-meaning, but naive, attempts to use IT as a blunt club to drive change. Multiple government administrations, of many political colours, have successively identified the desired political outcomes achievable through well-implemented technology-enabled public services, but successively struggled to make any meaningful or sustained headway – largely due to an underlying reluctance to make any major changes to the 'plumbing' of government. Perhaps small wonder when a report from an influential body such as the Institute for Government can be produced in 2013 that analyses civil service capabilities and yet contains no mention of technology or digital services: a revealing and damning omission in the internet age, when the civil service requires effective digital public management as part of its core capability.

These problems help illustrate why the modernization of government can never be about technology alone, but is about the more fundamental nature of democracy and the shape of public services in the digital age: about how outcomes can be better achieved rather than the lazy assumption that we can start with the organizational models inherited from the past. Some have made the argument that failures of IT are actually failures of policy – that some policies have been adopted that were never capable of being delivered since they were inadequately researched and evidenced. Yet equally it can be argued that failures of policy arise as a by-product of inadequate digital skills and implementation. Indeed, some policies might have been better framed in the first place if the data and skills had been there to provide insight and analyses of user needs prior to or during the formulation of policy.

As the private sector learned a long time ago, having high-quality, near-real-time data about users is an essential part of delivering better services – Tesco's Clubcard, for example, has been in operation since the mid-1990s. Whilst this is not a direct or perfect analogy for government, good, privacy-aware use of public data is something historically that has eluded the public sector, a problem that the ODI and the transparency programme are aiming to fix. Governments usually set broad direction through policy and expect to find capable teams around them to advise on the precise detail and its effective implementation: in turn, capable teams use information systems – their historic and current data – to help inform decisions and to implement intelligent service improvements. Copious evidence from the public record suggests that both the leadership capability and the quality of information required was largely missing for years.

Early evidence suggests that the programme of IT reform under the Coalition government is beginning to shift direction, but it will be a long haul to drive the depth and breadth of improvements required. A range of parallel, complementary measures include the use of commercial cloud computing and consultancy services available from the UK government CloudStore (discussed in more detail in Chapter 10); the impact of the spend controls on curtailing naive and poor behaviours; flexible resourcing frameworks enabling government to bring in the right talent; and the creation and impact of the GDS and the mandatory digital by default standard. But in many areas residual behaviours remain – the Department of Work and Pensions' flagship programme of Universal Credit (UC) is a topical example of a programme that was attempted in an outdated NPM fashion and, as a result, is now in the emergency room. The problems that have been encountered with UC may help to demonstrate that the biggest risk now is not change, but the failure to change: UC should never have been tackled as an IT-led programme, but as a business change programme.

If we have shown that, in the UK at least, the current programme of IT reform is finally applying the lessons learned to the timeless questions of 'What went wrong? Why did it go wrong? And why did it go wrong *again ... and again ... and again ...?'*, then where next for how governments can best benefit from the use of digital technologies? In what direction should governments head? What is the next big step for public services, to help them improve and better meet users' needs? We need a new approach in government to drive and deliver genuine reform in the way it is structured and operates. To help answer such questions, in the next chapter we review how the role of digital outside of government has impacted organizational structures and the role of technology in our lives – to explore how government might begin to close the gap between expectation and implementation.

5

Establishing a New Normal – Remaking Public Services for the Digital Age

So What is 'Digital' Anyway?

Whilst government was preoccupied with its repeated efforts to move online, elsewhere we have seen the emergence of some truly digital organizations. These digital organizations use new business models and operating approaches to take advantage of opportunities created by societal and technological changes – such as increasingly available high-speed connectivity, access to huge amounts of real-time information on every aspect of the organization's operating activities, and the convenience of digital media delivery models. However, a bit like other popular terms such as 'Cloud', 'Open' and 'Transformation', we recognize that 'Digital' is at risk of becoming meaningless through overuse, abuse and misunderstanding. We intentionally therefore use digital as an umbrella term for organizational values and practices that capitalize on the opportunities presented by the internet age.

It is also essential to separate the concept of digital *technology* from digital *transformation*. Technology is typically an enabler of transformation, but 'being digital' is emphatically *not* principally about technology. Successful digital organizations are much broader in their understanding of the implications of digital transformation. They understand the necessity to optimize their supply chains for digital delivery, evolve their business models to meet the expectations of digitally connected communities, and develop operating models clustered around speed and adaptability of their execution environment. They work closely with their product and service consumers through practices exemplified by maxims such as 'show don't tell' and 'done is better than perfect'. The thinking that enables organizations to work well in this way often contrasts strongly with today's accepted best practice in government. Digital transformation therefore requires redesign and re-engineering on every level – people, process, technology and governance. Full, enterprise-wide digital transformation appears similar to that shown in Figure 5.1.

Taking this journey to digital transformation is not easy. In fact, achieving fully digital status is particularly difficult for organizations that share one or more of the following characteristics:

- complexity, leading to entanglement of systems and processes and decreasing change efficiency;
- historic (brownfield) organizations (ones that have been in existence for many years) where there may no longer be a clear view of original rationale behind processes and systems;
- significant compliance or security considerations perceived as a barrier to agility;
- long-term employee base with low new-technology and customer-facing skills;
- low levels of understanding of digital ethos amongst senior leaders;
- lock in to long-term, inflexible technology contracts.

Unfortunately for many public sector organizations, the above list may read like a thumbnail description of their current limitations and constraints.

The Four Layers of the Digital Organization

The reason that the characteristics above constitute such barriers to becoming digital is that there is an obvious *horizontal* not *vertical* orientation

FIG 5.1 The digital public sector organization

to the digital organization shown in Figure 5.1, involving reuse, sharing and commonality across historical silos. These are the characteristics that government will need to develop and foster.

From our experiences in the public and private sectors, a simplified framework for understanding the key shared elements of a digital organization has been invaluable. It helps to think of this horizontal orientation within the digital organization in terms of four horizontal layers, shown in Figure 5.2.

The top layer consists of the users: people, communities and clients – those setting the *expectations* for digitally enabled services. One way to describe the transformation required for digital at the 'people' level is to look at it as a transition from external control to internal drive, from 'command and control' to 'climate control'. The emphasis shifts from managing the people to managing the things that help or hinder them in delivering results. The most important output of people management ceases to be the direction of subordinates and becomes instead the fostering of an environment and culture of healthy, self-directed achievement: one where experts are empowered to put their expertise into practice.

The 'communities' part of the top layer in Figure 5.2 refers to the depth to which an organization can open its data and make it available for public

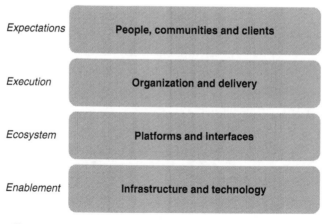

Expectations	**People, communities and clients**
Execution	**Organization and delivery**
Ecosystem	**Platforms and interfaces**
Enablement	**Infrastructure and technology**

FIG 5.2 / Four layers of digital

use. The more valuable that data is to users and developers, the more a community will form and more active engagement will follow as more value is derived from the data. To support this, datasets need to be made available in machine-readable formats, ideally in real time, direct from live systems or, if not, exported and refreshed when new data become available. Metadata, such as the information presented, collection method, timeliness, quality and other contextual information is crucial to allowing data consumers not only to understand available data, but to put them to appropriate use.

The 'client' part of the top layer in Figure 5.2 refers to the way that a digital organization is driven by the needs, requirements and feedback of its users (not its own imperatives). It's essential that the organization is designed around these needs and not its history – the convenience of current processes or the maintenance of the status quo. Figure 5.3 shows the order in which priorities and organizational effort should be focused to respond to the needs of users. Citizen needs and expectations will continue to evolve, driving enduring change in the services, capabilities and architecture needed to serve users.

However, simply implementing digital technology over traditional legacy processes and structures will not work: the last 20 or so years of 'online' government initiatives have demonstrated that eloquently. At the 'organization and delivery' layer of Figure 5.2, new, lighter-touch governance and assurance arrangements, a change to budgeting practices and flatter structures must be designed and implemented. These are a prerequisite for organizations moving quickly in their *execution*, responding flexibly to changed circumstances and pushing decision making and solution making further down the organization.

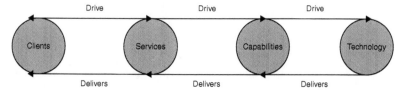

FIG 5.3 Digital drivers and delivery

The third layer in Figure 5.2 – 'platforms and interfaces' – is about creating an *ecosystem* of pre-built, reusable technology components as well as a marketplace of open integrations and innovative suppliers who are expert within that environment. Whilst digital organizations will still deploy some custom components and applications, the significant majority of basic and boilerplate functionality can be taken care of by adapting and reusing capabilities that are already available – either within the digital organization or elsewhere. This encourages the organization to think in terms of capabilities, business rules and components so that appropriate pre-built solutions can be used to accelerate delivery, allowing development effort to be prioritized and focused on business-specific needs. Governance needs to be able to support and enable the development of digital services, with governance of IT becoming the domain of public service management, who need to be able to gain and give assurance that investment generates value and reduces the risk of bad outcomes.

Finally, the fourth layer in Figure 5.2 – 'infrastructure and technology' – *enables* the others by providing the computing power and networking capability to support appropriately flexible, scalable and elastic solutions to fulfil business needs. As demand scales up and down, it is advantageous to correspondingly scale up and down with resource allocation, with cost determined by usage rather than fixed specifications under long-term inflexible contracts.

We recognize that these descriptions may not sound like or look like government in its current configuration – but, in a sense, that is rather our point. If governments are sincere about their aspirations to embrace digital, the implications are as profound as they seem.

User Empowerment through Digital

Digitization of service delivery in the private sector has spurred not just a technical revolution, but also a cultural shift in what people expect now in speed, accuracy and transparency of service delivery. Whereas people used to complete voluminous paper forms, which were then input manually by staff and processed by computers, consumers and citizens are now much more likely to input information directly into an online system through internet browsers and the growing plethora of mobile devices. Successful organizations such as Amazon encourage us to enter all the details required directly into their systems, allowing us to maintain and control our own data. As a result, we can check the status of any request, communicate with the service provider, and chat with other service users all with the click of a few buttons. In so doing, they have moved the cost of data maintenance and quality directly to us, in the process reducing their costs, bureaucracy and resourcing, and the complexity of their own operations. Government is well behind this curve.

One particular feature of the world of digitization, transparency and broader engagement is that the traditional model of 'doing it all yourself' – by letting outsourced or in-house teams build everything – has been increasingly replaced by a networked approach to assembling solutions from a variety of pre-existing components and services. Our digitally interconnected world means that organizations are now at the centre of a network of suppliers, consumers, employees, partners, analysts, competitors and various other stakeholders. As a result, the most envied and discussed organizations in the world are increasingly founded on open platforms, encouraging others to interact and innovate around them and form collaborative communities. Their ability to build and grow these ecosystems is fundamental to their success.

Below we highlight some of the biggest themes to have emerged over the past decade or so – from the speed of change to democratizing innovation.

The Speed of Change

Driven by the unprecedented interconnectivity of the internet, the proliferation of mobile devices and easy access to online services, the pace of change for most businesses is faster now than ever. A useful indicator of these pressures is the apparently unstoppable growth in online activities, which is well illustrated in a widely circulated infographic that examines the internet activity taking place in a typical 60-second time period.[1] This reveals that in an average 60-second period:

- 168 million e-mails were sent;
- 695,000 search queries took place on Google;
- US$219,000 of total payments were made on PayPal;
- 1,820 terabytes of data were created;
- 710 computers, 81 iPads and 925 iPhones were sold;
- ... and so on.

Business and technology leaders recognize that they cannot maintain existing practices if they want to prosper in this environment. Rather, they must respond to this accelerating pace of activity.

Management of Continuous Change

Traditional methods for co-ordinating and managing change (broadly defined as 'change management practices') involve a series of well-defined steps over a significant time period in which the change is understood, strategies for coping with the change are analysed, and supporting processes put in place to institutionalize the change into regular practice. Such traditional 'freeze–unfreeze–freeze' change models struggle to maintain relevance in today's fast-paced world, where changes are ongoing, fundamental and disruptive, the speed of adaptation to the change is critical, a wide variety of changes take place in parallel, or the environment in which the change is embedded moves too fast.

As a result, new change management practices are required, ones that better support rapid change scenarios. Consequently, we are witnessing a rebirth of change practices based on viewing change as a series of co-ordinated experiments. Such new practices will also need to be applied to public services and the agencies and organizations that run them as much as any other organization.

---

[1] Originally posted at GO-Globe.com.

New Citizens and New Expectations: The Impact of Mobile Technology

One particular pressure point for the adoption of more effective change management has been the growth of mobile technology and devices. Any successful organization must embrace this mobile-first, always-on world, and the freedom that mobile devices provide to participate in personal and business transactions regardless of where we are and what we are doing.

However, many organizations initially struggled to take advantage of mobile. The budget challenges encountered since the 2007 economic crisis have resulted in IT departments being unable to commit the necessary resources to manage disparate delivery channels for their services while dealing with a large backlog of mission-critical projects. Coupled with a lack of in-house skills to build efficient mobile services, the result has frequently been disappointing: limited delivery of custom mobile applications via long, complicated development cycles. These applications have been expensive to produce, and have largely failed to engage users with the enthusiasm accorded to many of the leading consumer-based applications, which have been built from the ground up for internet deployment and interaction by mobile devices.

A change of perspective was needed to break the status quo, and this materialized when organizations came to recognize that they no longer optimize decision making in terms of how they sell products and services. Buyers now place much greater priority on the experiences and outcomes enabled by these products and services. Priority is placed on improving the way products and services can be consumed, which accordingly becomes the focus of investment. For example, the user experience is significantly better if the right information is delivered to them at the right time, rather than overloading them with an endless stream of arbitrary real-time information that must be filtered, assessed and interpreted by each user. This form of journey mapping creates a focus on improving the user-centric experience, optimizing the user's activities across physical and digital touch points with the organization.

Offering greater connectivity and openness to a more diverse set of stakeholders is clearly one of the main strategic directions for many organizations. However, connectivity *per se* is not the aim. From a user perspective, the real benefit of a connected device is that it enables a different type of relationship with the people on both sides of that device. For the new generation of technology consumers, the expectations they have is that the technology is one link in a network that spans technology producers, other technology users and partners in an ecosystem of service providers. Remarkably, this expectation extends across a wide range of devices. Imagine, for example, a connected toothbrush that enables its user to improve communication with both their dentist (by automatically supplying usage data on brushing frequency and technique) and the toothbrush manufacturer (by logging performance data to improve the usability of the device). The user is placed in control of a relationship ecosystem focused on their needs, but which also brings significant benefits to the other participants too: this simple example provides just a small glimpse of the prize at hand for genuinely digital government.

Democratizing Innovation

Continuous innovation is increasingly essential to enable the creation of solutions that better meet users' needs, to develop channels that attract greater attention from the users served, and to reinvent supply chains to deliver more quickly, more cheaply and more effectively. But, what constitutes meaningful innovation in an existing 'brownfield' organization? To have real hope of meaningful improvements, the collaborative process from idea generation to solution delivery must be optimized, innovation practices enhanced to become flexible and repeatable, and leaders trained who are willing and able to lead teams in an innovation-focused interactive environment. In the past, innovation was slow and risky, and left to remote suppliers (if it happened at all). Today, there is an essential role for 'democratizing innovation' by establishing practices inside government that increase innovation speed while decreasing risk.

The focus in business is now on agility and openness. In much of the commercial world, consumers require organizations simultaneously to maintain a constant, open dialogue to monitor feedback and reactions to products and prototypes, whilst at the same time engaging in new forms of rapid producer–consumer partnerships such as co-creation, evolutionary design and micro-customization to ensure the business produces goods and services that its customers require at the speed necessary to maintain a market advantage. The goal is to deliver a rapid stream of new ideas to position the company as a leader in the vital knowledge-driven marketplace: governments now need to similarly improve the quality of public services by developing a more effective means of citizen feedback helping to inform and improve services – their quality, timeliness and cost-effectiveness.

However, substantial organizational and cultural obstacles need to be overcome if such innovations and insights about public services are to be brought into routine practice. Illustrations of the perils of these innovation challenges abound. For example, it has been estimated that possibly 80% of corporate innovations fail and only 10% of SMEs can sustain the innovation necessary to generate significant employment. In particular, *speed* is of the essence in introducing innovation: Intel Corporation, for instance, claims that 90% of the revenues the firm derives on the last day of the year are attributable to products that did not even exist on the first day of that same year.

Enablers of Change

Underpinning the above themes (and many more like them) is a set of core enablers common to the most successful digital organizations. We introduce these enablers briefly below since, as you will discover, we reference them repeatedly throughout the remainder of this book – and indeed we return to them in more detail in Part 3, as we believe that effective leadership requires an understanding of what lies below their surface.

Organizational structures and digital transformation

The move towards digital services is not just about using technology to deliver existing services on to a screen. Instead, it is about rapid innovation in solution delivery, a more agile organizational approach to decision making, a renewed emphasis on citizen-centric business models, and an architectural approach emphasizing openness to support shared service provision. The challenge in any digital transformation is to create organizations based on these kinds of adaptable behaviours: a set of characteristics in which the speed and effectiveness in adapting to changing conditions defines success.

Flexible architecture

Cloud computing has rapidly become a significant trend in the design and delivery of digital services. The main characteristic of a cloud computing approach is to deliver convenient, on-demand network access to a shared pool of configurable computing resources (such as networks, servers, storage, applications and services). The value of this approach is that it offers a great deal of flexibility to users of those resources. In particular, capabilities can be rapidly and elastically scaled-up when demands for those capabilities increase, and similarly they can be rapidly scaled-down when demand reduces.

The flexibility possible with cloud computing approaches is essential. Not only does this flexibility encourage dynamic relationships in the supply chain, it also provides much more explicit ways to look at infrastructure costs, to assign those costs to the role of each organization and team, and encourages delivery approaches more suited to today's highly diverse organizations.

Agile processes and practices

The long-standing challenges of traditional approaches to software development are moving organizations towards embracing agile software delivery techniques. Since the publication of the 'Manifesto for Agile Software Development' over a decade ago,[2] there has been widespread adoption of techniques that embody its key tenets. Agile practices are now the dominant approach in successful software delivery, yet have historically

---

[2] http://agilemanifesto.org/

been largely ignored in the public sector supply chain. However, these practices are not without their critics. Notably, agile delivery faces increasing pressure as software delivery moves from smaller co-located teams towards larger team structures involving a complex software supply chain of organizations in multiple locations – characteristics typical of a variety of public sector environments. In these situations the lighter weight management practices encouraged by agile software delivery approaches come face-to-face with the more extensive control structures inherent in any large-scale distributed software delivery effort.

The API economy, ecosystems and engagement models

APIs (application programming interfaces) effectively provide a specification for how software will expose a system's data and services – for example, how a system might enable someone using a mobile app to retrieve a full postal address after presenting the system's API with a postcode or zip code. The API acts as a control point between the system providing the service and those consuming it: the API provides a managed way both to enable access to data sources and to impose rules that guide and constrain how those data are accessed. API service consumers can take advantage of those services when constructing a new solution, so that delivery of a new capability by combing services assembled from several APIs becomes a faster, more predictable way to realize a solution. For example, someone developing a new mobile app might be able to use the APIs of several existing services to undertake some of the functions needed – such as reusing an existing address look-up service, existing authentication service and existing online payments service.

Summary: Characteristics of Digital Government

The last 20 years or so demonstrate why the benefits of digital government cannot be achieved by maintaining business as usual or merely by reprinting strategy documents with the same worthy political aspirations year after year. Technology will never deliver on its promise if it continues to be used merely as a 'bolt on' to traditional business practices, or to tinker at the edges of service design within current arbitrary organizational fiefdoms – to automate paper and the current way of doing things.

The real change is not about narrow definitions of online services or transactions or assisted digital. Rather, it encompasses the entire spectrum of public service culture, processes and systems in their entirety, not just a rebadging of old IT – although there is evidence that 'digital' is becoming a buzzword that masks exactly that. Digitizing government involves the redesign of public services, whether they are digitally delivered at their end point, or through a personal interaction delivered one-to-one in our homes. Digitally enabled public services have the potential to benefit everyone, from public sector workers through to those who are most excluded – the people marginalized and frustrated by the endless paperwork, broken processes and sterile computer systems that demoralize and dehumanize time and again. This is what digital government can fix – but only if the lessons are learned and the political will is there to tackle the more complex organizational and process issues that have long held back genuine reform, together with the entrenched interests with which any genuine reform inevitably conflicts. Let's be frank: digitizing government is revolutionary and will disrupt many cosy and long-established ways of organizing our public services – and unless we are prepared to engage in an honest, open discussion about how this will happen, and who will be affected by such changes, we will remain mired in the mistakes and extravagant waste of the past.

In this part of the book we have aimed to explore why government needs to move away from the failed approaches of the past: it needs to break the cycle of endless publication of strategies without clear mechanisms for delivery; to stop using technology merely to automate existing manual procedures and processes based on the movement of paper and because it is the *way it's always been done*; avoid the tendency for indiscriminate, undifferentiated outsourcing – and in particular the risks and problems of outsourcing elements that need to be part of government's own core operation; and challenge the lazy assumption that current organizational structures and processes are here to stay.

To see what is possible, we only need to turn to the best of the private sector: their focus on outcomes and how best they can be achieved rather than the maintenance of the status quo; the use of technology as part of a cultural shift away from functional business units and to restructure organizations around the processes that support services; the increased engagement of users, including enabling them to input, manage and control their own data; the need to recruit and maintain expert leadership, knowledge and oversight in-house; and the development of an open and competitive marketplace from which to choose suppliers, services and products.

These simple lessons are nothing new: a 1998 UK government planning document called for a wholesale transitioning from government's traditional silos to more horizontal, platform-based organizational structures, supported with the lifeblood of common information. If governments are sincere about moving beyond their much-repeated rhetoric, it is time to initiate the major reform programmes required, not merely continue tinkering on the edges.

Towards Reimagined Public Services and the Big Idea

In Part 2 and Part 3 we aim to provide an approach that combines the long-standing vision for better public services with a practical strategy for the next stage of reform. This is an agenda with the potential to deliver successful transformation and regeneration of the public service landscape: an agenda to deliver meaningful modernization of public services after more than two decades of failed political aspirations. But doing so will require not just a clear vision and direction – but a widespread understanding of how to make it happen and a robust political commitment to see it through.

2 The Big Idea

In Part 1, we reviewed the UK government's experience of trying to implement its long-standing political desire for public services to benefit from the use of technology. We found that, in common with many other governments, the UK experience for most of the past 20 years has been of multiple iterations of the same, long-standing political vision for improving public services, with little significant or sustained progress in delivering this on the ground. Instead, technology has been narrowly applied to automate existing processes, added to pre-existing, arbitrary organizational structures rather than being used as a catalyst for redesigning and improving services. We saw how this is in marked contrast to the way in which the best private sector businesses have successfully used new technology to create entirely new organizations, structures, systems, processes and business models that deliver services in compelling new ways.

Whilst there has been some recent, focused movement to tackle this historic malaise – in the UK, for example, through the work of the Government Digital Service (GDS) – government departments and agencies, and hence their services, remain largely based on inherited organizational structures and practices, siloed and inwardly focused. These departmental and agency silos are reflected in their use of technology, which is likewise largely vertically integrated in a series of separate silos, many of them providing similar capabilities. The legacy of indiscriminate outsourcing predominates, and public officials still often struggle to engage successfully with modern technology and smaller suppliers.

Finding the language in which to describe this wholesale reimagining and improvement of public services is difficult, although – as we have seen – there has been no shortage of attempts to do so in the policy announcements and publications of the past few decades. In this part, we therefore propose an agenda for a digitally enabled *real* transformation of our public services: nothing less than the chance to implement a radically better way of organizing and improving public services. An agenda that involves a wholesale shift in public resources away from the inherited way that services are operated and maintained now, to a world where public services are re-engineered and reimagined around citizens' needs. We do not pretend that this will be easy: to succeed, old organizations and institutions will need to change shape, or even disappear entirely.

In Part 2, we therefore focus on the role of *government* in delivering digital public services – what needs to happen to drive meaningful change and improvement. This involves two main elements:

- establishing the cultural framework (strategy and education);
- implementing a platform (delivery).

We then draw these together by considering the potential in local government.

6

Establishing the Cultural Framework

We describe in this book an approach to the design of public services that centres on citizens and the front-line employees who provide those services – not about digital as merely existing services delivered on a computer screen. To succeed, it will involve a strong political and leadership commitment to a meaningful untangling of the fractured services, systems, organizations and processes currently in place. This new approach to user-driven service design needs to be underpinned by a much better architecture – a set of digital building blocks that enable us to reforge public services around its users in much more flexible and relevant ways.

Almost all public services are enabled – and constrained – by back-office processes and transactions enshrined in technology: but what a shanty town architecture of technology it usually is. Current organizational structures and processes have often evolved over decades – even centuries – and are almost entirely hand-crafted using technology with no standard processes, and requiring armies of expensive repair personnel. Instead of using technology to redesign and improve our public services, we have built our technology *on top* of them, fossilizing their historic idiosyncrasies and making them even harder, and more expensive, to change. This is not conscious design – in fact, hardly any public services have ever been 'designed' in any meaningful sense of the word – and it is no one's fault: it is just the way it has happened. And this is the way things will continue if left unchecked.

This diagnosis explains the failure of previous responses, which were effectively back-to-front – they sought to achieve joined-up government by linking up *existing* vertical silos, rather than tackling and dismantling these silos to reimagine public services altogether. Over the past 20 years or so, this is why technology in this area has achieved so little and cost so much: it has been applied to solving the wrong problem and, in many cases, has made the situation worse, not better.

'Leaning' Government

Rather than start with the assumption that technology can help to automate and accelerate existing ways of doing things, prior to any update to changes in existing services, or the design and deployment of new services, a more fundamental series of questions needs to be answered. Instead of working within existing boundaries, government needs to consider the outcomes it intends to deliver and how best they might be achieved – rather than moving automatically into delivery of a particular solution based on the way things are currently done.

To do so, government needs to learn how to apply the lessons and practices of *lean* thinking: by 'lean' we mean the production-derived practice that, in this specific context, considers the expenditure of resources for any reason other than the direct creation of value for the citizen to be wasteful, and thus a target for elimination. So it will require a move away from inputs – meetings, paperwork, discussions, bureaucratic rivalries and the sheer frictional costs (in time and money) of current government organizational practices, systems and processes – into a resolute focus on outcomes: namely the most efficient and effective ways of delivering high-quality, timely and relevant services to citizens and businesses.

Let's use a simple example to illustrate what we mean as to how lean thinking might be effectively applied. In the UK, vehicle excise duty

(VED) has to be paid on an annual basis for every vehicle using public roads. Over recent years, this tax collection system has moved from a paper-based process to one that enables motorists to pay and renew their VED online. This system has been much lauded for being easy to use by developing some smart integration with the systems used by insurance companies (to validate that vehicles are also properly insured) and involves nearly 43 million transactions each year. The next step recently witnessed the removal of the paper disc currently sent to every motorist to put inside their windscreen to show that they have paid the tax – automatic number plate recognition systems long since made the paper disc a piece of theatre rather than necessity.

While this example demonstrates progress in digital delivery, digital transformation would also include a change in thinking to challenge the business models of the organizations involved. Lean alternatives to the current system that deliver the same outcome might include collecting the tax through a small premium on the price of petrol or diesel at garage pumps so that every time a driver refills their car they contribute towards the tax; or perhaps collection could be outsourced to the insurance companies, so that when drivers renew their vehicle insurance the VED is collected at the same time (in much the same way, for example, that employers collect the pay-as-you-earn (PAYE) tax from their employees on behalf of government through their payroll systems, or value added tax (VAT) is collected by retailers and other businesses). At a stroke, the additional 43 million annual VED transactions are removed, and with it a great deal of frictional inconvenience and associated organizational costs for citizens, businesses and government alike.

Could utility companies collect local taxes, payable per property? And what other vertically organized bureaucracies might usefully disappear via a similar sharing of revenue-collection transactional processes in this way? It is clear from these considerations that our thinking has much further to go. Whilst on the surface, therefore, VED appears as a story of successful modernization of an existing service, it is perhaps successful in the same way that Blockbuster video rentals was being 'successful' whilst Netflix and others came along and eventually ate its business by changing the rules of the game (moving film to streaming downloads rather than boxes of DVDs in a store). If government is concerned about the primary outcome – ensuring that every vehicle on the roads in the UK has paid tax – it could use lean principles to consider how best this might be achieved: developing and maintaining a system that requires 43 million citizens and businesses a year to transact with it just to pay this tax is not the only option.

The wider point we are making here is of course not about taxing vehicles, but about the *assumptions* that often seem to be made when public services are being considered for automation. The adoption of lean principles within government – something that appears to remain almost entirely absent – would ensure that robust consideration is given to examining all possible ways of achieving the desired outcomes in the most painless and least expensive way, rather than assuming that services have to carry on as they currently are merely because '*that's the way they have always been done*' – and that the role of technology is merely to help rub off some of the rough edges of those services. Advances in digital technology have opened up a huge set of options not just to speed up what is done now, but for redesigning the entire process. Lean needs to become an important and mandatory process in helping develop a wider cultural framework for truly digitizing government. It is only after the objectivity of a lean assessment has been completed that attention should turn to the most appropriate architecture to underpin the service and how it will be delivered.

Understanding how the Various Moving Parts Work *Together*

Just as one would expect a building or machine with no architectural blueprint to operate poorly, an organization with no common architecture detailing the relationship between its moving parts – mental, as well as physical – works at best sub-optimally, and at worst is dysfunctional. So here we discuss architecture in some detail: it is important.

Unlike houses or machines, which are relatively self-contained in their operation, organizations work more organically. In particular, they do different things, differently, with different people (supporting a range of different citizen relationships, different supplier relationships, different regulatory relationships, and so on). This observation is even truer of government organizations, because in addition to this complexity, government departments need to work effectively with one another. They need to do this, primarily, to deliver services that work effectively together in a joined-up way.

In criminal justice, for example, we need to join up policing with the Crown Prosecution Service, with the Courts Service, with the Prison Service, with the Probation Service, with Housing Services, with Social Services. Yet the consequences of the failure to design these services together in a joined-up way around those convicted of an offence are widely reported – and numerous attempts to use technology to overcome this poor, multi-organizational design to provide 'joined-up justice', such as the notorious Libra system (a case management system for use in magistrates' courts), have created huge costs with little benefit.

However, in addition to working effectively (joining up services around the citizen), government organizations also need to work efficiently. Although we have thousands of such organizations in the UK, they all have the same source of funding: the UK taxpayer. It therefore makes little sense for each of these organizations to procure their needs independently – as if all of their revenues came from independent, competitive sources. Although this might appear logical (and indeed be convenient) at the level of the individual organization managing its own fiefdom, it makes no sense at all from the perspective of a citizen using, and paying for, these services.

From an architectural point of view it would therefore be ideal for both effectiveness and efficiency if there were a clearer definition and understanding of the internal workings of our *individual* government organizations, as well as about how they all work *together*. Not some sort of egotistical, top-down masterplan: the pace of legislative, social, technological, economic and organizational change precludes any such top-down dreaming. Instead, it requires an ongoing dialogue between people within each of our organizations with a grasp of the needs of those they are there to serve and a general set of principles about how *all* public organizations will evolve, over time, so as to converge on more effective (better), and efficient (cheaper), ways of delivering public services. Individually, these organizations may provide different services, to different people, in different ways and will continue to require different business models. However, if we can start to agree across government on the underlying principles on which all of these organizations will evolve their business models, we will succeed in building a less brittle, more organically co-operative public system.

When we talk about architecture therefore we are speaking less of a thing (such as a plan or document) than of a clearly defined, communicated and widely understood set of underlying principles flowing through each of our differently evolving public organizations like DNA. Just as biological DNA rewards some behaviours and penalizes others within an ecosystem, so too will a set of common principles – expressed differently in different organizations, but operating in relation to the whole.

For example, if a set of common behaviours has evolved to standardize a particular activity (checking a citizen's identity, for example), then should someone else choose to operate a bespoke, idiosyncratic method for doing this within their own organization they will quickly become conspicuous in both their ineffectiveness (they won't be able to share information easily with other organizations) as well as their inefficiency (it will cost them much more to continue to do it this way and will also be more inconvenient to citizens, who will have to deal with a separate process from the one they encounter elsewhere). Such a waste of resource and self-indulgent effort – pointlessly duplicating something that already exists – will become progressively non-viable in evolutionary terms.

Open Architecture

Part of the cultural change in public services will require exploiting the move towards becoming open – by which we mean the movement that spans everything from open standards to open source software to open architecture.

UNDERSTANDING OPEN STANDARDS

The open model is starting to grow out of its traditional roots in hi-tech (think Amazon and Google's Android) and research and development (R&D) innovation (think crowd-sourced success stories from YouTube), and is now knocking at the door of almost everyone. As the open model grows, it is beginning to challenge the commercial viability of traditionally organized corporate functions such as finance and HR, which, whether outsourced or insourced, appear increasingly expensive as they ignore the emerging economics of doing things using common standards.

Open standards increasingly allow a dis-integration of traditionally integrated business functions and technologies into discrete components (think automotive industry). In turn, this allows you to standardize components more cheaply as commodities – high volume, low margin. They are not to be confused with 'open source', which is freely available software.

If government can move away from its traditional, department-based, siloed design, and start to cluster similar components together, it will take massive commercial advantage of its unique scale as a volume purchaser to create platforms around which suppliers of many different kinds will innovate, much more cheaply.

In an open marketplace, those who are prepared to componentize and standardize their businesses win in a number of ways over those who insist on maintaining an integrated, 'bespoke' way of doing things.

First, they free themselves from long-term, monolithic outsourcing/licensing contracts involving entire functions such as finance or HR, in which innovative activity usually remains frozen within contractual service levels for the lifetime of the contract: in other words, they become more nimble and flexible.

Second, by separating out those components that are standard and low risk, and which should be purchased as a utility or even consumed for free, there are major savings to be realized across the organization. For example, although you might previously have thought of 'finance' as a division to be outsourced, several components, such as 'payments', 'print services' and 'accounts receivable', are increasingly available as utility commodities that can be consumed like water, or electricity, via the cloud. Others – such as the desktop – are already following.

Third, and perhaps best of all, an open, component-based view of government offers unprecedented opportunities to build and deliver new services to customers, by literally reassembling or swapping out components like interoperable cassettes. For example, I can set up a fully functional outlet for, say, delivery of social services in a morning – and run this out of a library building, or a school after hours, by assembling a combination of standard components that include case management, HR and mobile IT. Such agility would have been unthinkable even five years ago.

As with the death of the old record industry – as new, digitally enabled ways of distributing and consuming music came along – the development and consumption of software is undergoing an irreversible shift towards a new business and commercial model enabled by technology, but where technology *per se* is increasingly unimportant. The best digital organizations have adopted open approaches and its associated philosophy as a core part of their organizational and technical culture. In a government context, the current battle is about whether government organizations will continue to be closed – bespoke, idiosyncratic, traditionally defined and non-organically related – or whether they will start to share much more, working more effectively and efficiently together as part of an organic whole. The move towards open standards battle is thus fundamentally about putting in place some of the building blocks for a new, open, architecture: about the future design of government itself and its ability to adapt and reconfigure itself without externally imposed constraints.

Figure 6.1 illustrates how government's traditional approach has situated itself in entirely the wrong quadrant to take advantage of this major industry shift.

The left-hand side of Figure 6.1 illustrates that by standardizing on the components of its plumbing in the upper-left quadrant ('business logic' and 'open technical standards'), government can start to be open (agnostic and plural) in its approach to technology, suppliers and commercial arrangements – the lower-left quadrant. This is like saying, 'We want a service that achieves certain outputs, and complies with certain open standards so we can switch easily. Providing you achieve these to the required standard, we don't care how you do it, or what sort of supplier you are.'

We have called this left-hand side the 'utility model' because it involves consolidating demand and standardizing the way in which these elements will be consumed across government. In other words, many of the things that government buys we can start to treat like a utility: a price-sensitive commodity to be consumed as and when we need it, turned on and off like a tap. Such an approach places government in a position of commercial

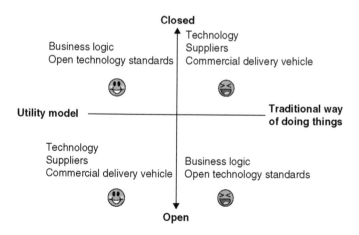

FIG 6.1 / Basic principles of open architecture

strength, exercising choice regarding technology, suppliers and the most appropriate commercial vehicle for services.

Compare this open architecture scenario with the right-hand side of Figure 6.1 – the 'traditional way of doing things'. This shows instead that government has generally maintained exactly the opposite arrangement, standardizing on bespoke technology, a handful of select suppliers, and uncompetitive commercial vehicles – for example, restrictive frameworks and constrained outsourcing contracts. This is like saying, 'We have standardized on company X's products and standards; we therefore purchase from company X; and we have a long-term licensing agreement with company X – and will adapt our own business logic and standards to fit their service.' No wonder government IT often became a byword for expensive, and inadequate, systems: once locked in to such a model, it becomes prohibitively expensive and complex for government to evolve and change. Within the current arrangements (the top-right quadrant of Figure 6.1), government is purchasing (technology) inputs rather than (service) outputs: it becomes locked in to proprietary standards and processes controlled by the supplier, weakening its commercial position.

This analysis may at first appear somewhat abstract. However, such thinking has real, tangible impact on how an organization operates. For example, one of the largest UK government departments has over 100 employees assigned to managing just one single software supplier who, ironically, has effectively been subcontracted to do their jobs for them via an outsourcing contract. The focus is in the wrong place – on technology, suppliers and contracts: in other words, inputs and overheads, not services for citizens. Our four quadrants show that achievement of an open architecture within government requires a significant – and doubtless painful – policy shift from the present situation. It encapsulates the only *real* transformation in town: that of the business model, and supporting architecture (the plumbing), of government. This is *real reform*, not the tinkering around the edges and throwing expensive IT at a problem that has characterized most government reform discussions to date.

In summary, government needs to say, 'We will provide certain common business outcomes (business logic) in a certain way so that they join up with everything else (open technology standards) from now on, regardless of who we are.' In turn, the very activity of government getting its act together, in volume, will create a platform for various people (others within government, citizens, large *and small* suppliers, third sector) to invest and innovate. This represents a major, and challenging, shift in the way government thinks and operates. Of course, government will need to evolve new governance mechanisms capable of coping with multi-supplier consumption models, based on compliance with open standards and delivery against service level agreements (SLAs). Models to consider in this respect are the utility companies, which also need to comply with regulatory standards regimes as well as delivery against SLAs.

Example: Replacing Silos with Component Reuse across Government

Let's dig a little deeper into what this means: it is important. Mark Foden of Foden Grealy Ltd, the change management consultants, has provided a helpful way of conceptualizing the way in which government plumbing – its technical architecture – needs to change, and why it needs to change at a pan-government level. In his four-minute YouTube video, 'The Gubbins of Government',[1] Mark begins with a picture of the current, siloed architecture of people, processes and technology within government, as shown in Figure 6.2.

Figure 6.2 shows how each department or service has its own entirely separate architecture, in which everything is treated in a bespoke or 'special' way. Each organization provides a separate, standalone service directly to the citizen (pensions, tax, driving licences, passports, and so on). Although this is of course a simplification, we can immediately see that it is a valid representation of the current model of public services – none of

---

[1] http://bit.ly/gubbinsvideo

FIG 6.2 / Mark Foden's government silos

which have been designed around the citizen, but merely around that of the providing organization.

Against this current, siloed architecture (which has never really been designed or architected in any meaningful sense, but merely blindly evolved), Mark sets out an alternative, pan-government architecture, divided into three layers (Figure 6.3). The first part, which he terms 'levers and dials', refers to those parts of the state with which citizens transact. Levers and dials comprise things such as websites, mobile apps, paper forms and telephone. We can immediately see that these have become standardized in the architecture, via common front ends such as the UK government's GOV.UK website. So whether we are talking about pensions, tax, driving licences, passports, or many, many other kinds of service, *all* government organizations use the same sorts of front ends instead of (re)inventing – and spending precious resources – on their own.

The second layer, which Mark terms 'gubbins', comprises two types: 'specific gubbins' (such as calculating tax or welfare, or printing passports) and 'common gubbins' (activities that we find across most government silos, such as collecting or paying money, or checking identity).

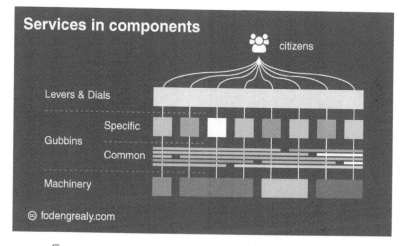

Services in components

Levers & Dials

Specific

Gubbins

Common

Machinery

☺ fodengrealy.com

citizens

FIG 6.3 / Open architecture involving reuse of components across government

It is the separation of these two types of 'gubbins' that forms the clever part.

In standardizing 'common gubbins', departments will benefit from three efficiencies: from the ability to share components (reducing cost); the ability to drive down the cost of these standardized components by purchasing them at volume (reducing cost again); and from the ability to swap out components easily when a better/cheaper one comes along, improving its competitive position (reducing cost even further). The citizen will benefit from government's ability to work more seamlessly, diverting resources away from wasteful internal administration and massively duplicated technology and resources, and into better service delivery, maximizing effectiveness.

Finally the third layer, 'machinery', contains the commodity elements: printing presses, post, computer servers and other hardware, data storage, networks, power, and so on. Because these are now a commodity readily available in the marketplace, there is even less excuse for government to effectively ignore this available commodity supply by continuing to own and provide them multiple times. Another way to consider this is to think about one of our most ubiquitous commodities: electricity. Were you to decide to run your own special voltage of 300v in your house instead of the UK's national standard 230v (with small tolerances either side of this), you would need to generate your own electricity using your own power station, instead of consuming power from the national grid like everyone else. This would be absurd, since it is obviously more expensive and less reliable than simply consuming a standard voltage from the national grid. But the problem gets worse: not only would you need to run your own power station – but you would also need to commission suppliers to build every appliance for your house on a bespoke basis, since there are no readily available appliances that run on 300v. You would also need to maintain and supply them with scarce and increasingly expensive spare parts – and would become quickly dependent on those few specialist systems integrators who understood the 'special' and one-off way in which they worked, who would charge accordingly. In fact, we can see how the adoption of common electricity standards has created a *platform* that underpins the activities of a vast and diverse industry. Government now needs to capitalize upon the same dynamic in the IT world.

We freely acknowledge that this transition will be disruptive and complex for governments to achieve for a wide variety of reasons – including the legacy of systems and processes already in place, the accretion of often idiosyncratic legislation over time embodied in those systems and in the related specialized knowledge retained by public officials, the complex inheritance of contracts and suppliers, the funding models involved (which will of necessity cut across traditional departmental funding silos), the decoupling of business and technology components required, the discipline of open technical standards and interfaces, and the skills and capabilities required to lead and deliver the results desired.

And yet – returning to the commodity machinery in Mark Foden's architecture – we can see that owning and running hundreds of bespoke versions of these in government silos appears equally absurd and will ultimately become unsustainable. Recalling our electricity example above, we can also appreciate that if the machinery (power station) is bespoke, then so too will be all the 'gubbins' and 'levers and dials' (appliances) that sit on top of it. If we would find it difficult to justify, or afford, an expensive bespoke, one-off suit when there is a ready market providing off-the-peg suits, then why should the situation be any different for the way we design, build and operate our public services? Commissioning bespoke luxury items when standard alternatives are readily available is an indulgent form of consumption undertaken from time to time by people using their own money – but surely not by those who claim to be serving others? If efficient modern private organizations consume from the commodity market, why should government be any different?

We believe it is not so much a question of *whether* government has to make this transition so much as a question of *when* it will recognize the need to do so – and commit the leadership, political capital and resources necessary to make it happen.

Innovate–Leverage–Commoditize (ILC)

We have looked at the initial lean-based decision process – relentlessly focused on how best to achieve the desired outcome – and examined Mark Foden's insightful explanation of how we need to approach the architecture required. With these stages successfully navigated, the question of how best to deliver the required service can be examined.

The three most obvious problems are: (a) How do we decide what should be provided as a commodity component and a common service? (b) Are components static – in other words, can specific gubbins become common gubbins? (c) How should we treat components?

The temptation when trying to determine whether a component is a commodity and suitable for a common service is to simply turn to Everett Rogers's diffusion curves. Described in Rogers's 1962 book *The Diffusion of Innovation*, these S-shaped curves explain how any activity spreads in society from early adopters to laggards. Hence it is tempting to argue that once laggards start to adopt something it must be common.

The problem is which S-curve do you use? For example, when something such as the phone appears, then you not only get diffusion of the phone but the release of ever-improving models of the phone. Each version has its own S-curve, which can differ in size of market and the time taken to spread. To illustrate this problem, Figure 6.4 provides five separate diffusion curves for an evolving activity from an early released product (A1) through various improvements (A2 to A5).

Each diffusion curve has an S-curve shape and achieves 100% adoption in its applicable market. But the size of the applicable markets and the timespan for diffusion is different between each curve. Hence when simply saying 'Ah, once the laggards adopt it, then it is common', then the problem becomes: which laggards do we mean? The laggards for A1 or the laggards for A5? When examining multiple waves of diffusion for an evolving product/service – such as the telephone, electricity or computing – we can comfortably state that as each improvement appears then the act becomes more ubiquitous and more mature. But can we measure this?

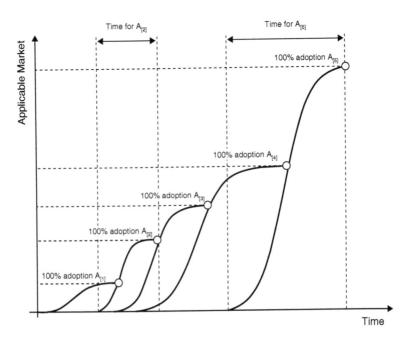

FIG 6.4 Diffusion of improving versions of an activity (courtesy of Simon Wardley)

The problem is one of understanding. When we take something that is mature, such as a brick, it is relatively easy for everyone to agree that a brick is a commodity. However, when we examine something that is relatively immature, such as a smartphone, then disagreement occurs over whether it is an innovation, or a product – or somewhere in-between. This issue can be visualized through a Stacey Matrix, a method of examining how groups interact based upon whether there exists agreement on what something is and how well understood it is (for example, how far or close to certainty we are). In the case of something mature, then all members tend to have experience of it (as in we are all certain of what it is) and there is a common and shared model of understanding: agreeing that a brick is a commodity, for example, is relatively simple. In the case of the smartphone, then neither of these two conditions exist – and hence agreement is fraught and complex.

Given that we cannot simply say 'once laggards adopt it then it is common', because we don't know which laggards to look for, and given we cannot simply say 'once it is mature', because groups will disagree about this as well – then do we have any way of determining whether something should be provided as a common component?

The trick is to examine both the ubiquity of something and the certainty issue highlighted in the Stacey Matrix. In 2007, whilst examining a previously identified pattern of evolution in business, Simon Wardley (a researcher for CSC's Leading Edge Forum) collated over 6000 publications related to various activities. He noted a recurring pattern in the style of publications, illustrated in Figure 6.5. In the early stages of an act, publications tend to refer to the wonder (for example, the wonder of radio). This would be followed by publications discussing building, construction and awareness (e.g. how to build your own radio set). Then the nature of publication would turn to maintenance, operations and feature differentiation between different examples, followed by simple guides for use (e.g. the *Radio Times*).

Wardley used the Type II and Type III publications to determine a certainty axis and then compared a large number of activities historically over

Type	I	II (key)	III (key)	IV
Publication Type	Refer to the **wonder of the thing,** described in terms of impact	Refer to **building, construction and awareness**	Refer to **operation, maintenance and feature differences** between different examples	**Dominated by use** i.e. what is built with this or on top of this including guides for maximizing use.
Measure		Volume	Volume	

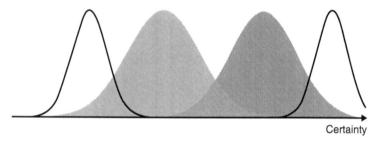

Certainty

FIG 6.5 Changes of publication type as an act matures (courtesy of Simon Wardley)

ubiquity (i.e. how widespread something was) versus certainty (i.e. how well understood something was). The result was also an S-shaped curve, which demonstrated a relationship between the ubiquity of an act and certainty (i.e. how mature and how well understood it is). Furthermore, by examining the different types of publications at various stages of the graph we can finally see how activities evolve, as illustrated in Figure 6.6.

In Figure 6.6, Wardley showed that for transactions, practices, data, and knowledge itself, the genesis of something is followed by custom builds and bespoking. It then becomes ubiquitous and well defined enough for products/services to appear where the concern becomes more with maintenance, operation and feature differentiation. Eventually the product/service becomes so widespread and well defined that it is more of a commodity and the concern is simply with use.

This model's usefulness lies in its ability to provide us with a way of classifying what should be 'common gubbins' – the commodity, the

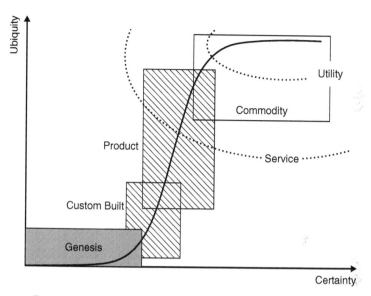

FIG 6.6 A pattern for evolution (courtesy of Simon Wardley)

best practice, the modelled and the universally accepted – as well as a mechanism for understanding how the novel and often 'specific gubbins' evolves to become common. What drives this process of evolution was later demonstrated to be simple competition – both supply and demand side: any class of thing (activity, practice, data or knowledge) where competition exists will follow the path.

The model also explains how we should treat things. Looking again at Figure 6.5, all the Type I classes exhibit common properties. They are novel, constantly changing, poorly understood, unpredictable, and sources of differential and future value. Appropriate techniques for managing this type include experimentation, a willingness to fail and agile methodologies. This 'uncharted space' of the novel, un-modelled, concept and genesis is what is commonly considered to be *innovation*.

However, the Type IV classes also exhibit common properties. They are common, well defined, measured, predictable, cost of doing business, tend towards low margin, and repeated. Appropriate techniques for managing this type include volume operations and methods such as Six Sigma. This industrialized space of the commodity, best practice, the modelled, and the universally accepted is what is commonly considered to be *commoditized*.

What should be noted is that any large organization or system will contain many components – some of which are innovations, and others that are commodities. Furthermore, the situation is not static, because supply-side and demand-side competition will drive components from innovation to commodity. In between these two extremes also exist components in a transitional state, in flux from innovation to commodity.

It is this recognition of how change occurs that led to the foundation of the innovate–leverage–commoditize (ILC) framework, developed by Simon Wardley with one of the authors. ILC helps break down complex systems into their component elements and considers how these might best be provided: Figure 6.7 encapsulates the principle of just such a framework. It helps government gain commercial advantage by developing a better

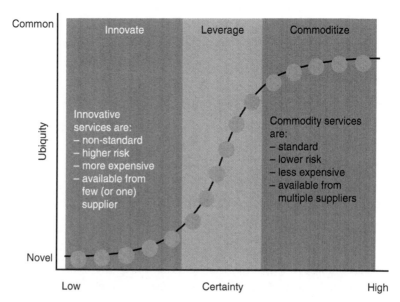

FIG 6.7 / The 'innovate–leverage–commoditize' (ILC) curve

understanding of the critical relationship between innovation and commodity, and offers a robust methodology for applying a set of common principles consistently across all architectural and commercial decisions within government.

The innovate–leverage–commoditize (ILC) curve makes two related points about the achievement of digital public services based on an open architecture. First, it shows that as common standards, business logic and resulting platforms are developed and shared across government we can expect to see costs decrease as services become less risky and more standard (commoditized: think ballpoint pens) and procured via utility commercial models – moving from bottom left to top right of the innovation curve. Second, and anticipating our discussion in Chapter 7 of the importance of platforms in driving innovation in Google's innovation ecosystem, it reminds us that such platforms are not needed merely to reduce cost: they are also required to incentivize and enable innovation. Taken together, these two points are a reminder that an open architecture is both a technical platform *and* a commercial model – promoting continuous, accelerated sharing of new services and supporting technology across government.

On the left of the figure, delivery of joined-up services to meet ever-changing legislative and citizen needs requires ongoing, multiple innovations, supported with a platform of open application interfaces, publicly available data and ring-fenced innovation funding, increasingly taking the form of rapid, iterative prototypes – where the cost of failure, development time and costs can be reduced dramatically whilst the rate of innovation in public services can be accelerated from months to days, significantly reducing development costs.

As pointed out by Wardley, many of the most successful organizations to develop ecosystems around core platforms and standards monitor new innovations and their reception by users. They then amalgamate those that appear successful into their core offerings: the middle column of Figure 6.7 reflects this process. It's the form of crowdsourcing practised by the standardized development platforms of Google, discussed in Chapter 7, as well as by others who encourage innovation around their platform: Facebook, for example, who provide an open platform around which an entire ecosystem of third-party companies develop; and Sales Force.com, who encourage direct customer engagement and innovation through IdeaExchange.

In these examples, new services (innovation) are developed into the platform and made available to other users (leveraged) – which in turn can often lead to wholesale integration and development of the underlying platform (commoditized). Government needs to build capability in the skills and approaches required to leverage successful innovations, and standardize these so that they can be delivered cheaply and efficiently at volume. To do so will require mature service and business management approaches such as ITIL (Information Technology Infrastructure Library) and Six Sigma, allowing specification, agreement and monitoring of service quality between commissioning and supply organizations.

Finally, the right-hand column of Figure 6.7 acknowledges the need to preserve a resolute focus on managing central, core platforms and services as commodities. In turn, this requires a separation of high-risk, bespoke activities from low-risk, commodity activities, ensuring that volume procurements such as outsourcing are used only for known commodities. As a matter of policy, there should be no outsourcing of undifferentiated services that have not had such components separated out beforehand, since innovations involving low certainty and ubiquity as shown in Figure 6.7 are likely to be more 'bespoke' and therefore expensive. In turn, ensuring that services are standardized and commoditized before being purchased in volume both creates a platform for innovation, as well as providing funding for innovation.

For the ILC dynamic to work, we need different skills within government: the skills and methodologies needed to foster innovation (on the left); those needed to identify promising applications and services and standardize, or leverage, these across government (middle); and those required to drive volume purchasing of commodities (right). This is summarized in Figure 6.8.

We acknowledge that these changes constitute a major, and painful, shift from the current modes of service conception and delivery. Given

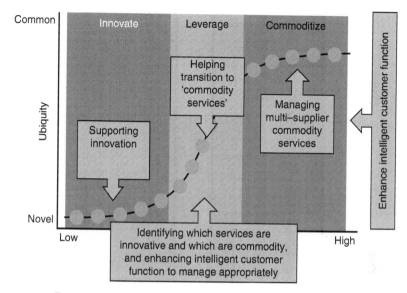

FIG 6.8 / New ILC skills needed within government

the risk-averse culture within government departments, and recalling the earlier discussion about culture change, a further, important component is therefore needed within the ILC model in order to drive open architecture behaviours: the concept of total cost of ownership (TCO). By establishing routine and frequent open (public) visibility of TCO across government for comparable applications and services, which should include full life-cycle costing (including the cost of exit, to help prevent lock-in to an incumbent supplier), it will become increasingly unsustainable for a department to insist on procuring a high-cost, bespoke service that perpetuates its legacy bureaucracy rather than modernizing it to take advantage of a low-cost, standard service.

A few more forward-thinking government bodies – for example the UK's Essex County Council – are already starting to make use of TCO as an explicit tool for driving a gradual organizational transition to a more open, commissioning-based operating model. If applied well, appropriate, rigorous, independent and transparent (openly published) TCO benchmarking by experienced practitioners will play a crucial role in driving acceptance of standardized 'utility' services by government – displacing the expensive indulgence of specifying bespoke, department-specific requirements.

But Who Sets the Standards? 'Tight-loose' in Action

The ILC framework recognizes the way in which the utility economics of open standards and cheap connectivity will increasingly determine how government moves to an era of digital public management. Not only is the achievement of joined-up services dependent on continuing innovation by an open marketplace delivered by the platform/innovation model (as opposed to large outsourcing contracts) – but it must also ensure it is in a position to take advantage of utility commercial models as these emerge.

An open architecture is characterized by a centralization/decentralization dialectic involving, on the one hand, a tight central mandation of open standards and interfaces by a core function that is positioned to leverage the innovation and cost advantages of, on the other hand, a plural, disaggregated delivery marketplace. The principles of such a dual approach have been acknowledged in the rhetoric of the UK Coalition government, with the Cabinet Office Minister's commitment to a strategy described as 'tight-loose'. This means taking strong central control over common, strategic elements such as communications, headcount, property, infrastructure and commodity procurement. Everything else is pushed out as close as possible to the edge – to the front line – to ensure the needs of citizens are met in the most appropriate and locally responsive way. Change of this magnitude requires a well-designed and executed pincer movement: highly capable, visionary and forceful top-down digitally competent leadership working hand-in-glove with the bottom-up, citizen-centric redesign of services.

It is this balance of a tight central core and a disaggregated, plural delivery marketplace that makes the platform/innovation model truly open. The role of government within this model is one of an intelligent enabler whose

role is to set the overriding framework across strategy, architecture, procurement and, especially, governance, in ensuring a continuance of public
service values. In this view, the question as to whether services themselves
are best delivered by public sector, private sector, third sector, mutuals,
hybrids of these, or by citizens themselves, will be determined increasingly
by the environment established by government at the centre, set against
the evolving ability – and willingness – of these actors to engage with
these incentives. Achieving this model can be seen, in simple terms, as the
dis-integration of tightly integrated, proprietary systems traditionally organized around the supplier and service provider – and their *reaggregation*, in
the form of services, around the citizen in such a way as to take advantage
of the utility economics of a rapidly evolving services marketplace.

The availability and mandated use of common infrastructure is critical to
this approach. This applies to the business as well as to the technology.
In addition to open *technical* standards governing data and interoperability, and clear *governance* standards enshrining public service values,
it is essential, as we have seen during our discussion of the quadrants in
Figure 6.1, that government converges progressively on *standard business
logic* – since standard processes themselves can become a commodity platform around which technology suppliers will invest, increasing innovation
and driving down cost. An example of such standard business logic is the
recently established Shared Service Centres, which reduce the plethora of
enterprise resource planning (ERP) contracts within the UK government
to two standard services provided by competing suppliers.

Whilst Shared Service Centres are a great start because they encourage
government to adopt standard processes where possible, they also risk a
new form of dependency, or lock-in, because ultimately they decouple
these services from the evolving, more transparent international marketplace of innovation and commoditization. A more significant step in the
longer term would be to adopt a set of core, simple back-office processes
across government around which the market will supply a range of increasingly cheap ERP modules that could eventually be rented by the hour
through a cloud-based delivery model with little to no vendor lock-in –
and potentially switched at will.

chapter 7

Implementing a Mature Platform

So What Is, and Isn't, a Platform?

We have briefly already touched upon the essential role of platforms. It's worth spending a bit more time on this discussion: the concept is an important part of achieving an open architecture. But we need to be precise in our use of the term, since the word 'platform' tends to get used (and abused) in different ways in different contexts. Let's begin with a review of several viewpoints of how different characteristics of platforms can help us understand the breadth of their application.

In an extensive study of platforms, London School of Economics (LSE) academic Annabelle Gawer has proposed an evolutionary model that differentiates among the various target communities for the platform. It comprises three stages:

- First, 'internal platforms': a set of subsystems and interfaces internal to the organization that have been intentionally planned and developed to form a common structure from which a stream of derivative products can be efficiently developed and produced (e.g. Sony's Walkman, Hewlett-Packard's modular printer components, Rolls-Royce's family of engines) – saving fixed costs, benefiting from component reuse and enabling flexibility.

- Second, 'supply chain platforms': which replicate these benefits across interfaces amongst *different* organizations within a supply chain – most notably, the automotive industry: for example, the Renault-Nissan alliance that developed a common platform for the Renault Clio and the Nissan Micra.

- Third, 'industry platforms': *'products, services or technologies that are developed by one or several firms, and which serve as foundations upon which other firms can build complementary products, services or technologies'*, such as Microsoft's Windows operating system, Intel microprocessors, Apple's iPod and iPhone, the internet, payment cards and fuel cell automotive technology.

In contrast, Tim O'Reilly has arrived at the notion of 'government as a platform', or GaaP, by focusing more on the basic values that a platform offers to consumers (in this case, citizens). It's worth reproducing in its entirety an example drawn from his chapter on GaaP in Lathrop and Ruma's 2010 book, *Open Government*, since it exemplifies the sort of options we face for the future of public services. O'Reilly first talks about 'vending machine government', where *'we pay our taxes, we expect services. And when we don't get what we expect, our "participation" is limited to protest – shaking the vending machine. Collective action has been watered down to collective complaint.'* He then contrasts it with:

> the idea of government as a platform [which] applies to every aspect of the government's role in society. For example, the Federal-Aid Highway Act of 1956, which committed the United States to building an interstate highway system, was a triumph of platform thinking, a key investment in facilities that had a huge economic and social multiplier effect. Though government builds the network of roads that tie our cities together, it does not operate the factories, farms, and businesses that use that network: that opportunity is afforded to 'we the people.' Government does set policies for the use of those roads, regulating interstate commerce, levying gasoline taxes and fees on heavy vehicles that damage the roads, setting and policing speed limits, specifying criteria for the safety of bridges, tunnels, and even vehicles that travel on the roads, and performing many other responsibilities appropriate to a 'platform provider'.

The key to all of these platform models is that they create marketplaces amongst distinct groups of users. In particular, two-sided (or more generally, multi-sided) markets are markets in which platforms offer interaction services to two (or several) categories of end users – such as eBay, Amazon and iTunes. A two-sided market serves two distinct categories of users, where each depends on the other in some important way, and whose joint participation makes the platform more valuable to each other.

In certain areas, government departments have used commodity markets for some time – such as energy, fuel, paper, bricks, pens: in fact anything that can be consumed in standard units across departments, and hence procured in volume, driving down costs. These things are all physical and benefit from the widespread acceptance that they can be *consumed in the same way everywhere*. This is the reason that they work as commodities: because we all use these commodities in the same, standardized way everywhere, we create a large market of consumers – and, in turn, this large market of consumers provides a powerful incentive for investment by suppliers. Finally, because of the size of the resulting market, investors will compete with one another to innovate, and to drive down cost: commodities are generally price sensitive. The *'platform'* underpinning all this activity is the standardized use. This is why our own understanding of platform places, if anything, even greater emphasis than O'Reilly on the role of open standards in bringing about common behaviours. In fact, we would argue that Gawer's platforms typology requires a fourth kind of platform:

- Fourth, 'open platforms': *'Freely available, standard definitions of service outcomes, processes, or technology that encourage multiple users to converge on utility consumption of services based on these definitions – which in turn encourages suppliers to innovate around these commodities.'* For example, the way in the UK that common acceptance of a 230v standard for electricity consumption constitutes a powerful platform for innovation and investment in a whole ecosystem of related products and services.

Fundamental to platform thinking is the creation, management and evolution of the platform. While many authors address these concerns, O'Reilly has also identified several key aspects of successful platform approaches – which can easily be seen to apply to government – that focus on their practical realization, evolution and adoption. Such practicalities are essential to their success:

* Embrace open standards: they encourage innovation and grow the market.
* Build a simple system – let it evolve.
* Design for participation.
* Learn from your users, especially ones who do what you don't expect.
* Lower the barriers to experimentation.
* Build a culture of measurement.
* Celebrate your developers.

So Where does the Technology Come in?

If government has been using commodity markets for years, you might be wondering about the relevance or novelty of all this platform stuff. Simple: the same platform-based principles now need to be applied to the design and plumbing of public services. Digitally enabled open architectures constitute a technological inflection point, enabling us to unpick the tangled mess of our current organizations into smaller building blocks, enabling cost comparison between commoditized components (in a manner that resembles our electricity market).

The open paradigm was initially confined to specific, technology-rich environments such as the open source software community, which has been capable of exploiting the commercial advantages of *technical* open standards. This is because these open standards did not transfer across to *organizational* processes and functions: they were restricted to chunks of developers' code, or technical protocols. So what has happened to change this?

Today, these same technical open standards are now capable of wrapping chunks (components) of *functional* business logic and workflow in such a way as to enable organizational processes and functions to be treated increasingly interoperably, like Lego building blocks. This technological innovation is nothing knew – as we review in Part 3, it has enjoyed various names from service-oriented architecture (SOA) to web services – and yet has unprecedented implications for organizational design. The ability to expose business logic via interoperable technical standards enables formerly vertically oriented business functions to be dis-integrated into small cassettes of 'common gubbins' and 'machinery' that can be reassembled around users in different ways to take advantage of the market. The more that the various elements of this plumbing can be treated as commodities, the more they can be commissioned and delivered very differently to the riskier, or higher-value activities ('specific gubbins', or face-to-face interaction), which can be treated in a more bespoke way. It is all about applying the right approach to the right parts of the organization and its needs – and about moving away from the one-size-fits-all mentality of the past.

The development of open standards offers the opportunity to extend the benefits of the open approach (in terms of innovation, crowdsourcing, agile services and cost efficiency) beyond its origins in software and technology business models, and to make them available to lower-tech, more mature organizations – such as government. Indeed, in seeking to dis-integrate traditional, vertically hierarchical bureaucracies – and re-aggregate them as agile, modular services around the citizen – business models and underlying service architectures for providers of public services will increasingly resemble the open architectures of a range of other service providers, from banks to supermarkets, that are seeking to implement similar changes.

PATHFINDER: NHS JOBS

NHS Jobs (www.jobs.nhs.uk), the online recruitment service for the NHS, is the largest, most successful example of a mass-subscription shared service in the UK, and has already generated savings of over £1 billion since its launch in 2003. The secret of

NHS Jobs's success is that it is a *platform*. In contrast to most UK shared services, in which two or more organizations typically vie with one another to impose *their* legacy, top-down bureaucracy on the other party – '*you* can share *my* service, but really *yours* is not suitable for *us*' – NHS Jobs was built from the bottom up as a platform to be used by over 500 NHS bodies in the UK.

Rather than build its own 'e-recruitment' system, Department of Health recognized that it could instead procure a single, nationally available commodity that would be 'consumed' on a transactional basis by NHS employers throughout the UK. It commissioned an SME to provide the complete service – including, critically, persuading 500+ NHS employers to forego their traditional, siloed processes to make use of it. NHS Jobs is now one of the top-four busiest recruitment portals in the UK and the biggest single employer recruitment site in Europe, with a unique visit every two seconds, 24 hours a day, and processing over 275,000 job applications per month.

Best of all, because of the power of NHS Jobs as a platform, the site has now become a valuable commodity. When the Department of Health re-tendered NHS Jobs in 2012, therefore, potential suppliers were asked to provide the basic platform to the department free of charge; instead, they competed on the quality of the *additional*, innovative services they would be able to offer NHS employers and applicants. An example of such a service is 'e-CRB': an electronic way of processing Criminal Record Bureau checks that looks likely to cut the process from several weeks to a few days, whilst reducing the current cost of CRB checking by two-thirds.

NHS Jobs is thus a poster child for the opportunity that government has to use its scale to trigger the development of commodity platforms. These platforms can be so valuable to suppliers that they are happy to provide the essential public service for nothing – and will compete to find new, innovative ways of serving the public that utterly transform the traditional ways of performing a particular function.

How Open Standards Create Innovation and Investment

So how do open standards help create platforms that in turn trigger innovation and investment? Open platforms have three distinct dimensions, which help to answer this question:

- First, a consensus around common standards for delivery enables growth of ecosystems of interrelated activities that are better able to handle the complexity of service delivery. This is the physical dimension of the platform, which gives rise to two behavioural dimensions.
- Second, as Karl Marx helpfully observed, diffusion of common standards has a commoditizing effect. It dilutes intellectual capital in a product or service and offers the opportunity to achieve economies of scale by spreading fixed costs over larger volumes of standardized activity, or fungible components. Such economies of scale provide organizations with the opportunity to commoditize what they buy – by promoting adoption of standard platforms – as well as to sell what they commoditize, by sharing their internal resources with others, as Amazon did very successfully, for example, with its web services business.
- Third, recognized common standards create market demand in which other organizations will invest for the future – exemplified, for instance, in the flurry of activity around the Android mobile platform. Significantly, once established, open platforms become widely available, generating commercial incentives to invest in 'upstream' R&D activity on these platforms. In turn, such open R&D activity facilitates 'crowdsourcing' of innovation, providing a more efficient, powerful and often cheaper way to innovate 'in parallel', rather than 'in series', against a commonly defined problem: examples of such crowdsourcing include the development of the Linux platform, or recent innovation models in the pharmaceutical industry.

In this way, it is hard to say whether it is consuming things in a standard way that creates commodities, and the investment around these – or if it is the market demand generated by all that standard consumption. In fact, it is both: common, standard ways of doing things, and the demand (and market) generated by all this standardizing, form two halves of a *platform* for further investment and innovation.

The Platform is a Dynamic, not a Thing

When we talk about platforms, therefore, we are *not* referring to some standard technology in the usual sense (as in an 'IT platform', for example). To be sure, open technology is part of the equation: but it is the demand created by standardizing things openly, and subsequent investment from the market, that is really important:

The platform is a dynamic – not a thing.

Google's innovation ecosystem offers a good example of the essential link between the openness of a digital platform and the innovation that can result. This example also illustrates the difference between traditional outsourcing mechanisms and utility, platform-based ecosystems. By providing a cheap, commodity platform, Google has encouraged a broad range of content providers, consumers, innovators and advertisers to build applications, share data and purchase services in a way that allows it to crowdsource ideas and then cherry-pick and invest in the best of these. The resulting continually emergent, innovative dynamic is clearly very different from a fixed supply contract owned by one, or a small handful, of exclusive suppliers. The economic power of Google's strong open platform is illustrated in Figure 7.1, where the emphasis is not the technological underpinning of Google as a tool, but rather the marketplace it creates between different communities (consumers, content providers, advertisers and innovators) to encourage purposeful interactions and exchange of goods and services.

Such open models are well proven within the commercial sphere, with numerous companies providing platforms around which third-party developers can innovate. Tim O'Reilly has observed that *'the secret to the success of bellwethers like Google, Amazon, eBay, Craiglist, Wikipedia,*

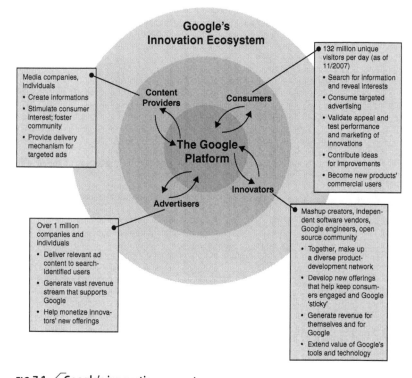

Google's Innovation Ecosystem

Media companies, individuals
- Create informations
- Stimulate consumer interest; foster community
- Provide delivery mechanism for targeted ads

Content Providers

Consumers

The Google Platform

Advertisers

Innovators

- 132 million unique visitors per day (as of 11/2007)
- Search for information and reveal interests
- Consume targeted advertising
- Validate appeal and test performance and marketing of innovations
- Contribute ideas for improvements
- Become new products' commercial users

Over 1 million companies and individuals
- Deliver relevant ad content to search-identified users
- Generate vast revenue stream that supports Google
- Help monetize innovators' new offerings

Mashup creators, independent software vendors, Google engineers, open source community
- Together, make up a diverse product-development network
- Develop new offerings that help keep consumers engaged and Google 'sticky'
- Generate revenue for themselves and for Google
- Extend value of Google's tools and technology

FIG 7.1 / Google's innovation ecosystem

Source: Iyer and Davenport 2008, HBR, reused with permission

Facebook and Twitter is that each of these sites, in its own way, has learned to harness the power of its users to add value to [... and] to co-create its offerings'.

Progressive convergence on open standards within an evolving open architecture will enable government to establish a sustainable platform for innovation, an open platform model that enables government services to become available to citizens when and where they need them: '*In this model, government [becomes] a convener and an enabler rather than the first mover of civic action*.' As a consequence, Tim O'Reilly's description of this as 'government as a platform' was both a statement of vision, but also an act of provocation – imploring government to be smarter about setting the enabling conditions for a myriad of locally appropriate social outcomes, rather than assuming that it will deliver everything from a limited, wasteful and ultimately self-serving, centrally imposed menu.

Avoiding Evolutionary Dead Ends: Blu-ray and HD DVD

It is important to emphasize that the platform-based marketplace model achieves its dynamic of continual innovation because it comprises both technical and commercial dimensions. In explaining why this is the case, consider the high-definition optical disc format war that took place in 2006–8 between the Blu-ray disc and HD DVD optical disc standards for storing high-definition video and audio. Because Blu-ray successfully became a common consumer standard for high-definition optical disc products, it was able to create a commoditized platform that drove down costs and allowed businesses to innovate: it created a vibrant market comprising commercial viability, low cost and choice.

In contrast to Blu-ray, HD DVD lost the standards war: it rapidly became seen as a proprietary standard relevant to only a limited – and dwindling – number of niche products and services, with the result that the market dried up; it had become an evolutionary dead end. Losing the standards war happens all the time: this battle closely resembles the VHS/Betamax video standards war of the 1980s, which saw Betamax similarly lose out. By analogy, government attempts to create joined-up government using traditional outsourcing instruments created its own evolutionary dead end: markets will only support outdated systems if they are paid an increasing financial premium, and because these systems are not a mainstream platform, the market will innovate elsewhere. Like HD DVD suppliers, government will be forced to turn back to the direction of mainstream platform evolution eventually – just more painfully, and much more expensively.

The evolution of open standards and cheap connectivity has allowed technical platforms and commercial markets to become inextricably linked. Modern IT needs to be light touch, open, agile and locally responsive – not as a matter of ideology, but because these are the characteristics of the successful technical platform/commercial model that has evolved. In this way, the transition required to create agile, bottom-up, citizen-responsive public services rests to a great extent on government's ability to execute successfully the move from closed to open standards (moving from the right-hand to the left-hand side of the illustration in Figure 6.1), in turn encouraging a shift from closed to open markets with their improved innovation and reduced costs.

Existing Public Services versus the Open, Platform-based Architecture

In many ways, an open architecture does not differ significantly from existing approaches to public service reform – with its intent to move from traditional, siloed bureaucratic forms towards disaggregation, competition and incentivization. However, although they may share similar aims, the respective models for achieving these aims are radically different. The current public services set-up has failed largely because it used technology to automate – not redesign – current services and substituted a monolithic, siloed private sector delivery model for a monolithic, siloed public sector delivery model. Crucially, although it aimed to disaggregate previously monolithic organizational *structures,* it failed to distinguish between, and thus to disaggregate, bespoke from commodity elements *within* services, as shown in Mark Foden's model in Figures 6.2 and 6.3, and was thus unable to generate the platform/innovation dynamic required.

The historic approach within government has been to continue operating within vertical silos of public service structures, rather than recognizing the potential of horizontal requirements (such as common, commodity services) where cost and complexity could be reduced. Because governments froze existing services and disaggregated at the wrong level, the desired competition and incentivization failed to follow. The result was a system with little incentive amongst a closed cadre of suppliers to simplify, and a proliferation of complexity.

In contrast to the focus on disaggregating *structures*, we will describe how the open architecture approach focuses on disaggregating a continuous *process* of innovation – exploiting and commoditizing services that never cease and cannot be locked down within long-term commercial arrangements. Open architecture can be considered as a digitally enabled, mature expression of the ideals of joined-up government with the capability to deliver it through a radically different underlying philosophy and approach, as set out in Table 7.1.

Given governments' long-standing desire to remodel themselves around the needs of citizens, they can no longer ignore the powerful technical/commercial dynamic of the platform/innovation model – which does just this. Yet the move to the utility economics of open standards and cheap connectivity challenges governments' traditional ways of sourcing its requirements. As Andy Burton noted in his comments to a UK government select committee on government cloud deployment:

> *A current barrier … is that procurement is not geared up, at this moment in time, to even define how those organizations move from classic outsourcing – build a data centre, build a unique application, manage*

TABLE 7.1 Same aim, different model: different approaches to disaggregation, competition and incentivization

Features of existing public service model	Features of open architecture model
Disaggregation at organizational level (such as agencies, arms' length bodies)	Organizational level disaggregation results from *disaggregation at service delivery level* into bespoke and commodity elements
Static, 'top-down' replacement of one bespoke organizational structure for another, rewarding complexity	Replacement of static structure with dynamic, 'bottom-up' process, rewarding simplification and platform reuse
Standardized technical solutions, suppliers and commercial arrangements	Plural technical solutions, suppliers and commercial arrangements
Plural business logic and technical standards	Standardized business logic and technical standards
Proprietary standards and technology platforms	Open standards and technology platforms

it 24/7 – to building something and saying 'it has got to conform to this standard; it has got to be able to work within this security framework and it has got to enable small businesses, from a software provision point of view, to be able to interface with local community groups', or whatever the case may be. The lack of framework is the biggest disabler today.

The above comment from the chairperson of the UK Cloud Industry Forum underlines the need for governments to manage the market effectively by driving open standards and platforms and encouraging competition, instead of concentrating it in the hands of a limited number of suppliers:

We can only achieve this post-bureaucratic ideal … if we don't view IT as an outsourcing solution. The fundamental thing that I keep hearing again and again is that we are looking at IT as something that is designed and built deliberately for a government department and managed by a third party. … Therefore the procurement process of making the IT uphold the bureaucracy is the wrong way around. There is not enough new thinking. (Burton 2011)

So far we have set out the key features of an open architecture (open plumbing) for public services. We have explained that, at root, such architecture is driven by progressive adoption of open functional and technical standards at component level – across government. Because digital technology now allows us to join up functional components as never before, we have the opportunity across government to create an open platform of unprecedented demand for standard types of plumbing, one that can trigger massive leaps in effectiveness and efficiency in our public services. We now turn to the basic mechanics of the way in which we can converge on an open architecture, and also explain how this fits with the notion of becoming a truly 'digital' government.

Culture Change from Closed to Open: Achieving the Open Stack

Encouraging new thinking and overcoming entrenched cultural barriers to the emergence and adoption of open platforms within the UK public sector remains a significant challenge. As an illustration of how difficult this can be, consider the differences between the two depictions (Figure 7.2) of the open stack, developed by one of the authors of this book in 2011 to explain the architectural *and cultural* change needed to bring about the open platform dynamic. It shows that there are various interrelated aspects that the public sector needs to address simultaneously.

Part A of Figure 7.2 shows the original concept that encapsulates the way in which open platforms are a dynamic comprising both technology and market behaviour. Moving down the stack from the apex, in order to achieve the aims of open government, the public sector needs to change the way in which it organizes itself. This form of organization needs to be established upon a set of firm architectural principles across the public sector that enshrine citizen-driven, standardized utility service delivery models. In turn, to achieve this, the public sector needs to stop developing and delivering everything internally, and focus more on the commissioning and consumption of service outcomes ('culture change from delivery to commissioning'). To do this, it needs to think much more about these end services, and worry less about the inputs ('service-driven procurement models and practices'). However, it won't be able to do this unless it is able to compare and contrast competing alternatives ('increasing transparency') – otherwise it will be comparing apples with pears. Moving downwards towards the technology base of the stack, increased transparency requires, in turn, commonly specified components; but these only work together if they are supported with standards of interoperability and shared data. Finally, in order for such interoperability to have credibility, it must be secure.

The way that the open stack appears in the UK Cabinet Office's *Strategic Implementation Plan* of 2011, shown in Figure 7.2 in part B, illustrates how difficult it can be to achieve culture change even within organizations that have embraced open principles. 'Culture change from delivery to commissioning' has been muted in part B of Figure 7.2 to 'innovative ways of working and strengthened governance', and 'service-driven procurement models and practices' have become 'commercial models and practices' – not at all the same thing. The hard fact is that achievement of open architecture and platforms within the UK's public services will require proper culture change, not an adjustment to business-as-usual. This

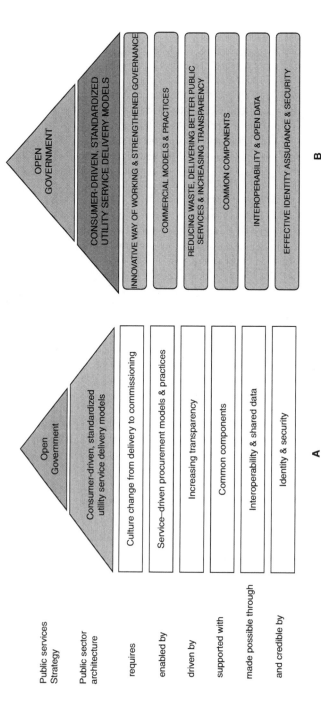

Public services Strategy

Public sector architecture

	A	B
	Open Government	OPEN GOVERNMENT
	Consumer-driven, standardized utility service delivery models	CONSUMER-DRIVEN, STANDARDIZED UTILITY SERVICE DELIVERY MODELS
requires	Culture change from delivery to commissioning	INNOVATIVE WAY OF WORKING & STRENGTHENED GOVERNANCE
enabled by	Service–driven procurement models & practices	COMMERCIAL MODELS & PRACTICES
driven by	Increasing transparency	REDUCING WASTE, DELIVERING BETTER PUBLIC SERVICES & INCREASING TRANSPARENCY
supported with	Common components	COMMON COMPONENTS
made possible through	Interoperability & shared data	INTEROPERABILITY & OPEN DATA
and credible by	Identity & security	EFFECTIVE IDENTITY ASSURANCE & SECURITY

FIG 7.2 Open stack – a mix of behaviours underpinned by technology

form of reorganization requires architectural principles across the public sector that enshrine citizen-driven, standardized utility service delivery models. In turn, government will need to stop focusing on building and delivering everything in-house, and focus instead on the commissioning and consumption of service outcomes. Deciding to develop platforms within government will happen only out of necessity – where the required services are not available for reuse elsewhere.

As a simplified example of how this works, imagine you have two icons on your desktop: Open Office (open source software that is free to use, but relatively basic) and a premium-priced office applications suite. If you click on Open Office, you consume these applications for free – providing you are happy to use the relatively limited menu of services, ones that you use 90% of the time. If you opt to click on the premium-priced icon, however, the meter starts running for every minute you consume the all-bells-and-whistles service (where you pay for all sorts of functions you never actually use). Assuming you are accustomed to using the premium service, which will you choose? The likelihood is that you're busy, and you will just click the premium icon, because it's easy and there are no consequences to you for doing so (the costs are hidden somewhere else in the system via the baroque mechanisms surrounding your organization's purchasing department, IT support team and departmental budgeting processes). Imagine, however, that your choices *do* have direct consequences to you in the form of an automatically generated consumption report and associated bill that is sent directly to your boss. During your biannual review sessions, your boss may be keen to understand the reasons for you ignoring the utility option. Did you *really* need to use the fancy document-formatting option with all those features? Which fancy features, specifically, did you use? Your survival of this interaction may rest with your ability to justify your continued use of premium features for which the utility option would have been adequate.

This illustration demonstrates two important principles. The first is that changing from *buying* more expensive components to *consuming* standard ones is as much about tackling entrenched culture as it is about providing transparent comparability between different offerings. The second is that it would be naive to believe that this culture will change simply because a boss expresses a preference for the standard alternatives: it will only change when transparent comparability exposes people's behavioural choices to internal visibility and to open, outside scrutiny. *This* is how the technology and the culture form two halves of the same coin.

This ecosystem understanding is fundamental to the open-architecture approach to delivering digital public management. Just as electricity is consumed as a utility platform *in the same way* across public and private sectors to run untold appliances, both sectors will consume standardized IT components as a platform for untold services, progressively challenging many traditionally held differences between the two.

Converging on Open Architecture

Government's attempts to date to deliver joined-up public services have floundered largely not because of technology but because of a continuing adherence to an outdated business model and culture, and an underlying (lack of) architecture that places it at odds with a global economy increasingly based on open platforms, open competition and rapid innovation. In response, we have outlined a guiding framework to enable public services to turn away from their evolutionary dead end of increasing reliance on ever larger suppliers offering proprietary closed solutions, and to reconnect with the mainstream economy heading in the opposite direction. We believe that this framework offers the public sector the ability to converge, over time, on similar ways of doing this wherever appropriate – with a radical impact on both the effectiveness and efficiency of our public services.

Based on the challenges already evident in the UK, transitioning successfully to an open architecture will require both a strong political will and an effective, lean and outcome-driven approach to implementation supported by complementary experience drawn from outside the existing skills base. We believe that our framework provides an effective means for government to transition, at both the policy and operational levels – to transform from the outdated existing ethos to the benefits of joined-up government. Open architecture emphasizes the reuse of existing infrastructures and services, rather than the historic focus on the duplicative acquisition of infrastructure and costly government systems. It provides an improved method of governance that can encourage new public service solutions to grow and succeed, by cultivating an open market that provides more effective competition. Government's ability to specify, procure and regulate public service delivery within this digital model is dependent upon its understanding and management of lean and outcome-drive thinking, its underlying dynamic, its expertise in separating niche from commodity requirements, access to open rather than traditional proprietary skills, and its ability to mobilize this understanding in its relations with service providers.

Spending More, or Less, on Technology?

Measuring the effective use of technology within the design, operation and delivery of public services is likely to mature into a comparative measure of how successfully governments have moved towards an open architecture model. However, organizations have often misused metrics as a deterrent to change, rather than providing a stimulus. For example, IT research company Gartner provides a range of industry global averages for IT spending as a percentage of total operating expense. Examples include '*3.2% across state and local government in 2010*' and ranging from '*7.9% of IT spend as a percentage of total operational expenses where total Operating Budget is above $10 Billion*'.

The value of such abstract averages can be limited when used in an attempt to demonstrate that IT delivers best value for money or that it is deployed effectively with a good return on investment. Visa Europe, for example, a technology-dependent and technology-centric organization, spends around 35% of its turnover on IT, a figure that may be a better indicator of whether an organization is in a *pre-* or *post-*digital services phase. After all, a digital public sector would eliminate many of the manual costs, internal bureaucracy and duplicated management functions, systems and processes – so as a *percentage*, expenditure on technology might well be higher but within an overall *lower* cost base.

Simplistically comparing one government organization with another utilizing generic averages doesn't work because it takes no account of whether an organization is attempting to deliver joined-up services using a traditional architecture comprising integrated systems, or aggregated services. Moreover, attempting to adhere to such benchmarks may drive perverse behaviour, mistaking IT solely as a cost rather than as a means of transforming the way an organization designs and operates its overall processes and services. A more focused approach to benchmarking would choose an appropriate peer group and conduct comparisons at the level of public services, rather than solely considering total IT spend.

Governments can learn from organizations about how IT enables processes and services to be fundamentally redesigned. Starting with an arbitrary percentage to be spent on technology is to start in the wrong place: the real issue is how to design and deliver optimal public services, based around citizen need, and the role of technology in that process. This might mean far more use of IT in the design and operation of public services, but an overall lower budget required as a consequence of the savings to be made elsewhere from improvements to public sector processes and systems. This is an essential and distinguishing characteristic in the process of becoming a digital organization.

Getting Started – Digital Profiling

We have seen how digital is about using the capabilities and mindset of internet-based organizations, methods and processes to separate out silos into lateral layers that enable us to reconfigure all those old organizational boundaries around the citizen. So how does government get started on this journey? We suggest a simple digital profile as a way to separate out organizational capabilities that may currently be vertically integrated, and map them out horizontally into their various shareable/reuseable components along the ILC model, explained earlier in Figures 6.7 and 6.8.

As a simplified example, consider the different profiles created by applying our ILC framework to produce a digital profile of the human resource

(HR) functions within a large, blue-collar recruitment agency, on the left of Figure 7.3 below, and again to the HR function within say, a niche, high-end strategy consultancy (on the right).

In our hypothetical example, both companies have a traditionally organized HR function operating in a siloed manner, performing all of its roles in-house. However, by using the ILC framework to generate a digital profile of the various activities/capabilities of the recruitment functions in their respective HR departments, very different patterns emerge. In the case of the HR function on the left, both advertising and training can be procured on the internet (commodity): the interview, induction and appraisal functions can all be performed by an external company specializing in such standard functions for service organizations (onboarding of blue-collar workers is a relatively standardized, low-risk activity). The result of this profiling activity is that there is very little justification to retain most of the HR function in-house. Much of it will be provided by third parties taking advantage of various digital media to provide these services seamlessly and cheaply.

In the case of the niche consultancy on the right, however, the digital profiling exercise has yielded a strikingly different result. Advertising can certainly be pushed out to the internet – quite a bit of training might reasonably be provided by externals specializing in basic consulting capabilities (such as project management and basic MBA skills). However, the interviewing is always performed by at least one partner: a time-consuming activity, by expensive people. However, in the consultancy's case, such 'bespoke' expenditure is entirely appropriate: the consequences of recruiting an incompatible employee for the consultancy far outweigh those for the blue-collar agency. However, some of the savings achieved by treating some of the more mundane, standardized activities as commodities to be pushed outside the organization mean that there is more money available to spend on a really thorough interview. In summary, Figure 7.3 illustrates that the application of a consistent set of principles (ILC) to two different businesses can result in very different digital profiles. This shows how open architecture can use tight consistency to support greater diversity than we have at present.

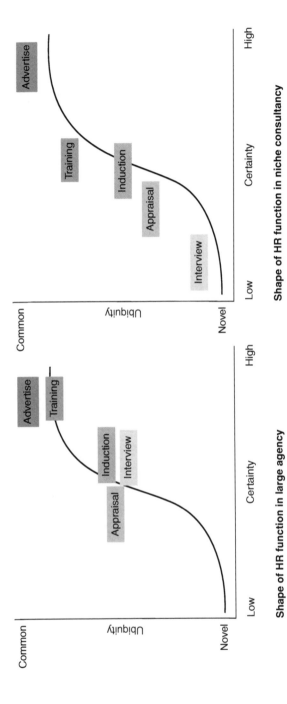

Shape of HR function in large agency

Shape of HR function in niche consultancy

FIG 7.3 Using ILC to profile a vertical silo, separating it into components

PATHFINDER: LAND REGISTRY

Land Registry needs to respond to rapidly changing customer expectations. Customers are starting to compare their experience of Land Registry to their other digital interactions with consumer organizations such as Amazon and eBay, business services such as Google Apps and application developer services such as Stripe Payments.

In response to these expectations, Land Registry had experimented with several digital pilots and projects. Quite rightly, the Land Registry Digital journey originated from the 'outside in'. It has allowed the organization to experiment with digital technologies, start to understand what digital means, assess where there is most work to be done and explore the art of the possible. However, because these initiatives were undertaken outside the core technology architecture, Land Registry realized that, although successful in their own right, they would have limited ability to improve fulfilment, efficiency and data exploitation right across the enterprise.

In response, Land Registry has begun to plan a transformation journey to becoming a digital organization, where business services and technology services are in sympathy and componentized. Learning from early concept explorations, using agile techniques, work has begun to plan a portfolio of change that will fundamentally rebuild, rather than externally repaint the way the organization works and the way services are offered.

Land Registry's business is centred on customers, and it achieves excellent customer satisfaction ratings. Historically, however, the business has grown up around different data. As in all government departments, the result is that it is difficult to share its informational lifeblood in a fluid, natural and transparent way, seen from the point of view of what a customer is trying to achieve. This can manifest itself in customers having to re-enter a name and address for each interaction, or, for caseworkers, a need to manually go in and out of multiple applications to deliver a single user journey.

As a result Land Registry is considering adopting a service-based platform approach, to manage interactions with the core information asset so that customers are able to get the result they seek without needing to understand the register processes. The strategic selection of linked platforms can support both the transition to the new environment and the development of components using open standards or openly documented interfaces to avoid vendor lock-in. Such a platform-based approach might appear as follows:

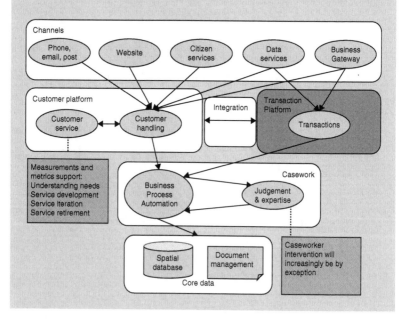

chapter 8

Future Digital Public Services

The Opportunity in Local Services

For many citizens, local services are our closest and most common interaction with government, and the public authorities who provide them are an important bedrock of local democracy and accountability. In the UK, this local landscape is surprisingly complex: there are hundreds of principal authorities: 27 county councils, 55 unitary authorities, 32 London boroughs (plus the Corporation of the City of London), 36 Metropolitan boroughs, 201 districts, 32 Scottish unitary authorities, 22 Welsh unitary authorities, and 26 Northern Ireland districts.

Despite this tiered structure, it is not unusual for many of these organizations to carry out slightly different versions of precisely the same administrative tasks: collecting local taxes, and spending them on the provision of a spectrum of local services ranging from the built environment to social care. In this respect, local government resembles a group of companies. However, were a group of private companies to duplicate their administrative functions hundreds of times over in this inefficient way, shareholders would demand change very quickly: indeed, there might even be a shareholders' revolt. As taxpayers, we need to start to hold local government to account in the same way: after all, it belongs to us and we pay for it. We are not meant to be paying for internal infrastructures and processes, but rather the *outcomes* that local government promises to deliver to us: if there are ways this can be done more efficiently and effectively, we should expect local administrations to do so.

The impetus to address all this duplication has become even more acute in recent years with the need to absorb progressive cuts to funding while at the same time starting to work collaboratively alongside other organizations, including the health service, criminal justice and housing associations. Although most councils have at least one 'transformation' programme on the go (many of these are now into their second or third iterations of transformation), closer inspection reveals these to be almost always variants of the endless undifferentiated outsourcing disease described earlier.

In consequence, many local authorities are now in significant trouble: lured by the prospect of cutting cost, many have tied up entire vertical functions with outsourced service providers for up to 15 years, in many cases simply transferring their own staff to run the same inefficient technology and processes under another organization's control. Because they have usually handed over a messy organizational function to the outsourcer – lock, stock and barrel – they can expect to be told that it is progressively expensive to run, recalling our earlier example of Blu-ray/HD DVD. They can also expect to pay a high premium for the smallest adjustment to specifications that may have been laid down a decade ago – such as a necessary response to new legislation. In such cases, local residents who are being asked to choose between keeping open their libraries, day centres or their playgroups, are unwittingly paying some organizations large amounts of money for alterations to services for which they are already paying excessively high fixed fees.

A lack of flexibility and agility really matters in local government because, in common with most politically led organizations, councils are required to comply with and implement changes in legislation and policy both at a local and national level. At a national level, legislation that impacts on local government is often poorly defined, unclear and late in its delivery – in the UK such examples include Universal Credit and the localization of council tax. Such examples leave the Revenues and Benefits Team within a council needing to adapt its processes, job descriptions and technology at the last minute, something that is not easy or cheap given the state of current local government business, information and technical architectures.

Locally, policy decisions are often set in direct opposition to the council's stated business strategy, or developed on the hoof in response to local issues that an influential local councillor might face. So, for example, a local authority business plan may state that saving money is their main goal. Then, seemingly counter to this goal, the council's cabinet may decide to offer a free green waste collection service to residents with large gardens. This may sound trivial, but at short notice the Waste Team needs to find money to deliver the service, citizens need a facility to book the collection, and citizen service agents need to track performance and deal with, record and escalate complaints and issues.

Existing business architectures across local government make implementing new legislation and policies expensive, failure-prone and protracted. The existing situation significantly constrains policymaking and can contribute to an unhelpful breakdown of trust and co-operation between elected members and council officers.

The need for change-ready business design is heightened further by the requirement on local authorities to be 'event driven'. If a child dies whilst under the supervision of the council or there is a major chemical spill within the region, then organizational resources will be diverted at short notice to deal with the situation and its aftermath. All organizations are event driven to some extent, but extreme events that force businesses to change direction are exceptions rather than the norm. The range of areas covered by local government and its societal position as a kind of 'safety net of last resort' means that the ability to respond easily and cost-effectively to unexpected events is critical. On top of this, local government is subject to the same change pressures as all other private and public organizations – cultural change, technological advances and economic trends.

Of course, technology is only one element of business architecture and it is clear that even the most sophisticated, well-designed technology landscape cannot on its own deliver an agile and flexible local authority. So, for example, modern technology does not on its own deliver a more flexible workforce or leaner business processes.

However, when the problem is expressed from the opposite perspective, the importance of technology becomes clear: without well-designed, user-centred, platform-based and increasingly open technology architecture, all other initiatives aimed at creating a more flexible, responsive organizations will fail or be severely hampered. It is therefore critical to understand the current design of local authorities, and the role that technology plays in that architecture. There are 433 principal local authorities in the UK so it is impossible to generalize as if they all follow the exact same model. However, they do share common characteristics. James Herbert, managing director of Methods Digital, has developed an overview of the differences between the way that local government is currently designed and how it might look in the future, as shown in Figure 8.1.

The first two columns of Figure 8.1 broadly describe the current situation of most local authorities at all levels – County, District, Unitary, Metropolitan or London Borough. The defining feature – as with many organizations – is of functional silos. This in itself might not be a problem if the silo operated at a strategic or commissioning level; however, the silo approach diffuses all the way down through each professional stack, permeating its way into staff, processes and ultimately into the technology supply chain for each of these areas. The technology supply chain comes to replicate these silos so closely that it mirrors it back to the organization, enforcing its continuation.

Such replication occurs because each silo is locked into long-term contracts for specialist software; even if the software has become anachronistic or comparatively expensive, it is usually too costly and complex to move to other solutions. Similarly, if a particular silo does secure the funds to adopt a different technology product, it will likely choose a slightly more up-to-date application but one that keeps it locked within its silo. Scant regard is given to wider strategic architectural principles when these buying decisions are made. Such a choice is not made with any malicious

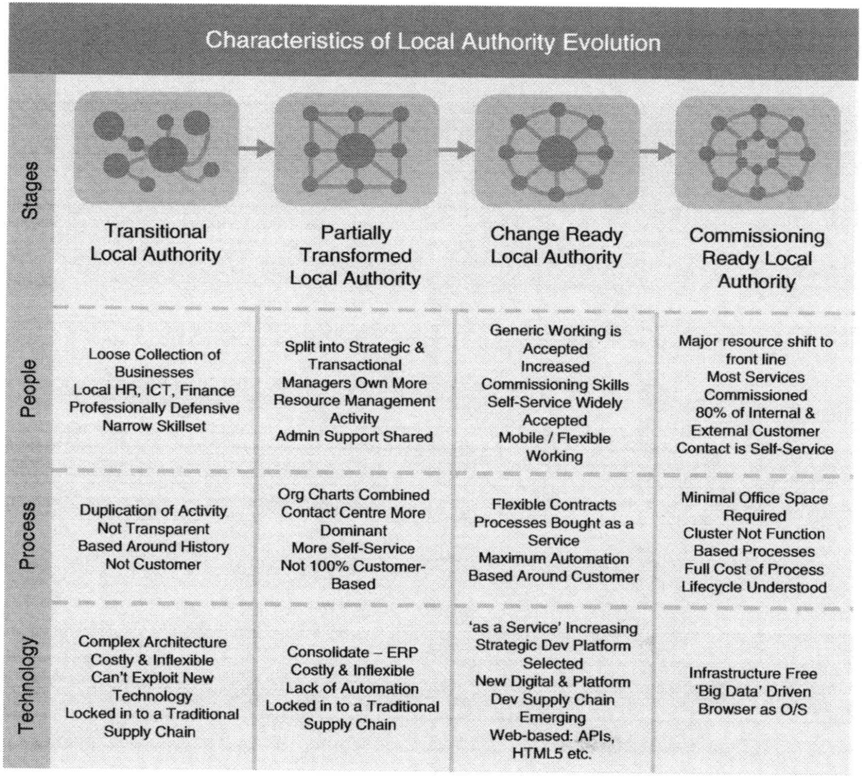

143

Characteristics of Local Authority Evolution

Stages	Transitional Local Authority	Partially Transformed Local Authority	Change Ready Local Authority	Commissioning Ready Local Authority
People	Loose Collection of Businesses; Local HR, ICT, Finance; Professionally Defensive; Narrow Skillset	Split into Strategic & Transactional; Managers Own More Resource Management Activity; Admin Support Shared	Generic Working is Accepted; Increased Commissioning Skills; Self-Service Widely Accepted; Mobile / Flexible Working	Major resource shift to front line; Most Services Commissioned; 80% of Internal & External Customer Contact is Self-Service
Process	Duplication of Activity; Not Transparent; Based Around History; Not Customer	Org Charts Combined; Contact Centre More Dominant; More Self-Service; Not 100% Customer-Based	Flexible Contracts; Processes Bought as a Service; Maximum Automation; Based Around Customer	Minimal Office Space Required; Cluster Not Function Based Processes; Full Cost of Process Lifecycle Understood
Technology	Complex Architecture; Costly & Inflexible; Can't Exploit New Technology; Locked in to a Traditional Supply Chain	Consolidate – ERP; Costly & Inflexible; Lack of Automation; Locked in to a Traditional Supply Chain	'as a Service' Increasing; Strategic Dev Platform Selected; New Digital & Platform Dev Supply Chain Emerging; Web-based, APIs, HTML5 etc.	Infrastructure Free; 'Big Data' Driven; Browser as O/S

FIG 8.1 Local authorities' evolutionary journey

intent: rather, the pressure is on the team to make progress locally within the governance and funding model that drives them towards overcoming the problems at hand.

As an example, a local authority may procure its Adult Social Care application and its Revenues and Benefits application from different divisions of the same company. Each system will have components – workflow, case management, payment engines, and so on – that are common to both, but the authority will in effect pay for each component twice to the same supplier. Multiply the cost of buying these components many times across the 180 to 300 applications that local authorities typically manage – and the cost to council tax and business rates payers becomes clear. Then replicate this redundancy across each local authority, and the broad scale of the waste and inefficiency takes on an even more significant scale.

Furthermore, as many of these are traditional applications built from the ground up on proprietary technology, it is costly and difficult to integrate them, resulting in a sprawling technology architecture through which it is difficult to facilitate a positive citizen and user experience. As a simple analogy, imagine if screw heads, nuts and bolts had not been standardized. How many tools would be needed to carry out relatively straightforward DIY projects – and how much frustration would this cause? In effect, this is the lot of many of the staff and customers of local government today.

The supply chain is incentivized to maintain this situation as it can secure revenues for many years to come by making each silo dependent on its products and services. The supply chain will look for opportunities to lock the silo down, and can charge high rates for extra work that is required when the siloed business area needs to work with or share data with a different silo: this might be across the local authority, or even externally into partner organizations such as health, or the third sector. Innovation is locked out, and other companies cannot bring their products and thinking to the table. In this sense, therefore, most of the technology suppliers in local government could be defined as the opposite of 'platform businesses'.

The future local government business architecture has four key drivers at its heart:

- It is designed with the expectation of change.
- It is flexible enough to cope with unanticipated change.
- It enables services that are cheaper, better and faster.
- It enables services that are good enough.

These drivers have three implications. First, the business model or architecture needs to accept that local authorities are subject to a wide range of external forces beyond just legislation, policy and events. We illustrate these external forces in Figure 8.2 via a business model canvas outlining the key drivers for local government.

Second, the business model needs to be *designed* to be change-ready. We do not propose designing any single, detailed business architecture for all 433 local authorities, but tools such as the 'Local Government Business

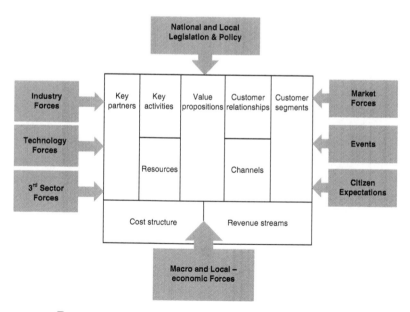

FIG 8.2 / How external forces shape the business model

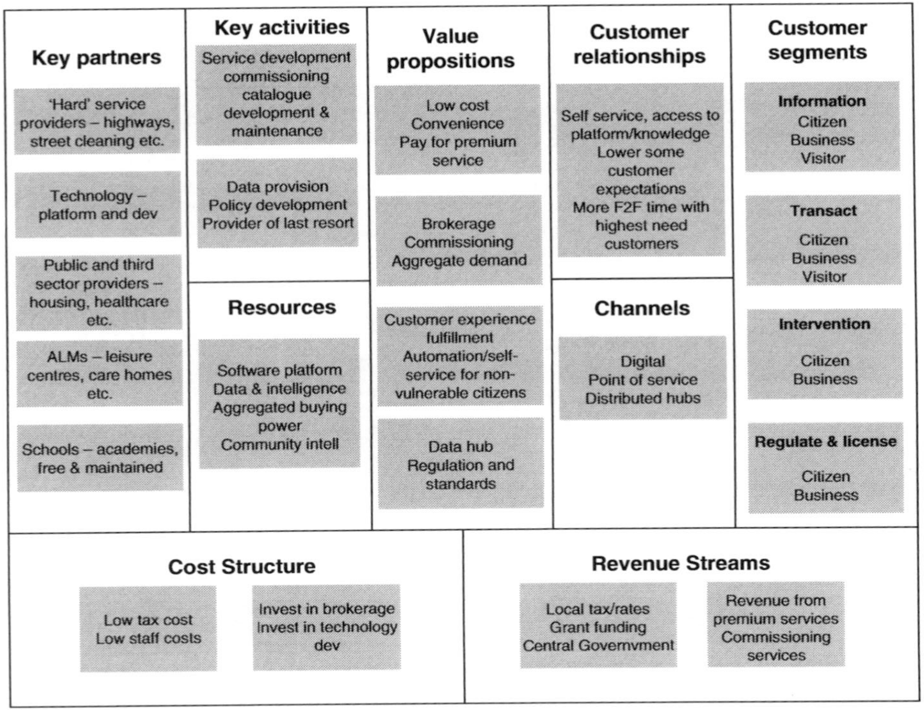

Key partners

'Hard' service providers – highways, street cleaning etc.

Technology – platform and dev

Public and third sector providers – housing, healthcare etc.

ALMs – leisure centres, care homes etc.

Schools – academies, free & maintained

Key activities

Service development commissioning catalogue development & maintenance

Data provision Policy development Provider of last resort

Resources

Software platform Data & intelligence Aggregated buying power Community intell

Value propositions

Low cost Convenience Pay for premium service

Brokerage Commissioning Aggregate demand

Customer experience fulfillment Automation/self-service for non-vulnerable citizens

Data hub Regulation and standards

Customer relationships

Self service, access to platform/knowledge Lower some customer expectations More F2F time with highest need customers

Channels

Digital Point of service Distributed hubs

Customer segments

Information
Citizen
Business
Visitor

Transact
Citizen
Business
Visitor

Intervention
Citizen
Business

Regulate & license
Citizen
Business

Cost Structure

Low tax cost
Low staff costs

Invest in brokerage
Invest in technology dev

Revenue Streams

Local tax/rates
Grant funding
Central Government

Revenue from premium services
Commissioning services

FIG 8.3 Developing a change-ready architecture using the business model canvas (courtesy of James Herbert)

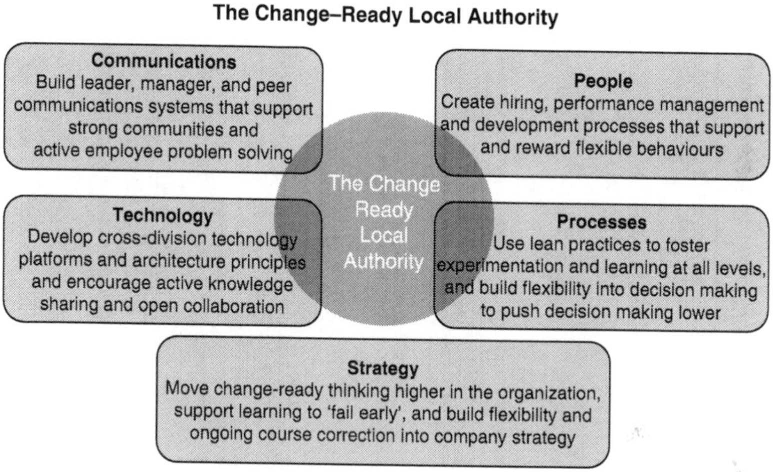

The Change–Ready Local Authority

Communications
Build leader, manager, and peer communications systems that support strong communities and active employee problem solving

People
Create hiring, performance management and development processes that support and reward flexible behaviours

Technology
Develop cross-division technology platforms and architecture principles and encourage active knowledge sharing and open collaboration

The Change Ready Local Authority

Processes
Use lean practices to foster experimentation and learning at all levels, and build flexibility into decision making to push decision making lower

Strategy
Move change-ready thinking higher in the organization, support learning to 'fail early', and build flexibility and ongoing course correction into company strategy

FIG 8.4 / Achieving change-readiness across several dimensions simultaneously (courtesy of James Herbert)

Model Canvas', shown in Figure 8.3, can be developed as a useful first step in defining a change-ready business architecture.

Third, the key drivers underlying change need to permeate every dimension of the local authority simultaneously. As illustrated in Figure 8.4, this includes addressing communications, technology, people, processes and strategy.

Change-ready Business Model

Clearly, across 433 principal local authorities, there would be many flavours of the business model canvas and associated business architecture. What remains, however, is that many local government organizations have lost their way and are spending significant amounts on outdated technology and inefficient organizational structures that are locked into inappropriate and expensive long-term contracts. Ironically, they are presenting the problem to residents as a need to shut down or curtail front-line services – when in many cases, better architecture and management would have enabled them to spare residents such choices altogether. Were our local authorities each to undertake a digital profile based on ILC, we would see that we have hundreds of 'HD DVD organizations' paying through the nose for bespoke services to prop up lots and lots of slightly different versions of *the same* local services. It would be possible to overlay most of these digital profiles on top of one another, and they would look the same.

Note that what is broken here is not the front-line services themselves (though like most services, these could usually do with some improvement and are being starved of resources because of the money being spent inefficiently elsewhere). No, what is broken and sucking the lifeblood from these services is all that back-end bureaucracy: Mark Foden's 'gubbins' and 'machinery'. This is a major reason why our libraries and leisure centres are closing, and why our healthcare visitors may only have ten minutes to spend with us per visit. It is that old plumbing again – the architecture. That is why we say it is so important to get this right. So let's look at how things could be so very different – at why no one would need to make that unnecessary and often artificial choice between their local library and their playgroup.

A Better Outcome

Let's start right down at the level of an individual service, to show how things could be in a platform world. Let's imagine that you run the Revenues and Benefits service at CityTown Council. In the majority of cases, your job involves managing an outsourced service supplier to do this for you: specifying and managing their delivery of service outcomes, along the lines set out above.

During your biannual performance reviews with your chief executive, the conversation will centre around your management of the particular contractual bind in which CityTown is likely to find itself: perhaps, if the contract is nearing its end, discussions about which of the limited menu of available alternative large suppliers CityTown might be able to turn to next. Now consider the radical – genuinely transformed – alternative, shown in Figure 8.5.

In Figure 8.5 (admittedly much simplified) we have applied the ILC from Chapter 6 to profile the integrated stack of Revenues and Benefits. Looking at the overall 'utility' area, we can see immediately that some functions typically found inside these services are now available as utilities in the cloud. We simply don't need to pay bespoke prices any more for these components. By using standard components – say document management – across other functions (say, Housing, and Social Care) as well as Revenues and Benefits, we can seamlessly share documents between these traditionally separate silos, yielding a faster, cheaper and far more joined-up service to the citizen. We will just consume these as services as we need them: when a better one comes along, we can simply slot one out and replace it. They are utilities, which means that there is nothing special at all about them: they are used by large and small organizations, public or private sector, just like electricity. Why would anyone want to use them any other way?

The reality is, of course, that some of these functions – the ones in the inner, 'shared' area of Figure 8.5 – are not yet common enough to be

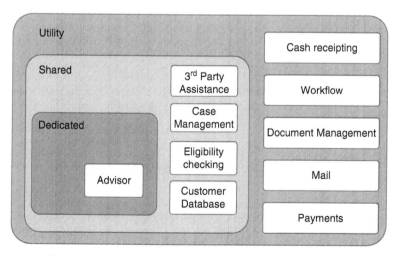

FIG 8.5 / Applying ILC to reimagine Revenues and Benefits

consumed as utilities: not enough people will ever use them to produce a viable market.

However, these will be common to every single local authority that provides Revenues and Benefits services – as well, of course, as to many of the other services that all these authorities provide. So why pay for them again and again all over the country?

In this reimagined future, these components will be shared and consumed commonly wherever possible. Recalling the quadrants in Figure 6.1, councils will have slowly converged on a position in the top left, where they are able to say to the market: 'We will progressively perform eligibility checking in a certain, ordinary way across all of our operations, supported with certain open technology standards.' With demand like this, councils would have a range of solutions from which to choose, and a rate of innovation in this area that local government can currently only dream of.

Significantly, we have left one function – Advisor – in the 'Dedicated' area of Figure 8.5. This is the face-to-face service – the *real* part of the public service for its users, not the gubbins and machinery. CityTown quite rightly wants to retain this so that it can provide the best possible service and keep its ear to the ground with regard to how the service is performing. Happily, because it is saving so much by treating the gubbins and machinery as it *ought* to be treated, having first separated it out, it is able to increase the number of face-to-face workers it employs – as well as give them a lighter case load, which means they are able to spend more time with every citizen. By getting its act together architecturally, CityTown has quite simply shifted its resources away from HD DVD bureaucracy to the front line, where it should always have been.

PATHFINDER: LONDON BOROUGH OF HOUNSLOW

Hounslow's organization has grown organically over the years, underpinned with proprietary 'best of breed' systems: siloed data making interoperability between services challenging. By 2012, the council had limited enterprise-wide capabilities and a lack of centralized customer data. Anthony Kemp, executive director of Resources, realized that rather than just replace point systems, there was a growing need for radical change at an enterprise level.

The reason that Kemp's approach is radical is that there was no attempt to embed new technology into old processes. In contrast, Hounslow has been implementing a platform-based approach: a very new way of working in local government and the wider public sector – that builds progressive capability around a small number of common platforms – in their case, the core platform is Salesforce.com and Force.com. The emphasis is on standardizing business processes, underpinned by a single platform, rather than adapting technology to existing processes. The advantages of this approach are huge opportunities for process improvements and information sharing across the council – accompanied by a systemic shift over time from a dependency on third-party suppliers for support and maintenance, as was historically the case, to controlling these activities in-house. Accordingly, the in-house development team has become the new centre of the ICT department – and processes are grown out from here.

Hounslow has discovered that platform-based approaches such as this one offer a step change in ability to put the customer in charge, which runs in stark contrast to traditional outsourcing-type arrangements, which continue a cycle of dependency by the public sector on large suppliers. In contrast, Hounslow assembles and shapes its own enterprise-wide services from standard 'building blocks', and is empowered to own and maintain these. This 'building block' approach is immediately obvious from Hounslow's platform-based architecture, as follows:

File-sharing Box.com	DMS	Service Cloud Salesforce	Marketing Cloud	Identity Services AmazonAWS	IaaS
Collaboration	Scanning Repository	Force.com	database.com	Database Services	Drupal WebCMS	Data Warehouse
Office365	Kofax	Heroku	Jitterbit	AirWatch	Aerohive
ExchangeOnline	ScanningEngine	Pure PaaS	IntegrationaaS	MDM	wifi
GIS	Docusign	IAR	JIRA	Quest One	Bime
Gazetteer	Electronic Signature	Info Asset Mgmt.	Agile Dev Mgmt.	RBAC Mgmt. PW self-service	BI Analytics

Perimeter Control

Firewall	VPN
Load Balancing	IPS

Desktop		Line of Bus Systems		Corporate Systems		Networks & Comms	
App Delivery	Session Delivery	LOB	LOB 2	Finance	FS	Switches	Telephony
Image Delivery	Thin Client Mgmt.	LOB 3	LOB 4.	HR	Payroll	Printers	Scanners
Tactical Desktop stack satisfies the short to mid term aspiration whilst the application portfolio is reduced and rationalised and capabilities are developed onto the core platform.		Agile development teams operate in this space to create LoB capabilities on the Force.com platform and decommission legacy LoB systems once migration is complete.		Corporate systems are integrated with the core platform via integration as a service engines such as Jitterbit. Local assets are migrated to IaaS or alternative SaaS products are consumed		Local assets reduce over time in terms of telephony networking. Local scan & print assets continue to be required.	

Platform and component-based architecture at LB Hounslow

One of the main challenges of rolling out this project has not been the technology itself, but building awareness within the organization of quite how powerful an enterprise platform can be for improving service delivery. In this type of transformation, many system users initially find it hard to fully embrace the tremendous opportunities now presented to them in being able to tailor and evolve the standardized 'building blocks' of their own system to the enterprise's needs – on a self-sufficient basis. However, once 'the penny drops', and they see why the council has taken this approach, people become enthusiastic about getting involved and aiding the creation of their new platform.

The example of the pathfinder London Borough of Hounslow shows what we believe to be the first enterprise-wide attempt to implement just such an architecture based on ILC. Many of the components in the architecture (for example, file-sharing at top left) are standardized, consumption-based, shareable across the council and easily swappable: everything is consumed from the cloud, and wherever the market permits it consumes all those parts that can be consumed as a utility, such as hosting and compute – with more to follow.

This is, however, just the start of a game-changing transformation and reinvention of public services that is achievable in the local services space. The same rigour can be applied to the new operating models that are starting to appear across local government, as councils struggle to reconceptualize their organizational structures to enable them to deliver services in a more diverse way. Figure 8.6 shows how ILC can be used to generate robust thinking that is *consistent and defensible* across all of the delivery vehicles that a council may wish to adopt.

In this example, we can see that CityTown has applied consistent principles across its various operations. It has distinguished between those parts of its future operating model that it wishes to retain and those parts that it wishes progressively to consume as a utility. In the middle are those parts for which no mature utility market yet exists – but which it nonetheless seeks to share with other, similar organizations. In turn, we would expect each of these functions to be able to produce a digital profile like that shown in Figure 7.3: the entire council 'drills down' consistently right to the bottom. Significantly, were every one of the authorities in the UK to perform such a profiling and make these available to one another, this would immediately trigger a frenzy of urgent discussions, as authorities

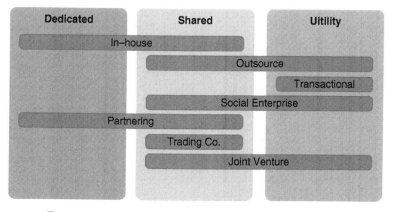

FIG 8.6 / Applying ILC to generate a consistent local services delivery model

started for the first time to apply a consistent set of principles to their operations, and to realize the significant benefits that are available.

The wholesale convergence on ILC by local authorities as a way of progressively converging on open architectures would create massive new platforms for innovation, investment, and consequent savings and improvements UK-wide. For example, how many councils moving to the top-left quadrant in Figure 6.1 – adopting standard ways of doing various gubbins and machinery activities, within a common set of technology standards – will it take before this market takes off and spreads through the entire local service market? Before councils joining the bandwagon are enjoying costs for services, such as revenues and benefits, of less than half the others? And why stop there? Do we really think that other providers of local services (we have already mentioned blue light, healthcare, housing, third sector and citizens themselves) will ignore what is happening, and not join in?

Imagine solving all of the current integration, data mining/sharing, evidence-based policy headaches at a stroke. Being able to respond quickly and cheaply to new legislation. Regaining control of our architecture, our budgets and our suppliers. Retaining our essential front-line staff. Being able to offer new services, cheaply, which draw seamlessly on all of the old vertical silos. And, best of all, spending much, *much* more on the things that we should be spending our money on.

DIGITAL LOCAL SERVICES

Google, Apple and Toyota are some of the most discussed and valuable organizations on the planet. As exemplars of the platform-based business model, they enjoy the advantages of commonly accepted ways of doing things, huge cost savings arising from aggregated demand and runaway innovation from a plural marketplace that is attracted by all this commonality (we are commenting here on their business models only). Current local government is the opposite. Vertically integrated into silos, it reinvents the same wheel again and again and is offered very little real choice. Perhaps worst of all, services are not designed for residents or the workforce and do not join up easily with other services and partners.

Converging on common ways of doing things, supported by open standards, would enable UK local government to become much more like Google, Apple and Toyota. Benefits include unprecedented joined-up sharing of information across the councils, their residents, partners and suppliers. This commonality would support custom apps built by the community, single-dashboard performance management, evidence-based analysis and commissioning, data mining and fraud detection, demand forecasting, integrated portfolio planning and management, open access data, supporting greater democratic engagement, wiki-style content management and self-serve business intelligence – right across council lines of business.

But Digital thinking can be extended across local services as a whole. Hundreds of local government organizations, surrounded by many thousands of other local service providers (healthcare, blue light, charity, housing and so on) could combine demand to create a very different market dynamic. This would require *all* providers of local services to work together to map their businesses and identify those common standards upon which they could all converge over time. Rather than choosing from a limited menu of bespoke suppliers, local authorities and service partners would assemble far more personalized services around residents from a varied menu of standard building blocks. Resources consumed by unnecessary duplication could be redeployed into face-to-face services. Partners could use many of the same building blocks, too – solving many of the looming headaches around joining up services (for example, between health and social care).

In short, the business model for local services as a whole will also start to look more like the platforms created by Google, Apple and Toyota. This requires much greater commercial agility and risk sharing across a portfolio of commercial contracts, with the local services always acting as the intelligent customer in this contracting portfolio.

Digital Profiling: How to Start a National Conversation

How, then, could we encourage all our local service providers – local authorities, housing associations, health service providers, blue light services and so on – to start generating their own digital profiles, and (better still) to start looking at other people's digital profiles, to identify all those missed opportunities for commonality?

Within the UK, and recalling our 'tight-loose' principle about the role of the centre in catalysing discussions about convergence on open standards, we suggest that a lead owner, such as the Department for Communities and Local Government (DCLG), makes available standard, web-based digital profiling and supports local service providers as they start to build a picture of their services using ILC.

In this process of entering digital profiles into a common service, service providers will start to expose clusters of services and components that actually look very similar, but which they are currently paying over the odds for. These data can be published automatically and openly as a continually evolving conversation on a website, so that digital profiling gathers momentum as service providers start to see the benefits of a visibly evolving national landscape of service demand. Such a bottom-up, emergent landscape of demand actually constitutes the open architecture itself: user-driven, open, fast-moving and collaborative. In rendering visible all of this currently similar but invisible demand, digital profiling will trigger conversations everywhere about shared *capability* (in contrast to existing discussions about top-down shared services, which usually descends into petty stand-offs about whose service is to be shared), as suppliers and service providers start to identify opportunities – and emerging markets – for standardized service components.

Finally, government can then link this evolving open architecture more explicitly to the marketplace by joining it with a suitable commodity procurement vehicle (in the UK, this is government's G-Cloud framework and its related CloudStore). Rather than a static catalogue of relatively random services, as is the case now, such procurement vehicles could become the intelligent commercial dimension of a vibrant (inter)national open marketplace for components and services.

/ Open Architecture and Agile: The Yin and Yang of Digital

We have explained how open architecture, as the updated plumbing of public services, will enable service providers progressively to converge on standard ways of doing things. This in turn will generate aggregated demand for consumable, commodity services – a marketplace that will attract investment and innovation from suppliers. We have called for a new iron discipline – digital profiling – essentially a dialogue in which all service providers can look at their requirements for standardizable components in the same way – since the power of open architecture lies in consumers' progressive adoption of commodity standards.

Remember: *open standards are the foundational principle underlying an architecture of consumption.* Open standards don't care where the technology comes from, in the same way as you probably don't care which version of Google you're running today: providing it meets standardized service outcomes and overarching technical/security criteria, you're happy to just consume it. And government IT could be the same: if we could only have the self-discipline to standardize our demand across government for common building blocks, we would create a ready market, in which a host of large and small suppliers would willingly innovate and compete.

A properly architected government would create huge demand for standard functions, and would then simply be able to sit back and consume, as the market responded. No more painful and intrusive upgrades, maintenance or supplier lock-in: as a general rule government wouldn't build and maintain much stuff itself any more, but would opt instead to consume the best, most innovative stuff from a rapidly evolving, globalized marketplace. It would get its act together, stop bespoking things and join the mainstream – benefiting from innovation at commodity prices.

We believe it's also worth calling out an important difference between open source software and an open architecture. In contrast to the consumption architecture underlying open standards, open *source* is different, because it *does* care where the technology comes from. And because of this, a government architecture founded on reuse of open source can never be an architecture of utility consumption: instead, the logic becomes one of in-house development and maintenance (the stuff doesn't exist 'out there', so you need to build it). The tail wags the dog once again, as happened with the earlier outsourcing model to big suppliers who likewise built everything (although they mainly chose proprietary technology to do so).

And this is where 'agile' comes in. In the context of an architecture of consumption, agile delivery is an extremely powerful approach, since it allows the recombination and reuse of standard building blocks, closely customized to users' requirements. However, the local approach is always tempered by the iron discipline of consumption and reuse wherever possible: the principle of open standards. In contrast, in the context of an approach involving in-house development and maintenance, agile delivery becomes potentially dangerous, because untempered by the open discipline of consumption and reuse, the local approach can run amok: new systems and applications are spun up with little regard for the overarching ecosystem in which they will need to exist. Being 'agile' becomes the end rather than the means, and government starts to build its own proprietary solutions yet again – although this time badged as built on open source. Something written in Ruby is little better than something written in Visual Basic if it commits government to a lifetime of bespoke building, maintenance upgrades and catch-up, whilst outside the open standards world moves on at a faster pace. There is currently an emphasis on agile delivery approaches within UK government that threatens to overshadow the more fundamental architecture of consumption upon which such agile practices need to be built. We address this tension below.

Build or Consume?

The debate about build versus consume is possibly the greatest challenge for governments' digital strategies. Put simply, where a government department or agency requires a particular system or service for which there will be little demand elsewhere, it obviously makes sense to build or commission this, with all the flexibility that an agile development and delivery approach supplies. Recalling Gawer's typology of platforms, this is her third definition: 'Industry platform', in other words, where government thinks of platform as a piece of software that needs to be built and operated from the centre. Although in time others may innovate around the services provided by this platform, the platform itself remains a common asset.

However, it is immediately apparent that this constitutes a different type of platform than the open platform discussed above – the proposed fourth definition of platform that we added to Gawer's typology. Here, instead of the flexibility promised by agile practices, we require the rigidity and discipline of open standards and open architecture: where appropriate, we need people to refrain from building their own 'special' service, and instead to assemble their own locally relevant service using standard, commonly available components. For governments, the challenge of digital is to understand when one type of platform is appropriate, and when, in contrast, we need the other. Both are *complementary* rather than competing notions of government as a platform (GaaP). Why should government assume for a minute that it is capable of innovation in a top-down, command economy style? As in the Google model, it is the great mass of citizens that innovate; government's job is to provide the enabling infrastructure, market incentive, protocols and governance. Digital is not about building *per se* – via agile practices or otherwise.

We suggest, therefore, that a mature understanding of the relationship, or tension, between the 'yin and yang' of digital demands greater recognition by governments, since it is superficially easier to focus on individual requirements – albeit using an agile approach – than to encourage everybody to consider the iron discipline of commonality. In this way, agile delivery should not become synonymous with digital: a government internal development team that builds lots of bespoke and 'special' software is, from the perspective of open standards, not much of an advance on the previous outsource arrangement: both detach government from the open, digital mainstream – and from the lifeblood of innovation, consumption and commoditization that this offers. In reference to Eric Raymond's widely known analysis of open source approaches, both are cathedral visions rather than bazaar ecosystems. We must ensure that applying agile practices does not become a fetish: something imbued with additional symbolic charge over and above its actual meaning. Amidst the growing noise of crowds enthusiastically chanting 'agile!' we must ensure that the signal of open standards is not allowed to grow fainter – and with it, the possibility of any genuine services revolution.

Summary – Characteristics of Digital Government

In Part 2, we have made the case for a wholesale commitment to radical digital transformation across our public services. We have attempted to take the long-standing political aspirations and recent digital developments of Part 1 to develop a framework that can successfully deliver the long-awaited era of better public services, reimagined and reinvented through what technology now makes possible – but only as part of a wider cultural and organizational shift.

In so doing, we acknowledge the efforts, and successes, of a great many people who have been working in the digital space for several years. However, we also hope that we have made the case for an urgent national discussion about the need to adopt a 'lean' mindset that asks necessarily frank and sometimes awkward questions about our current assumptions regarding the outcomes required of public services and how best they might be optimally delivered. Following from this, we have highlighted the necessity of *profiling* public services, using the innovate–leverage–commoditize framework and the power of open standards. By explaining the linkages between open standards, platforms and innovation, we have shown that open architecture is ultimately not a matter of minor tweaks to processes here and there, whilst leaving the fundamental service organization unchanged in its bricks-and-mortar form, cushioned in its comforting public/private sector blocs.

Achievement of digital public services will require nothing less than a lean-thinking mindset that helps underpin a wholesale dis-integration of these organizations, and the reaggregation of their various functions in the form of digital profiles, in the way we have explained. The reaggregation is around information and data, the lifeblood of all modern service organizations, clustered around the citizen, not the corporate. Digitizing government is thus an organization-wide undertaking, not a niche activity for technologists. It is for the minister, the chief executive, the permanent secretary – the citizen.

But there is more. We have illustrated how the public sector is large enough to be able to reap many of the benefits of digital organizations such as Google, if its myriad organizations could only start to de-duplicate standard ways of doing things. This calls for individual public organizations to develop enterprise-wide digital profiles enabling them to evolve over time, as well as maintaining continuous dialogue with the evolving profiles of others – perhaps initially within their sector, then nationwide. The taxpayer could sit at the centre of a powerful ecosystem of platforms and innovators, and our public services could better utilize these resources. There would be fewer managerial and bureaucratic opportunities within government, and more technical expertise.

Of course, the state is not like Google in many ways: it is both provider and consumer of services, it can never outsource risk to suppliers, and it undertakes many activities that are either too sensitive or commercially incompatible to place outside the public domain. That said, it is not so different from the likes of Google in terms of the way it can become more efficient at designing and running its services, its internal processes and its operations. We have provided a clear framework for enabling this vision of government as a platform (or, more accurately, government as platforms) to become reality, based on lean thinking, digital profiling and open architecture.

Overcoming our natural inertia requires a national debate. If our public organizations were not shielded by the taxpayer and in the position of being monopoly providers, in our increasingly digital age most would have gone bankrupt years ago. As with the example of the record industry, we need to understand that the structural reconfiguration of our existing public services will come anyway, sooner or later, as they become financially unsustainable, and/or simply irrelevant to the way in which people live. As the shareholders of government, we just need to make the choice about whether we want to be in the driving seat as this happens.

Service Providers
and Digital Delivery

We have been clear from the beginning of this book that digitizing government is not *primarily* about technology – but technology does have a fundamental role to play in the development of a digital organization. In our experiences of dealing with many different organizations, one particular problem we have encountered time and again is the lack of a common understanding of the core technology principles that underlie and enable many digital organizations. Far too frequently we have seen management decisions that unwittingly have a major impact on digital technology costs and efficiencies, or that lack understanding of the opportunities for much more effective services delivery if the digital technologies were employed with greater care.

In Part 3, we therefore devote time to setting out in more detail the technological aspects of digital public management in government being constructed by service providers (such as government departments and agencies). Our aim here is to close the gap in knowledge around the technologies that can help bridge the gap between intent and reality, building on the lessons learned in Part 1, and the 'Big Idea' framework and approach set out in Part 2. Hence, the focus in Part 3 is on providing more detail behind the core building blocks of the framework – drilling down into aspects of digital organizational structures, flexible architectures for large-scale systems, agile processes and practices, and the connected infrastructure required to realize a platform vision. The main elements of the discussion bring depth to the steps required to implement the kind of meaningful digital transformation we espouse.

For those feeling comfortably familiar with the topics we discuss here, we make no apology: without bringing everyone up to the same level of understanding about these critical technological developments it is hard in any organization to make much headway. It is by helping to establish both a common, consistent understanding of these topics, and a common vocabulary in which they can be discussed, that the move towards a truly digital organization can begin. For those feeling uncomfortable with the technological viewpoint expressed here, we equally implore you to spend the time to delve below the surface of these solutions in order to gain insight into how the needs of today's digital generation are being addressed.

In deciding what to focus on here, we have drawn upon the successful culture and practices of other organizations where digital initiatives are having a profound and significant impact. We therefore ground these discussions in a context that recognizes several important characteristics for digitizing government:

- **A blend of public and private systems**. The breadth and depth of services that must be delivered in a digital government cannot be developed exclusively by government-funded projects solely for the use of government-employed service providers.
- **A constant focus on cost-efficiency**. Costs must be contained by using standardized technologies wherever possible, forcing adjustment in government practices to be in line with commercial practices, or adapted to the specific needs of government.
- **An open architecture for flexibility and growth**. Advances in open standards and open systems offer the possibility of taking an 'open architectural' approach that encourages convergence around common standards and local innovation, as different local groups recombine these standard 'building blocks' to deliver new, more people-centred services.

Organizational Structures and Digital Transformation

The Foundations of Digital Transformation

Throughout this book we have defined digital transformation quite broadly, encompassing everything from the cultural and organizational changes required to the related use of new digital technologies in order to enable major improvements – such as enhancing user services, streamlining operations or creating entirely new services. Fundamental to this intentionally broad definition is the realignment of technology and business models to more effectively engage users. Restating our argument, our contention is that this breadth of view is an essential element of any viable digital transformation strategy, and that limiting the concept of digital delivery is both naive and harmful – and likely to condemn governments to repeat the cycle of self-similar rhetoric of 'better public services' of the past 20 or so years.

The challenge, then, for most governments is how best to plan and execute the strategic changes necessary to survive the disruption that digital technologies bring. Government is not alone: the vast majority of organizations lack the structure and experience with digital technologies to make significant progress in this transformation. In fact, the lessons from the past decade point to the three areas in which digital transformation causes particular disruption: how you understand your customer (or citizen), what you consider to be your key service outcomes, and who has insight and influence on your data, processes and practices. Approaches in these areas differ significantly depending on the maturity of the organization with respect to digital technology deployment.

Examining the digital maturity of an organization (via maturity frameworks such as the MIT Sloan School digital maturity index, Table 9.1) can provide insight into the emphases, thinking and current actions being undertaken, helping to understand the journey towards adoption of digital technologies, and consequently the likely capacity and speed of further activities in this direction. A first step, therefore, is for government agencies to undertake an honest baseline assessment of where they sit against such a digital maturity model – and understand where and how they can expedite their transition to a genuinely digital culture. Mapping the current landscape before deciding where to head – and why – is an important part of the initial process, but one often neglected.

Digital-based operating models are important to government because they offer increased access to information, transparency of business

TABLE 9.1   MIT Sloan School's digital maturity model

The MIT Sloan School recently created a simple digital maturity index for examining the adoption of digital technologies and their impact on practices in those organizations. It consists of four levels, with the following characteristics and indicated levels of occurrence in private sector surveys:

- **Beginner (65%).** An organization has deployed basic email and enterprise software, but has been slow to adopt digital technology in areas such as social media and analytics.
- **Conservative (14%).** An organization has good vision and strategy for digital technologies, but is slow in adoption and avoids any digital leadership activities.
- **Fashionista (6%).** An organization quickly adopts new digital technologies, but without a well-defined strategy or vision for its use across the organization.
- **Digirati (15%).** An organization with a strong shared vision for digital technology and the internal structures to execute effectively to realize business benefits.

As we see from this analysis, almost 80% of organizations can still be classed as low maturity in terms of digital transformation, where they may have made efforts toward adopting digital technologies but without doing so in the context of the broader transformational implication of such a move. Clearly, even in the private sector there remains a long way to go in digital transformation.

processes and greater customization to a variety of needs. These elements are perhaps most succinctly summarized in the simple digital business model framework devised by Peter Weill and Stephanie Woerner, shown in Figure 9.1.

In this framework, a digital business model has three components: content, customer experience and platform. The content component reconsiders what the customer (or citizen) consumes. This may be digital products such as software or electronic documents. It may also be other forms of information such as product details, service descriptions and comparison data. The customer experience component explores the best way to package the content to meet a customer need. The result may be a community experience, a personalized product experience, an open information access experience and so on. The platform component offers a way to deliver that experience. It may be via well-defined data management practices, an open interface, through the operating system on a mobile device and so on.

Through this simple three-layer framework it becomes possible to explore elements of any digital business model. For example, in the private sector

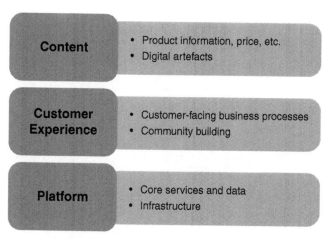

FIG 9.1 / Digital business model framework

Source: adapted from Weill and Woerner 2013

we can view the direction of publishing companies as much more than putting documents online. Rather, through this lens we see how proprietary, tightly integrated packages of content such as articles, photos and news items have been unpacked to offer wide collections of community-provided or syndicated materials accessible through many different channels. The experience offered to consumers is highly personalized to different consumer tastes and profiles, and delivered on demand or at the user's specified time frame to various devices that the user owns. The infrastructure supports the curation, co-ordination, and management of all these data sources, made accessible through a flexible software platform supporting many possible delivery models.

In the public sector the situation is similar. In the case of the UK government, for example, much of the current emphasis is on enhancing community interaction across a platform of public services. Efforts to open up public data sources (such as the large collection of data sources available at data.gov.uk) aim to offer content in new ways that encourage a variety of user experiences. For instance, the portal and dashboards presented at GOV.UK offer a unified user experience for the websites of all government departments, and many other agencies and public bodies. Here the user can see all UK government policies, announcements, publications, statistics and consultations. In parallel, restructuring of the underlying infrastructure is taking place to enable greater transparency in the way the public sector operates, and to support flexibility in how the content is made available for consumption (many of them described in the UK government's blog pages at gds.blog.gov.uk).

PATHFINDER: GOVERNMENT DIGITAL SERVICE

The Government Digital Service (GDS) was established in 2011, following the agreement of a new approach to public sector IT within the Cabinet Office (see Part 1) based on progressive adoption of open standards. Responding to the need for a tight central core to consolidate and agree standards across government, GDS has had two primary thrusts. First, it pushed for the adoption of a central 'publishing platform' (website) across government, and in gov.uk has succeeded in consolidating a messy and expensive web estate into a single, award-winning channel that has proven widely popular.

Government Digital Service

Design Principles

Listed below are our design principles and examples of how we've used them so far. These build on, and add to, our original 7 digital principles.

1 **Start with needs***
2 **Do less**
3 **Design with data**
4 **Do the hard work to make it simple**
5 **Iterate. Then iterate again.**
6 **Build for inclusion**
7 **Understand context**
8 **Build digital services, not websites**
9 **Be consistent, not uniform**
10 **Make things open: it makes things better**

Second, GDS has begun turning to issues of architectural consolidation within government, identifying 25 government organizations with whom they are working to transform legacy processes using principles based around simplification and reuse, as in their website, above. We like GDS's design principles very much. Whilst we could say nice things about all of these principles, two are especially relevant for the wholesale digital transformation of public services discussed in this book. The most relevant of all is number 9: 'be consistent, not uniform'. We have explained how the application of a consistent approach (open architecture using ILC) across all government services will succeed in generating untold variety from standard components. In designing public services, open architecture enables us to *design for variety*, enabled by *standard components*, selected and configured locally using *consistent thinking*. This tension between standardization at component level, and enormous innovation and variety at service level, lies at the heart of digital thinking.

Principle number 3: 'design with data', also deserves special mention. By accepting that information is now the lifeblood of the modern organization, our ability to collect, share and rapidly make sense of it quickly becomes a paramount design consideration. We only understand what organizational plumbing we need when we know what lifeblood sustains different parts of the organization. Much of our organizational life centres on performing transactions and transformations of data, from one part to another. Once we start to focus our attention on the data, rather than the bricks-and-mortar structures, many of these old structures start to look increasingly redundant.

The value of this thinking, however, is to remind us that the most significant change in any digital transformation is the effect it has on the way the organization is designed to deliver the best possible customer experience. Digital transformation takes advantage of technology to question major assumptions we make about the users we serve (be they citizens or consumers), the experiences we offer to them, and the most efficient ways to deliver those experiences in a co-ordinated, consistent and cost-effective way. However, to understand the true extent of what 'digital transformation' means, we need to shift our perspective away from the specific *technologies* inherent in a digital world and towards the *principles* on which digital-driven organizations operate. Companies lauded for their digital credentials demonstrate a way of working that distinguishes them from their competitors. These characteristics lead some people to refer to such organizations as 'elastic enterprises', where their distinguishing features are not specific choices of technology or strategy, but their ability to adapt rapidly in the face of change: the very characteristics long desired by governments struggling to adapt more efficiently and in a more timely fashion to ever-changing socio-economic demands. So let's now consider this notion of 'elasticity' of an organization in a little more detail.

'Elastic' Principles of Successful Digital Organizations

A number of organizations have found ways to become more flexible in their ability to absorb growth, and to react to changes in market conditions – moving quickly into new areas, adapting to different delivery channels and forming new alliances as necessary to deliver more efficiently. Vitalari and Shaughnessy propose that such elastic enterprises are based on five principles, as set out in Table 9.2.

The result of applying these five principles is the development of organizations with a more dynamic, agile approach to change, and with the flexibility to adjust to unforeseen circumstances: the very characteristics that governments need in order to maintain their relevance to citizens in the twenty-first century. True digital transformation is therefore about rethinking business strategies and adjusting organizations to be more flexible and responsive to change, not about deploying new technology within existing processes, problems and practices.

However, this need for greater elasticity requires significant reshaping of an organization, particularly with regard to the way digital technologies are deployed as an enabler to broader digital transformation. With such a large percentage of organizations at the early stages of this journey, it's

TABLE 9.2   The five key principles of 'elastic enterprises' (Vitalari and Shaughnessy 2013)

1	A clear business platform where business rules and relationships are well aligned to address customer needs and support supply chain opportunities
2	The development of a healthy business ecosystem where interacting participants in the platform are motivated to deliver major functional capabilities and services in support of the organization's business goals
3	Explicit creation of universal connectors to services offered by the organization through interfaces that encourage and leverage business partners
4	Cloud infrastructure for rapid deployment and low overheads in internal management of critical core services, and external delivery of capabilities to clients and partners
5	A leadership style and approach that recognizes the transformational impact of digital business, and is unafraid to drive the organization in new directions toward reshaping its role, purpose and operating model

useful to consider at least three elements fundamental to the success of government in successfully transitioning to a truly digital culture:

1. Adopting an experimental approach to organizational agility based on lean principles.
2. Reshaping the business model based on the new opportunities brought by digital technologies.
3. Establishing an adaptable organizational culture appropriate to fast-paced digital change.

We take a look at each of these in a little more detail below, as they play an important role in helping to move an existing organization to one with a digital culture.

Experimental Approaches to Organizational Agility

Surviving short-term pressures inevitably means that building the next generation of services in any organization often takes a poor second place to supporting current day-to-day activities. It is no surprise, then, that most technology-dependent organizations focus the majority of their activities towards core processes aimed at efficiently controlling the management, upgrade and repair of their existing systems. In fact, typically, up to 80% of all IT costs are consumed in such tasks. Consequently, an understanding of digital transformation must ground its work in approaches that recognize and deliver efficiency in existing environments.

Lean

We have already mentioned the importance of a 'lean' mindset in Chapter 6, where we explored the cultural framework required for digital govern-ment. For many organizations, *lean thinking* provides the basis for effi-ciency approaches. Lean techniques are a manufacturing and production practice based on the lessons from the manufacturing domain in the 1980s and 1990s. Expenditure of resources for any goal other than the creation of value for the end user is considered wasteful and thus a target for elimination. Value is defined as any action or process that a user would be willing to pay for – and hence lean thinking is centred on preserving value with less work. A lean style aims to optimize flow, increase efficiency, decrease waste and use empirical methods to decide what matters, rather than uncritically accepting pre-existing ideas.

The original lean practices used by Toyota in car assembly plants have been adapted to many other organizations. However, the key elements of lean thinking remain true to the original vision, as shown in Table 9.3.

In the move towards digital public service delivery there is a need to focus on lean practices with the aim of ensuring fast cycles to improve feedback and learning across the value chain. The result is an agile innovation practice viewed as a series of experiments governed by well-defined hypotheses, a focus on speed of testing those hypotheses, and recognition that a clear approach to measurement and management is essential to ensure any experimental approach converges towards meaningful decision making.

Some key principles in this area are emerging, summarized by Eric Ries in Table 9.4.

These lessons are important: in the digital age, government services (whether government explicitly recognizes it or not) are realized through software-intensive business processes. Redesigning those services requires

TABLE 9.3   Key elements of lean thinking

Define Value	Specify value from the customer or citizen perspective
Map the Value Stream	Identify the value stream for each product or service and challenge all of the non-value adding steps (wastes) currently necessary to create and deliver this product or service. Add nothing except value
Create Flow	Make the product or service creation and delivery process flow through the remaining value-added steps
Establish Pull	Introduce pull between all process steps where continuous flow is possible
Pursue Perfection	Manage towards perfection the number of steps and the amount of time and information needed to create and deliver this product or service

TABLE 9.4   Key principles of agile (Ries 2011)

Agility is management	Too many people associate an agile organization with a chaotic, 'anything goes' attitude to governance and planning. Nothing could be further from the truth. In any agile approach there must be a very strong management dimension to ensure progress is co-ordinated and aligned. Large numbers of small incremental changes must be made based on analytical data. That cannot occur without discipline and rigour.
Validated learning	Agile decision making requires constant feedback, and is consolidated through frequent reflection. Any agile organization must learn from the experiments it undertakes, and validate that learning with real-world inputs.
Innovation accounting	Measuring progress in conventional ways (for example, source lines of code delivered, function points coded, and so on) offers little value to an agile organization. Rather, the organization is optimized to rapid decision making, flexibility in adopting new capabilities, and ease of adaptation to evolving feedback from early consumers. Consequently, a new view of innovation accounting is required that focuses on establishing benchmarks for these areas and accelerating the pace of delivery based on managing those measures.
Build–measure– learn cycle	The most critical life cycle process in an agile organization is the 'build–measure–learn' cycle. A great deal of attention is directed towards its definition and execution. The speed and acceleration of executing that cycle are determinant factors in understanding the agile organization.

a disciplined approach to allow changes in the business processes that realizes them. Ries (2011) observes that what distinguishes more successful organizations from others is that they welcome and embrace change, making many adjustments in the business processes as they learn what works and what doesn't – changes in value proposition, customer segment, business model, partner network and so on. Their key attribute is their ability to *pivot* when they gain feedback contrary to their expectations: they change direction but stay grounded in what they have learned. Furthermore, they focus on validated learning and employ a rigorous method for demonstrating progress through positive improvements in core metrics and key performance indicators critical to their business. This is a very different model for government services, which have generally been put into place and then left largely as they are without a continual process of user-centred refinement and improvement.

Reshaping the business model

We recognize that the changes we are discussing will not be easy or quick to achieve: successful change of any kind requires a substantial investment in people and culture. Without careful analysis and planning, even the best-intentioned transformations rarely have the impact expected, and almost certainly not at the pace anticipated. Many recent studies into high-performing organizations have highlighted the dominant factor played by people and team dynamics in any technology-driven delivery success. Yet in spite of these studies, many organizations fail to take adequate account of the human elements of an improvement programme, and focus a majority of their attention on the more mechanical technological and process aspects. Just such a technology-led approach has characterized many governments' efforts to move online – and in part explains the large-scale failure of such initiatives.

For inspiration, it is useful to consider the recent revolution in software delivery practices – inspired by the need to place people at the centre of the creative process of any digital transformation effort. In fact, the agile manifesto issued over a decade ago was explicitly aimed at placing the focus of attention on the impact of people in software-intensive activities.[1] Several agile software development methods produced as a result of that thinking provide guidance on how to motivate teams to encourage greater emphasis on the importance of cultural change rather than mechanical processes. Jim Highsmith offers perhaps the most straightforward advice on successfully changing delivery culture by creating self-directed teams: get the right people; articulate the project vision, boundaries and roles; encourage interaction; facilitate participatory decisions; insist on accountability; and steer, don't control.

Such simple guidance presents an obvious starting point for those governments embarking on a digital transformation to improve their culture with flexible development capabilities. However, their interpretation and implementation can be much more challenging in practice and they may appear 'soft' in comparison to more systemic changes, and yet harder to

---

[1] http://agilemanifesto.org/.

manage (or measure) than the simplistic project management checklists, documents and charts of the past. Much more radical management principles are required to prevent this thinking from being isolated at development levels within an organization, and made more widely applicable across all levels in the organization. Within a broader organizational culture and context, two dimensions are particularly critical to success: organizational and individual.

Establishing an adaptable culture – organizations and individuals

At the *organizational* level, the major pressure on digital transformation is the need to constantly adapt to meet the demands of changing environments. Although it is tempting to believe that such adaptation can be driven through high-level corporate initiatives (the top-down approach adopted during the e-government and t-government eras), the most common approach in organizations successful in digital solution delivery involves building the visibility and credibility of digital leaders throughout the organization, and to encourage communities led by those elected by the community itself (so-called meritocracies). In this way the organization builds an environment that encourages action from the bottom up and naturally develops employees who embrace and share new ways of thinking and working.

A recent study emphasized six findings that underscore the importance of organizations encouraging this kind of thinking in individuals and teams:

- Organizations require significant time to absorb changes, and react to new norms. Typically it takes more than two years for major organizational shifts to be accepted. Attempting more rapid change in organizational structures frequently has negative impacts that overwhelm the improvements they introduce.
- Where organizations are experiencing fast-paced changes in their environment, their employee's ability to adapt to change is more significant to success than their productivity and performance. Not only do they enhance their own impact on the organization, but they also learn from others, seek feedback and support their peers.

• Agile organizations must improve communication, increase the transparency and focus on sharing information that helps employees be self-directed autonomous and develop their own solutions to problems they encounter.

• The highest-performing individuals and teams in an agile organization create strong networks, and use these networks as a primary source of communication, problem solving and social interaction.

• The enablement role assumed in most software-driven businesses must be revisited for agile organizations. They must prioritize coaching, connect employees to the right networks and communities, and emphasize honest retrospection and feedback to improve all aspects of the organization.

• The focus on agility is a cross-functional effort. It affects all aspects of the organization, including its approach to hiring and training employees, performance management models, external communications and public relations, strategic planning and technology investment.

At the *individual* level, any major change in a digital transformation must be supported with education, training and ongoing support. Many approaches are possible: using online or classroom-based techniques, through specific coaching sessions or in-project support, employing external consultants or using in-house experts and mentors, and so on. Each organization must make its own choices based on their context and experiences. However, based on our experiences with organizations making substantive digital transformations in service delivery, we feel the need to highlight two particular educational dimensions that are often overlooked and yet which provide value in this context: variation by role and by project type.

The first, varying the education and training by role, may seem obvious, but we have found that careful attention should be given to the needs of certain roles within an organization. For example, in one situation digital transformation involved substantial agile practice training for practitioners, and similar efforts were under way for project managers. However, the resistance in supporting large-scale change in behaviour was coming from a lack of senior management understanding. Little attention had been paid to how to discuss digital transformation and its implications for the broader organization with key personnel in critical functions such as contract management, human resources and financial planning. Basic understanding of digital technologies and their implications for these roles was important because the broad adoption of new practices inevitably had major impacts on many of the core processes; how each individual's performance is assessed; how project time and effort is accounted; processes and practices for hiring new staff; how contracts between organizational units are defined; and so on. By excluding individuals in key roles across the organization it inevitably led to misunderstandings and misalignment of goals, with consequent impacts on organizational effectiveness and morale.

The second is varying the education and training by project type. In many digital transformation situations we see clear distinctions among project categories such as front-office or back-office projects, maintenance projects, mainframe projects, on-line channel projects and so on. The initial danger is that education about digital transformation is considered only important for some of these categories (typically those focused on digital media or digital delivery channels) and not for others. In such cases, an immediate two-tier perception is created, resulting in friction between the different groups. Alternatively, the temptation is to provide a uniform approach to education across all roles. While a core set of education and coaching needs may be broadly appropriate, there will undoubtedly be requirements for specific topics to be addressed, with different people working in these project categories. For example, we have seen significant resistance to adopting various agile practices in software delivery teams responsible for mainframe software maintenance projects. Closer investigation revealed that the education and support for those teams was being given by external consultants who were very skilled in the latest agile methods for small web-based systems but with very little background, understanding or experience in the challenges of maintaining business mission-critical application on a mainframe. The mismatch of cultures led to very poor results.

Consequently, for digital transformation success, our experiences suggest that each public sector organization must spend time assessing its organizational structures, categorizing the key roles, and laying out a model for improving digital knowledge across all levels. A comprehensive education programme is an essential component of this model, addressing themes relevant to the needs of all key roles across the organization.

Some Challenges – and How to Overcome Them

We have discussed how public sector organizations are looking to accelerate the delivery of citizen and business value through better-managed, rapid change cycles, but their complex structures, processes and environments make this tough. In particular, governments typically face at least five challenges, namely how to:

- overcome badly designed and inconsistent processes;
- increase speed and efficiency while simultaneously increasing value;
- be flexible and creative to meet user needs but get measured on utilization;
- deploy and support multiple technologies, platforms, languages and tools that drive transparency;
- accommodate a 'flattening world' that drives collaboration across agencies, services, geographies and cultures.

So just how should governments respond? We believe that governments need to adopt the following principles:

1. *Agile change management,* because it accelerates time-to-value and:
   a. enables a better understanding of – and a rapid response to – user needs;
   b. organizes work efforts according to the principles of time-based competition;
   c. adds a management system focused on delivery acceleration.
2. *Open collaboration,* because it increases collaboration while recognizing individual achievement and:
   a. enables the formation of high-functioning teams;
   b. moves the focus beyond utilization;
   c. increases the visibility of individual achievement;
   d. leverages the value driven by external input and open collaboration.
3. *Platform-based architecture,* because it encourages flexibility in design and delivery and:
   a. allows the evolution of a service architecture based on a service-oriented view;
   b. supports an ecosystem of providers around a core set of capabilities;
   c. opens up access to a broad community through standard interfaces.

TABLE 9.5   Technical challenges to success

The people break	Resistance to change is commonly experienced with any new way of working. Agile, open team practices can deeply affect the culture and values that are in place, and result in strong pushback from disoriented individuals.
The tools break	Most business processes are not targeted at rapid delivery cycles and extensive experimentation in creating new products and services. Tooling can be a severe inhibitor to agile ways of operating if not aligned with the innovative practices.
The governance breaks	The measures and metrics used to govern assume a traditional view of project progress and success. Adjustments are required to provide a balance between governed progress and the need for fast learning cycles.
The customer breaks	Any rapid delivery cycle demands more frequent feedback with customers and other stakeholders. Getting the input needed to learn is essential. Yet many consumer–supplier relationships do not readily support such interactions.
The financial controls break	Product funding cycles are frequently based on progress through various stage-gates such as 'design complete' and 'first customer shipment'. In more agile delivery cycles flexibility is required to fund activities with different risk profiles, delivering functionality in small slices.
The organizational structure breaks	Eventually the whole management structure of the organization becomes stressed when empowered teams interact directly with consumers in rapid iterations of new product features. The command-and-control view of decision making can be directly at odds with the shifting priority-based delivery model of the agile teams.

Source: Adapted from Richard Durnall, Thoughtworks

Implementing these principles supports service innovation using rapid prototyping and ongoing improvements that remain responsive to changing organizational needs. These constitute important early steps in a move towards processes of continual innovation and improvement. However, sustained and successful innovation of public services will require a broader view of agility and openness in government. Many governments have seen their ambitions thwarted by overbearing and slow-moving cultural, engineering and management practices. In any real project, substantial effort is invested in essential activities such as liaising with users, arbitrating conflicting demands, hiring staff, obtaining and setting up test equipment, interacting with project and programme management co-ordinators and training teams on new capabilities. Without care, the gains from agile and open delivery methods become insignificant in the daily cut-and-thrust of a project, or else become choked by the broader organizational inertia and inefficiency that surround them. Good ideas are repeatedly sucked back below the waves.

Richard Durnall, a principal analyst with Thoughtworks (a leading global software delivery organization), has summarized recurrent challenges to the successful adoption of innovative approaches within large organizations. He observes that the challenges encountered follow a familiar pattern, and the substantive culture-change inherent in digital transformation faces a common order of failures: starting with the people involved in the change, the locus of concerns then moves to tools, governance, customers, financial controls and, finally, to the organizational structure itself (see Table 9.5).

Summary – the Elements of Successful Digital Transformation

Driving innovation is critical for the success of digital initiatives in the public sector. However, lessons from agile software delivery experiences have taught us that it is fatal for an organization to become over-enamoured with the mechanisms and sheer excitement of the innovation process itself. For success, the focus of attention must be on innovation management practices that yield results, and based on techniques that address the most common failure points.

Our experiences have made us well aware that defining and executing a digital transformation strategy is neither straightforward nor without risk. Many organizations have taken the first limited steps on this journey through the adoption of digital media for communicating with customers, engaging in pilot projects built with new open technology stacks, and by updating parts of their back office with lighter weight technology infrastructure consumed as a service.

Through our experiences with many organizations undergoing the trauma of digital transformation, we have identified several areas that help these organizations to maintain their momentum and focus in a time of constant change and challenge. Those enjoying most success demonstrate three clear traits: they encourage an experimental mindset based around lean principles; they actively explore digital business model alternatives; and they assist the organization and its people to become more change ready. In this way, they bring to the organization the agility and flexibility necessary to embrace digital transformation as a way to become more elastic, so that their scale and growth is a positive force in delivering an excellent customer or citizen experience.

Furthermore, this digital transformation cannot take place in a closed, proprietary environment. Former CTO of the US Aneesh Chopra, in his book *Innovative State: How New Technologies can Transform Government*, describes how the focus on open innovation has been essential in US government, and how new technologies that underlie the digital economy can realize Tim O'Reilly's vision for government as a platform (GaaP). Chopra provides a wide range of examples to support his discussion, illustrating how platform-based thinking can revolutionize service delivery in government.

A primary inspiration for Chopra is the pioneering work on open innovation practices by Berkeley professor Henry Chesbrough. His seminal work on how to understand open approaches to innovation in the private sector is well known. However, he also has looked to apply his work to public institutions such as US government agencies. Government's role, according to Chesbrough, is to 'do enough to liberate or harness the energies of the private sector' and use this to drive the public and private sectors closer together. Chopra has worked to realize this approach in several government agencies, with some notable successes.

Chopra's experiences over the past few years led him to develop an 'open innovation toolkit' that he has used to consolidate how open government can be realized in practice. His focus is on the change in culture necessary to open up thinking around the options available to policymakers to achieve their aims of providing more effective services to citizens in a more collaborative way, and to do so as efficiently as possible. He identifies four key elements of this toolkit:

- **Open data**, to enable public access to more of the information currently closed to external scrutiny, and inaccessible to new service deliveryo pportunities.
- **Impatient convening**, to drive the private and public sectors towards the necessary open standards that increase competition and open up markets to suppliers of all sizes.
- **Challenges and prizes**, as incentives to focus potential providers of services on the issues critical to government, and to change the procurement processes from long-term risk avoidance to shorter-term value creation.
- **Attracting talent into the public sector**, by specifically recruiting entrepreneurs from the private sector into public sector roles, and by inspiring a new generation of digital-aware public sector employees.

The results of pursuing these changes have been significant: most notably across healthcare, tax management and veterans' affairs. However, much work remains to bring greater alignment across public and private sectors. Chopra notes that *'open innovation is about handshakes and handoffs: the handshakes between powerful, enabling entities that allow for the handoffs to those with the hope, ambition, inspiration, and ideas to make our country better in every conceivable way'*. We could not be more in agreement with this sentiment, and this book provides our response to how this can more readily be achieved.

The rest of Part 3 explores three specific practices and techniques for use in the public sector that are an essential part of the transition towards digital public management: flexible architectures for large-scale systems; agile processes and practices; and the connection of open interfaces in an 'API' economy.

chapter 10

Flexible Architectures
for Large-scale Systems

In the past, public services often procured information systems that were 'built to last' when in fact the real requirement was that they should be 'built for change'. Their tight vertical integration meant that modifying any part of a system often impacted upon the entire system. What should have been a simple update of a business policy, calculation or rule requiring a few hours' work turned into a complex, bureaucratic and code-intensive process that instead took months of tedious effort. Such brittle systems built on 'telephone book' lists of upfront requirements ironically made it harder for policy to be nimbly adapted, yet the one certainty in government is the need to be flexible to meet constantly changing requirements and alterations in policy.

Successful digital organizations have adopted more flexible and iterative approaches to a key area of their technology: its software architecture. This need to adopt better software development and deployment approaches has been recognized by the UK government through the creation of the Government Digital Service, which is introducing to the public sector the techniques and approaches that have long been successfully used in the private sector. But software does not exist in a vacuum: as we have seen earlier, it needs some sort of architectural framework within which it can live and breathe.

In any meaningful discussion on software architecture, two elements must be addressed: the services being provided, and the infrastructure that supports and interconnects those services. As a result, here we first consider the services perspective and provide a real-world example of the digital profiling we discussed in Chapter 7: it provides an essential precursor before important decisions can be taken about which aspects of an architectural model can simply be consumed from an existing service, and which may need to be custom-built in-house. We then explore some specific aspects of different architectural approaches for large-scale systems delivery.

Digital Profiling

In Part 2, we discussed the important role of digital profiling and the innovate–leverage–commoditize (ILC) model. Prior to any work looking at how a new or existing public service might best be (re)designed, built or acquired, we emphasized how its requirements must first be properly profiled. Having previously demonstrated the principle, we now look at a real example of the use of the ILC framework to take the first step towards a digital profile.

The High Speed 2 (HS2) railway infrastructure programme is, as its name suggests, an investment programme to construct a high-speed railway, between London and areas to the middle and north of the UK. Its CIO, James Findlay, has profiled the technology capabilities for the new organization, shown in Figures 10.1–10.4. The technique used by HS2 is known as a Wardley Map, after Simon Wardley who first used and described the technique in 2005. This technique combines two elements in order to create a visual landscape for a complex system. The first element is the value chain, which in this case is described as a chain of needs from visible user needs to the underlying (and hence invisible) components required to meet those needs. By way of illustration of this approach, Figure 10.1 provides a simple (but incomplete) example for 'making a cup of tea'.

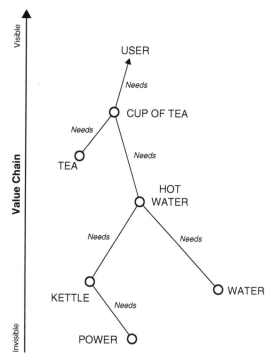

FIG 10.1   Value chain of needs (courtesy of Simon Wardley)

Whilst an organization can be described in terms of a set of value chains, the problem remains that value chains aren't static and the components within them evolve. Hence the second element of a Wardley Map is to add in Figure 6.6 from Chapter 6 – the previously described pattern for evolution, reproduced for convenience in Figure 10.2.

Figure 10.2 reminds us that the overall purpose of a digital profile is to separate out, and then profile, the various elements of a technology estate according to the basic ILC logic: is it something we should be treating as a utility (consuming) or maybe a basic commodity (purchasing in standard formats)? Is it something that only a few people use, but on which we might collaborate with them to bring down cost? Or, finally, is it something that for the foreseeable future will remain a bespoke item for our organization? Bear in mind that, given technology's increasing role as a

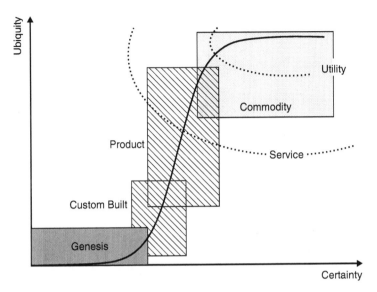

FIG 10.2 / Evolution of an activity

'Trojan horse' for embedded ways of doing things within an organization, these choices will affect the way in which the entire organization functions – because we are effectively talking about re-plumbing it in an entirely different way. By combining both value chain and evolution together then you can create a map of the landscape – and since evolution is applicable to activities, practices, data and knowledge, then all of these components can be visualized.

Figure 10.3 shows this principle in operation at HS2. In this example we can see that some of the obvious elements (power, computer processing, standard HR, website and so on) are treated as commodity/utilities to be either consumed on demand (like electricity) or purchased in standard units (like pencils). We can see that some of the ERP-type functions (finance, customer relationship management, risk management) are not yet widespread enough in the market to be consumable as utilities – but these are things that we should nonetheless consume in a standard way wherever possible (the UK government has recently established shared service centres to support this aim). Next, the 'custom built' column

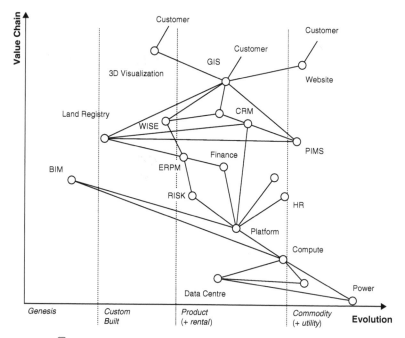

FIG 10.3 A Wardley Map of HS2, separating out different technology capabilities

contains those elements that we know we need, but which to our knowledge remain reasonably unique to our organization, or one or two others. Finally, the 'genesis' column shows those 'known unknowns' where we will need to work iteratively in an agile manner to discover and evolve what it is that we need, and build this capability within the organization.

Having separated out the technology, which would previously have been treated as a vertical stack, into its discrete components and distinguished carefully between them to generate a digital profile using the ILC principle, it then becomes possible to build out a procurement strategy that underpins these principles, to allow the sourcing of every component in the optimum way possible. Thus HS2 is using the UK government's electronic property and information mapping service (PIMS), which it is consuming as a commodity; a single ERP platform, consumed from one of the government's shared service organizations, to cover finance, HR and customer relationship management – but within individual functions supported via the new standard service catalogue G-Cloud. Note that Figure 10.3 shows which of these functions, such as HR, lie at the commodity end of this spectrum, giving clarity about where this consumed service really needs to demonstrate value.

We can see that there are several functions (risk management, ERPM, WISE) that are purchased through specific suppliers, either consumed via a bespoke contract or purchased on an individual basis. This is the model that most closely represents the traditional 'systems integrator' way of doing things, with little or no commonality across government. Finally, HS2 is building several functions in-house – interactions with Land Registry, 3D visualization for customers, geographic information interfaces for customers and the customer website. The customer, as the stakeholder at the top of the value chain, is receiving the bespoke attention (recalling Mark Foden's 'levers and dials') – whilst the heavy lifting (ERP platform, data centre, power, compute – Mark Foden's 'machinery') is consumed as a common service wherever possible. In the middle, we have Mark Foden's 'specific gubbins' (Land Registry interface) and 'common gubbins' (PIMS, standardized ERP applications such as finance, HR and so on) – which HS2 can do in the same way as other government organizations simply by applying this methodology and exercising a little self-control. This approach to acquiring services is highlighted in Figure 10.4.

The HS2 example demonstrates the power of the ILC approach in enabling government organizations to dis-integrate previously vertically integrated silos of impenetrably linked technology and business process, and start to profile them in ways that allow accurate distinction between their various components, with appropriate sourcing strategies against each one. In turn, treating commodities for what they are avoids paying bespoke prices for off-the-peg suits – as well as allowing individual components to be updated or replaced easily, and combined with those of other organizations. Although cost-saving is a good thing, it's only really when the advantages of working with other people's systems and data become clear that the *real* benefits of digital organizing start to become apparent: delivering a transformation in the quality, relevance and maintainability of the services.

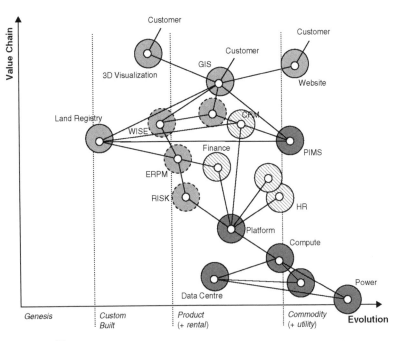

FIG 10.4 **Using appropriate procurement routes for different capabilities**

The use of this profiling is essential before rational decisions can be taken about which elements of the architecture might best be built – and which procured. However, successful execution of this approach requires a more detailed understanding of the underlying software architecture issues that must be faced. In particular, most government systems have been conceived, designed, delivered, evolved and maintained over many years. Disentangling them is a formidable exercise that should not be underestimated. In the end, the complexity of the technology will have a major influence on what is feasible and how best change is to be managed and phased. Closely related to these concerns is how the development and integration of software components from the bespoke and hand-built to the reuse of existing commodity elements are to be managed. To address these issues, we now turn to look at different approaches to software architecture in order to understand the challenges that must be addressed, and to identify those best suited to support the move to become a digital organization.

Approaches to Software Architecture

Traditionally the pressure on software and service delivery has been to balance activities across four main dimensions:

- **Productivity** of individuals and teams (including the suppliers running the teams on government's behalf), typically measured in terms of lines of code or function points delivered over unit time.
- **Time-to-go-live** for projects to complete and deliver a meaningful outcome. This can be measured in average time for project completion, project overruns or turnaround time from request for a new capability to its delivery in a product.
- **Process maturity** in the consistency, uniformity and standardization of practices. Measurements can be based on adherence to common process norms or by maturity approaches such as the capability maturity model (CMM) levels.
- **Quality** in shipped code, errors handled and turnaround of requests. Measures are typically combinations of defect density rates and errors fixed per unit time.

However, with the increasing pressure for governments to respond more quickly, finding an appropriate balance across these factors is increasingly difficult.

Traditional approaches to enterprise software

Building an enterprise-scale software system has always been (and remains) a complex undertaking. It's not just government that has a track record of large IT-related projects running into problems: similar problems are commonplace in the private sector too.

In spite of decades of technological advances, the demands imposed by IT systems and their users frequently stretch to breaking point an organization's ability to design, construct and evolve mission-critical solutions. In particular, few new government systems have the luxury of being designed from the ground up. Usually they involve extending the life of an existing solution by describing new process logic that manipulates an existing repository of data; presenting existing data and transactions through new channels such as web browsers or smart devices; integrating previously disconnected systems supporting overlapping business activities; redesigning a complex algorithm to take account of a new operating context; and so on. Consequently, a primary focus for any software architect is to describe and realize the key elements of the system and their interactions. This provides the clear architectural framework necessary for understanding and analysing the system's behaviour.

For more than a decade, the blueprint for describing traditional large-scale application architecture approaches has been based on an 'n-tiered' approach – one in which an application is segregated into a number of tiers to allow changes to be made independently in each tier. For example, a typical three-tiered view may distinguish as separate layers the presentation (user interface), the business and process logic, and the data management elements to be implemented. This is similar to the early government portal architecture we discussed in Chapter 3, which proposed a three-tier model.

In practice it is common for each tier to be implemented by a specific technology solution – for example, one or more products can be used for defining and managing the business logic layer. This has resulted in vendor-specific application servers appearing for particular technology implementations: these have become common middleware (middle tier) solutions widely used for supporting major application deployments. As a result, the business logic that forms the core of an application is implemented in a specific technology and executes within the appropriate application server. A typical n-tiered solution is illustrated in Figure 10.5.

Over time, the middle-tier layer became progressively more complex in many organizations –in part a by-product of the rich variety of different

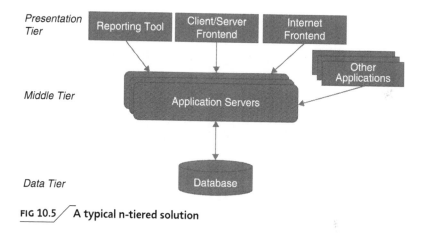

FIG 10.5 A typical n-tiered solution

technology solutions, standards and implementations that became available. To overcome this challenge, many organizations employed an 'enterprise service bus' (ESB). An ESB is effectively a vendor-neutral way of connecting together different supplier products in the various parts of an n-tier solution in order to hide complexity, simplify access and to allow developers to use generic, standard forms of query, access and interaction. As illustrated in Figure 10.6, its main roles include:

- Distributing information across an organization quickly and easily.
- Hiding differences among underlying platforms, software architectures and network protocols.
- Ensuring that information delivery is consistent even when some systems or networks fail, or go offline.
- Re-routing, logging and enriching certain kinds of interactions and information flows without requiring applications to be rewritten.
- Providing support for partial service solution implementations to test potential solutions quickly, and to enable incremental upgrade of enterprise services and applications.

To design solutions across multiple tiers, a new design approach was needed that allowed the behaviour of the overall solution to be described and analysed based on its numerous interactions across the different

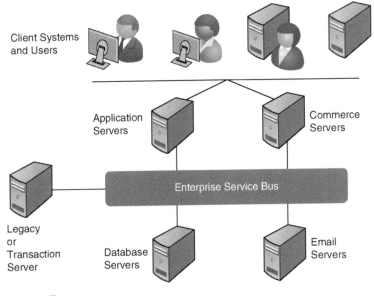

FIG 10.6 / An enterprise service bus

components. The result became known as the service-oriented architecture (SOA) model since it provided a way to define an application as a loosely coupled collection of service interactions that performed a specific activity. The SOA model allows a wide measure of flexibility in how specific components can be developed, acquired, reused and updated without redesigning the overall application.

While SOA-based solutions improved the ease with which applications could be designed and implemented from a number of component parts, a number of limitations were found in practice. First, services are often large, complex and stateful (they need to remember, for example, where somebody is when they are in the middle of a lengthy business process). Hence, they require significant management to ensure they meet the needs of a diverse user base, and extensive overhead to manage changes to interfaces and implementation of the services. Once constructed and operational, there is very limited flexibility to replace services. Second, typically there is no consistent, managed set of interface definitions. As a result, users of a service cannot rely on the availability of that service over significant periods of time. Finally, use of the ESB requires excessive overhead to marshal, transform, manage and co-ordinate the many requests among the components. Unfortunately, the advantage of overall management via an ESB is often at the expense of speed and efficiency, and constrains potential users from experimenting with new services.

Despite these limitations, SOA-based solutions became widely implemented in many organizations. They were typically used where the requirements were well known, highly predictable or governed by substantial change management practices. With the fast-paced requirements of today's world, the limitations of traditional SOA are often seen as too restrictive. Much lighter weight, more dynamic forms of service interaction are required where new inter-organizational relationships can rapidly be formed and services created (and re-created) in rapid, controlled cycles. As we will see when we discuss open platform interfaces in Chapter 12, there are now more lightweight methods of achieving what SOA once tried to achieve – and these form an important part of modern, agile and elastic organizations.

The emergence of lighter weight practices

These long-standing challenges of traditional approaches to software development are moving organizations towards embracing agile software delivery techniques. Since the publication of the 'Manifesto for Agile Software Development' over a decade ago there has been widespread adoption of techniques that embody its key tenets. Agile practices are now the dominant approach in successful software delivery – yet have historically and notably been largely absent or little used in the public sector. However, these practices are not without their critics: in particular, agile delivery faces increasing pressure as software delivery moves from smaller co-located teams towards larger team structures involving a complex software supply chain of organizations in multiple locations – a characteristic that typifies some public sector environments. In these situations the lighter weight practices encouraged by agile software delivery approaches come face-to-face with the more extensive control structures inherent in any large-scale software delivery effort.

Over the past decade many different opinions and viewpoints have been expressed on the term 'agile software architecture'. However, no clear consensus has emerged. Fundamental questions remain open to debate: how much effort is devoted to architecture-specific tasks in an agile project? Is the architecture of an agile software system designed up front as part of an overall blueprint, or does it emerge as a consequence of ongoing development activities? Who participates in architectural design activities? Are specific architectural styles more appropriate to agile software delivery methods? How are architecturally significant changes to a system handled appropriately in agile software delivery methods? And so on.

Regardless of this debate, the reality is that how organizations use applications is changing, and partly as a consequence the way the public sector designs and delivers its applications must also change. Driven partly by mobile and cloud application design needs, application design is increasingly granular in functionality, special purpose in design, and lightweight and platform optimized. The result is a new approach to the problems of enterprise application architecture – one that is much better suited to government's fluid and ever-evolving needs, and in particular its long-standing desire to be able to move at speed when socio-economic demands necessitate.

Next generation enterprise application architecture

Over the past few years the pressure for new, more responsive applications has continued to increase. SOA-based solutions encouraged a design approach based on the assembly of components. Yet the push for supporting new devices, new business models and more agile delivery practices could not readily be addressed using existing architectural approaches.

Attention turned instead to successful web-based solution providers such as Amazon, Facebook, eBay, Google, Yahoo and Apple. These companies demonstrated that they could create massively scalable solutions based on web technologies. They quickly built systems that were able to operate on distributed technology platforms, manage many millions or even billions of transactions, support huge varieties of user needs, and evolve rapidly through both planned and unplanned delivery cycles: a description that well fits the needs of many government services. A number of technologies and techniques were emerging from those communities that could be adapted to meet the needs of enterprise software delivery and, given their proven scalability, would easily accommodate the needs of most public sector agencies and organizations.

The basis of this next generation of application architectures has been to focus on the gap between the legacy underlying infrastructure at the heart of brownfield environments such as government and the fast-changing world of web, cloud and mobile computing technology. As illustrated in Figure 10.7, the main approach is to consider enterprise applications to consist of two main parts: an infrastructure services (IS) layer and a business services delivery (BSD) layer.

The *infrastructure services* (IS) layer contains the stable, long-lived elements of the solution. In particular, most services contain large amounts of data, application interfaces and other back-end elements that are typically managed and governed by dedicated teams within the IT services organization. For example, the data definitions and data management services are central to many functions. The IT organization spends significant time ensuring that the large amounts of data being managed conform to these definitions, and maintaining data quality while undergoing continual change.

The IS layer helps move towards greater flexibility in the maintenance and accessibility of those services by virtualizing storage, infrastructure and access. The elastic capabilities of cloud services are used to enable the

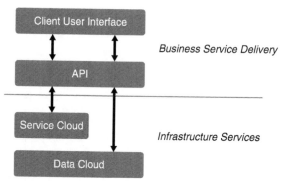

FIG 10.7 / Enterprise applications

existing elements to be organized for greater efficiency in storage costs, access and control. Through using a combination of cloud capabilities, the IS layer exposes the legacy back-end services to users in more usable ways, and prepares for rapid increases in data storage and data transfer as the quantity and diversity of users expands.

For improved flexibility in practice, the IS layer addresses three main concerns:

- Standardization of access requires the selection of a small number of standard formats and protocols for data.
- Open data access provides publicly available data definitions and published data sets for third parties to use. Security of data and data access is critical for many systems. Consistent mechanisms for classifying and controlling access will determine the openness possible. In addition, support is required for external auditing and review.
- Governance of data evolution determines the quality and currency of available data. Flexibility of changes to data definitions and operational data must be balanced with the need to control who has access to change these elements. Updates and evolution of data sources will require clear policy guidance.

The redesign of back-end data and services is allowing many organizations to adopt open standards and solutions for the IS layer, and to re-evaluate their dependence on home-grown infrastructure and data management technologies. Where they see no business advantage to developing their own infrastructure, many IS layers now rely on scalable infrastructure designed for large-scale web access from third parties such as Google, Amazon and Dropbox: in other words, they are consuming existing capabilities rather than building their own.

The *business services delivery* (BSD) supports the agile delivery of services to users. The goal of separating this set of capabilities from the IS layer is to provide it with much greater flexibility for change, diversity and experimentation. In particular, this layer must cope with a much faster pace of change in user needs, business models supported, connected device characteristics and so on.

There are two main aspects to the BSD layer. The first, the presentation aspect, deals with the many different concerns of display and user interaction. The technologies supported by this layer may vary widely, but will include support for multiple web browsers, different mobile devices and their operating systems, multi-language support, different formats and interaction styles, accessibility issues and so on. Typically, a great deal of experimentation takes place in this area requiring additional support for instrumentation, feedback, and split testing (i.e. varying what is seen by different user communities to validate potential changes).

The second, the interfaces (or API) aspect, provides the co-ordination of access to the capabilities of the system from external sources. An API provides the access point for different user communities to construct solutions that use, or consume, the services provided. Opening up a system to greater external use requires a set of well-defined APIs with different characteristics: they will be used by a variety of users internally, with suppliers and consumed by partners. Chapter 12 discusses the importance and relevance of APIs in much more detail: they are an essential component of digital service delivery.

Into the Clouds

The arrival of cloud computing is by far the most conspicuous trend in recent times, and is already having a widespread impact on software delivery, making inroads in private and public sectors alike. Whether viewed as a natural extension of internet-based computing or a completely new phenomenon, high-bandwidth interconnectivity and cheap processors and storage serve organizations by creating large computing centres that may be distributed around the globe. These centralized computing centres can be created by a single organization, shared between organizations, or be provided by third parties as a resource that can be acquired as necessary. All of these give rise to digital technology infrastructures that can be co-ordinated more effectively via shared service centres, and can be supported more efficiently using a flexible set of hardware and software services that can expand and contract as the organization's needs evolve.

This move towards a centralized approach for greater flexibility and efficiency in service delivery is not new. From the earliest days of computing there have been moves to centralize computer resources, share access to costly infrastructure, increase flexibility of access to common services, improve responsiveness to peak demands for capabilities and so on. What is new in the recent move towards cloud computing is the technology infrastructure that now makes that possible, the business environment that is forcing efficiencies across digital service delivery, the expanding global nature of many organizations and their supply chains, and a broader business re-evaluation of the role of digital services in support of the organization's value to its stakeholders.

There are many primers and insightful analyses published on cloud computing and its impact. Rather than replay those themes, we provide here a short overview of cloud computing and then focus on the most important implications of this trend in the context of public services. We summarize three common dimensions of cloud computing that help describe the breadth and impact of this approach: the characteristics of a cloud approach, cloud deployment models and service models for the cloud.

Characteristics of a cloud approach

The main characteristic of a cloud computing approach is to deliver 'convenient, on-demand network access to a shared pool of configurable computing resources (e.g. networks, servers, storage, applications and services) that can be rapidly provisioned and released with minimal management effort or service provider interaction'.[1] The value of this approach is that it offers a great deal of flexibility to users of those resources. In particular, capabilities can be rapidly and elastically scaled-up when demands for those capabilities increase, and similarly they can be rapidly scaled-down when demand reduces.

Supporting this elasticity of capabilities are two enablers essential to make the approach practical. The first is to allow the users of the resources to

---

[1] The US National Institute of Standards and Technology (NIST) definition of cloud computing: http://csrc.nist.gov/groups/SNS/cloud-computing/cloud-def-v15.doc.

be able to self-provision the capabilities they need, and to obtain (near) immediate access via a set of automated provisioning services. The second is a monitoring and measurement approach that allows pay-per-use accounting for those resources being consumed. The richness of these two enablers helps to distinguish cloud computing from previous attempts to offer pooled virtualized services – they were typically restricted to a very limited set of options and required expensive and time-consuming interventions from a service provisioning team.

The flexibility possible with cloud computing approaches is essential. Not only does this flexibility encourage dynamic relationships in the supply chain, it also provides much more explicit ways to look at infrastructure costs, to assign those costs to the role of each organization and team, and encourages delivery approaches more suited to today's highly diverse and rapidly evolving organizations.

Private and public clouds

There is a wide variety in the way that cloud computing services are made available to users. Two significant variations have emerged that polarize ends of the delivery spectrum: public and private clouds.

For organizations with teams requiring access to common capabilities, it can be effective to create a *private* cloud computing solution: it can be acquired and dedicated to that organization's needs. A private cloud computing approach enables teams to have quick access to its services, and metering provides accurate accounting (and even allows cross-charging) of those services to their users. Private cloud computing services can be created by organizations when they require the flexibility offered by shared, virtualized capabilities but are not able (or are unwilling) to accept the implications of sharing those capabilities with other organizations. Private cloud is not the same, however, as an existing supplier merely re-badging their existing data centre, full of existing hardware and software, as a cloud service. Traditional data centres and cloud computing centres provide very different features and characteristics in how they provision, manage and account for their services.

The more significant development in cloud computing is the emergence of *public* cloud capabilities, which are readily accessible over public infrastructure such as the internet. Multiple organizations share the use of that infrastructure (so-called 'multi-tenancy') and thereby reduce costs for both the cloud users and cloud supplier. The use of a third-party provider of resources over a public infrastructure can offer great cost savings to the user (in the manner of a utility), increases the flexibility and availability of the services, and eliminates wasted investment in infrastructure acquisition, set-up and service administration.

Various hybrid models of cloud computing are also possible. For example, some organizations use private cloud capabilities for the most bespoke and idiosyncratic aspects of their business, and make use of public cloud services where their needs can easily and more cost-effectively be met by standard services.

Service models for the cloud

There is a huge array of cloud-based offerings, and a wide variety of ways of packaging, delivering and charging for those capabilities. It is worth highlighting the three predominant categories of capabilities being offered through cloud computing models. These are illustrated in Figure 10.8.

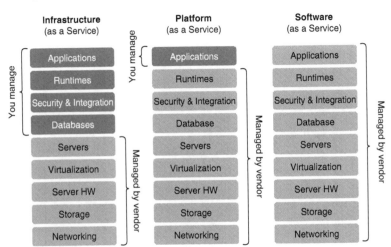

FIG 10.8 The three key cloud-computing models

Infrastructure-as-a-service (IaaS)

Infrastructure-as-a-service (IaaS) provides a starting point for offering cloud-based services. It provides the organization with dependable, scalable and expandable hardware (e.g. processors, storage and networking). These capabilities may be offered directly as the service that the end users consume, or be used as the foundation for building virtualization layers and higher-level services. For example, if a team requires an additional terabyte of disk space to manage the temporary data needed for a series of system tests, a cloud-based solution would be able to accommodate that request (whether implicitly or explicitly made) rather than having to look for an available machine or go through a complex acquisition approval process.

To support IaaS requires a number of services that may include the ability to pool highly available CPUs and storage (perhaps differentiated by particular kinds of hardware characteristics), to meter the capacity and utilization of resources, to bill and chargeback for consumed services, to audit and analyse for compliance to specific norms and standards, and so on. The IaaS services must guarantee that particular functional and non-functional requirements will be met in areas such as performance, response time, availability and so on.

Platform-as-a-service (PaaS)

Platform-as-a-service (PaaS) delivers a more complete computing platform for developing and delivering applications. In particular, a PaaS offering will include operating system and other middleware capabilities, typically with the latest versions of the software, updates and patches applied. For example, often when an organization wants to test a new application they need to acquire and configure each computer platform on which the application must be tested. This may mean several different platform variations with combinations of operating system, database, web server and so on. In a PaaS approach, specific platform combinations are requested and provisioned using a cloud computing model. Typically, a limited set of PaaS solutions is available for use by default. In addition, a user may be able to define specialized stacks of software that combine the available platform elements to provision a specific PaaS solution that meets their needs.

An important variation on the PaaS approach is that the platform may itself be a development and delivery platform for new cloud-based services. For example, the Amazon Web Services platform (AWS) includes a PaaS offering that delivers a fully functional development and delivery capability for organizations wanting to deliver solutions that run on the Amazon IaaS offering, called the Amazon Elastic Compute Cloud (EC2) and that integrate with a set of solution components they have created to execute on that infrastructure. Similarly, Salesforce.com provides force.com as the PaaS offering for creating new solutions that integrate with its Salesforce.com solution elements.

The PaaS approach is very appealing to two kinds of organizations. First, smaller organizations can take advantage of PaaS to access a wide set of platform variations without the capital investment necessary for each of them. Second, for larger organizations the PaaS approach offers standardization to ensure that teams use the same technology base with appropriate versions of each component of the platform installed there.

Software-as-a-service (SaaS)

Most organizations interested in the cloud computing model are not software development companies: they use the software as a means to support and differentiate their businesses. They are looking to have business- or domain-specific capabilities offered as a service where they simply make use of that service as and when they need it, in the quantity they need at the time. This has resulted in a very large set of offerings now available in a software-as-a-service (SaaS) model.

Again, both public and private cloud approaches are possible. In the public cloud category there are now some very well-established examples of SaaS. One example is Gmail, Google´s e-mail service that provides a SaaS e-mail capability that is widely used by individuals and increasingly deployed in businesses and other organizations, including universities. Another well-known example is the cloud-based sales management service from Salesforce.com. Both of these examples exhibit the key characteristics of today's SaaS offerings: internet-based access to a core organizational capability provided on a pay-per-use model with a great deal of elasticity in the underlying technology. This kind of simplification of service provisioning is very appealing to organizations that see no value in the investment and administration required to maintain close control of that capability in-house.

Impact on Government

There is already a high level of interest in cloud computing in government and the promises that it brings to reduce cost and increase flexibility of service delivery. Many public sector bodies are already involved in pilots, or even actively using cloud technologies and cloud-based services. Over the coming years this interest will probably become tempered with the reality that in some respects cloud is 'just another deployment platform'. Hence, the use of this platform will require a wealth of supporting capabilities to both create solutions *for* the cloud, and to take advantage of solutions and services *on* the cloud.

Initially, we have seen many traditional solutions ported to the cloud platform. This is an important starting point for use of the cloud. However, it is very limited in terms of many of the important usage scenarios for cloud technology by governments. There is less understanding of which new software capabilities, services and approaches will be needed in much more complex scenarios. For example, we are already seeing interesting scenarios that raise new challenges:

- Several teams are deploying applications on to a public cloud infrastructure for access by users. How do those teams collaborate to share information to ensure that they do not place sensitive data on the public infrastructure? What co-ordination is given to the teams to ensure that the management of shared content is handled effectively?
- Multiple system integrators and specialist vendors must deliver different solutions as part of a software supply chain that must be integrated to be delivered into production. How can the cloud be used as the delivery platform to co-ordinate and govern delivery and integration of these components?

These, and many more such scenarios, are stretching conventional processes, skills and technologies for software delivery. Many organizations are actively working on new deployment approaches that provide the additional governance, visibility and control that is demanded in such situations.

Several showcase examples of the use of cloud computing technologies in government now exist. In the UK, for example, the G-Cloud (Government-Cloud) initiative consists of a simplified set of procurement practices and a cloud-hosted catalogue of marketplace services that conform to those practices. Consequently, UK government agencies can find competing services providers by searching this catalogue, and more readily contract with the suppliers listed as they are already approved against the contracting regulations in force. As of March 2014 the government reported the following stats:

- £124,066,998.46 total contracts awarded via G-Cloud to the end of 28 February 2014.
- 59% of those contracts by value and 58% by volume, from all reported sales to date, have been awarded to small–medium enterprises (SMEs).
- 78% of those contracts by value were through central government, 22% through the wider public sector.
- 74% of those contracts by volume were through central government, 26% through the wider public sector.

In a second example, the UK Government Digital Service (GDS) has hosted its main information portal site, GOV.UK, on a cloud-based infrastructure for several years. It recently demonstrated the commodity nature of cloud-based services by re-hosting the GOV.UK site from one cloud implementation to another. They blogged after this move:

We migrated:

- *100,000 items of content (webpages)*
- *250GB of attachments (downloads from webpages)*
- *20+ databases (ranging from 6MB to 6GB in size)*

The noticeable effects were:

- *for ordinary users: Applying for a Vehicle Licence was disabled for 2.5 hours (between 6.00pm and 8.30pm)*

• *for government users: Content could not be published for 90 minutes (between 6.00pm and 7.30pm) without manual intervention by the migration team (available by phone in emergencies)*

The significance of cloud on producing notable operational efficiencies can be seen in the example of the UK government, which has been reporting average savings of 50% on a like-for-like basis by moving services to the cloud. This shows the potential of commodity services to reduce costs compared to those incurred in the past. One of the guiding principles of G-Cloud has been to avoid multi-year contracts, recognizing the need to be able to take rapid advantage of improvements in both technology and price. The current approach is to use 1–2 year contracts for IaaS, with an option to extend, or the ability to switch to another IaaS provider, as and when desired.

The UK government's early experiences of adopting cloud for its main web presence are but a small sign of things to come and an insight into the benefits that could flow from the smarter use of commodity elements. It provides an illustrative and important first step on the journey we set out in this book: a journey that we believe all governments will eventually want or need to follow.

chapter 11

Agile Processes and Practices

Change cannot mean chaos: in most organizations all activities, and change activities in particular, are governed by a plethora of formal and informal procedures, practices, processes and regulations. These governance mechanisms provide an essential function in managing and controlling how software is delivered into production. However, we have also seen first-hand an overabundance of these controls in many organizations – to the point that they can severely limit the organization's ability to be effective.

Members of one large enterprise software delivery organization joked that they had recently completed an analysis that showed that even if they were to deliver the 'null project' (a project where there was no new software produced) they would still require almost six months of elapsed time simply to write all the documents, go to all the meetings, and obtain the formal signoffs for the project to be considered in compliance with local procedures and placed into production. Such a scenario is likely to be painfully familiar to many in the public sector, where overly formalized models based on methods such as TOGAF and PRINCE2 can involve even the simplest, minor change generating a significant workload in terms of governance, process, meetings and paperwork.

This anecdote illustrates the pressure on software delivery organizations to balance their delivery capabilities across four key dimensions, as we highlighted earlier:

- **Time-to-delivery** for projects to complete and deliver a meaningful result to the business. These are often measured in average time for project completion.
- **Productivity** of individuals and teams, typically measured in terms of lines of code or function points delivered over unit time.
- **Process maturity** in the consistency, uniformity and standardization of practices. Measurements are gathered based on the number of waivers to common process norms or through use of maturity approaches such as the capability maturity model (CMM) levels.
- **Quality** in shipped code, errors handled and turnaround of requests. Measures are typically combinations of defect density rates and errors fixed per unit time.

Finding an appropriate balance across these delivery success factors is a constant battle. Increased flexibility, or agility, in delivery is becoming an essential element of enterprise scale software delivery – and indeed of organizational culture. In this chapter we analyse this broader view of agility. After initially considering the change in thinking about software delivery that agility requires, we focus on the ways in which this agility can be scaled and adopted in a public sector organization.

Agility in Software Delivery

Agility has been summarized as:

> An iterative and incremental (evolutionary) approach performed in a highly collaborative and self-organizing manner with just the right amount of ceremony to frequently produce high quality software in a cost effective and timely manner which meets the changing needs of its stakeholder.[1]

---

[1] This definition is in line with many similar that exist in the literature.

Captured in this rather dense definition are several concepts that we see as essential to the spirit of agility:

- Activities necessary to adhere to process rules, governance and conformance (broadly defined as 'ceremony') should be kept to the minimum necessary for the context of development.
- Focus on quality is consistent and continual, with early definition of testing criteria, constant test execution and clear validation of test status.
- Interaction and collaboration among the team is fundamental and must be made as rich and simple as possible to ensure high-quality communication.
- Changes are expected and demand clear visibility, early intervention and rapid response.
- Stakeholders and customers have a critical ongoing involvement in the project.
- Frequent delivery of working software is essential and is the primary means of understanding and measuring progress.

A majority of the work around agility has focused in the software development area, with new approaches and techniques for accelerating coding and testing, understanding requirements changes and co-ordinating code-test-build activities. But a broader perspective on agility delivery is also important: organizations are now shifting their thinking towards applying agile approaches in *all* aspects of their delivery.

Rethinking Enterprise Software Delivery

Important advances in enterprise software development have enhanced the productivity, quality and effectiveness of delivery organizations. However, the challenges of delivery have forced organizations to rethink aspects of how they perform their task – and focused attention on three fundamental observations.

First, the value an organization derives from a system is frequently not clearly understood in relation to the investment in the development and maintenance of that system. Second, systems undergo constant change, both during their design and construction as the true needs and necessities of the system become better understood, and after delivery when end users start to exercise the system. The ability of these systems to evolve is a core quality that is poorly addressed in principle and expensive to support in practice, particularly with many old management methodologies.

Third, most costs in systems delivery occur after a system's first release to production, with substantial rework, changes and continual evolution of capability over a long period of time. Yet much of the attention and investment in many organizations is focused on detailed descriptions of a system's assumed initial requirements, and an expectation that software delivery will be 'built as defined', fielded into production, then slowly evolved and updated.

These observations will be familiar to anyone working in government, where current computer systems can often – ironically – act as the most significant barrier to updating and maintaining public services in a timely and cost-effective fashion.

From Software *Development* to Software *Delivery*

In response to many of these challenges we have seen the emergence of a change from software *development* to software *delivery*. This change affects several dimensions, as illustrated in Figure 11.1.

A software delivery perspective focuses on a number of important concepts and practices, as set out below.

Continuously evolving systems

Enterprise software – much like public policy – undergoes a continual process of change. Traditionally, the goal is to optimize the development of the first release of the system. But the critical phase actually comes *after* first release. This evolution should be the focus of attention, and investment should be placed in techniques that support and encourage software

Software Development Perspective	Software Delivery Perspective
Distinct development phase	*Continuously evolving systems*
Distinct handoff to maintenance	*No distinct boundary between development and maintenance*
Requirements–design–code–test sequence	*Sequence of released capabilities with ever increasing value*
Phase and role specific tools	
Co-located teams	*Common platform of integrated process/tools*
Standard engineering governance	*Distributed, web based collaboration*
Engineering practitioner led	*Economic governance tailored to risk/reward profiles*
	Business value and outcome led

FIG 11.1 Contrasting a software development and software delivery perspective

to evolve to meet changing user needs. This is a particular requirement in many public sector systems, where, for example, taxation and welfare rules, processes and calculations may be subject to frequent remodelling and change: systems must be built with this expectation of change, not 'locked down' with an illusory set of 'final' requirements documented at an arbitrary moment in time.

Blending of boundaries between development and maintenance

A clear distinction is normally made between development and maintenance, often involving organizational, process and cultural implications for a 'hand over' of the system into maintenance. With an evolutionary view of software delivery, the distinction between these two activities is blurred to the point that development and maintenance are just two aspects of the same need to create and deliver the system. Any live system that is to remain relevant will undergo a continuous process of development and maintenance.

Sequence of released capabilities with ever-increased value

A traditional development view operates from the understanding that after a deep analysis, the requirements for a system are signed off and development of the system begins with the goal to 'fulfil' those requirements and place the system in production. But in the real world requirements emerge and evolve as more is discovered about the needs of the stakeholders and as understanding of the delivery context grows. A more realistic approach to delivery views the system not as a number of major discrete releases, but as a continuous series of incremental enhancements with increasing value to the stakeholders.

Common platform of integrated process and tools

The old siloed delivery approach is generally supported by processes and tools optimized within the boundaries of each silo or existing business process. This occurs because most parts of government define processes and acquire the tools individually, function by function, administrative unit by administrative unit, with little thought for the end-to-end flow of information and artefacts. A delivery view recognizes the predominance of the interoperation of these processes and tools to optimize system value.

Distributed web-based collaboration

Teaming and teamwork is a focus within functional areas for a development approach. A delivery view defines the team more broadly, recognizing that stakeholders in software delivery may vary widely in function, geography and organization. Technology support to include all those stakeholders in team activities is essential. While a variety of collaborative, web-based technologies have emerged in recent years, many organizations have deployed them in an ad hoc way, and invested little in any concerted approach to adopt them across their organization.

Economic governance tailored to risk/reward profiles

To manage software development most organizations use a collection of processes, measures and governance practices that focus on development artefacts such as the business case, software code, requirements documents and test scripts. A delivery view moves the focus of governance towards the value of what is being delivered, aiming to optimize features delivered and time-to-value of delivered capabilities, increase burn down of backlogs of new requests, reduce volatility of systems and sustain velocity of delivery teams.

Business value and outcome led

Many organizations have prided themselves on their technical skills and the depth of their knowledge in technologies for software development and operations. These are vital to success. However, at times this emphasis on development has created the perception in the broader organization that the delivery organization is constantly in search of the latest technology solution with little regard to where and how such technology investments help the business achieve its goals. A focus on software delivery gives greater emphasis to the business value of those investments and creates a more balanced view of investment.

The Basis for Agile Government

The changes we have briefly outlined here radically alter the way governments can approach the design and delivery of their services. They encourage styles of software delivery that move away from early and artificial lock-down of decisions to reduce variance in software projects towards controlled discovery, experimentation and innovation: this transition is important if government is not to continue repeating the project delivery failures and costly overruns of the past.

The growing interest in and literature around agile development practices has been the primary source for much of this evolution in thinking and practice. Drawing from the practices of high-performing teams, a philosophy of software delivery was defined that was captured in four principles in the 'Manifesto for Agile Software Development': (1) the importance of individuals and interactions over processes and tools; (2) working software over comprehensive documentation; (3) customer collaboration over contract negotiations; and (4) responding to change over following a plan.

These four apparently simple principles contradict almost every tenet of existing ways of working in government. The repercussions of these simple yet radical beliefs have been profound, and we have seen a great deal of subsequent analysis and activity in defining new processes, methods and tools that support these beliefs. There are many important implications for large-scale government projects, most notably for the organizational control structures in place to guide and manage the projects. To illustrate this, consider two particular approaches: waterfall and agile project delivery.

In a waterfall-style delivery model there are successive stages of requirements and analysis before construction, test and delivery activities can take place. In addition, these activities are largely executed in sequence, with little opportunity for overlap. The involvement with and handover to operations staff occurs once the system is complete. This creates a very stable, sequential flow to system delivery, with clear handoff between teams, inspection criteria and control points. For stable, well-known problem domains with experienced teams, this approach is very effective in managing progress and delivering to predefined schedules and budgets.

In contrast, an agile delivery approach recognizes the evolutionary nature of the development and delivery tasks and aims to involve all project staff in decision making as early as possible. While it is not an option to 'avoid' essential design and delivery tasks, such as requirements management or testing, the approach overlaps these tasks so that they occur concurrently, with the involvement and co-operation of the whole team throughout the lifetime of the project. Consequently, the approach must consist of tools and services that facilitate and support common teamwork with specific attention to collaborative interaction, visibility and status management, and co-ordinated planning.

The agile delivery approach seeks to shorten the time-to-delivery through optimized concurrency, early visibility into problems and blockages, reduced late rework through continuous feedback and greater co-operation at all stages. A common software delivery automation capability is essential, because agility is possible only if high-bandwidth communication and co-ordination among teams is supported to realize the distributed collaboration that is necessary; if decision making is based on real-time information on current status; and if early insight into problems allows quick diagnosis and immediate intervention through continuous measurement and transparency into individual, team and project progress. For rapidly changing scenarios, or where there is uncertainty as to the user needs, agile delivery approaches offer the flexibility required to evolve the solution towards a viable solution.

Agility at Scale

The rigorous control structures of waterfall approaches are particularly useful when a variety of teams (perhaps from different organizations) work together on progressing a solution through a pipeline of activities from requirements through design and implementation, and on to deployment. However, with the fast-paced changes of the digital age, many more projects require the greater flexibility and more incremental delivery exemplified by agile practices. This results in a key question often asked in government about agility: 'Does the flexibility offered by agile approaches scale to the distributed management needs of complex government projects?' To answer that question, we explore two critical dimensions of the scalability of agile approaches. The first examines the context in which agile practices are applied. The second describes the key scaling factors and their impact on agility.

Agility in context

Although the principles of agile thinking may remain consistent, their application in practice can vary widely: governments need to understand the complexity of the particular delivery environment in which agile thinking will be applied.

As illustrated in Figure 11.2, it's useful to highlight the context for agility in two dimensions: organizational drivers and technical/regulatory drivers. These dimensions help us to explain the implications of increasing complexity on how agility is applied in practice within government.

At the bottom left of the diagram, where the organizational and technical/regulatory aspects are least complex, we typically see co-located teams with small numbers of developers building applications of limited complexity and minimal deployment risk. Many of the initial agile approaches began in this context, and techniques such as 'extreme programming' find their majority of use in this context.

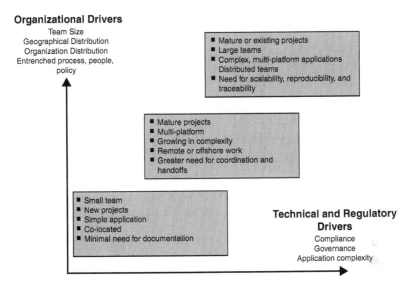

Organizational Drivers
Team Size
Geographical Distribution
Organization Distribution
Entrenched process, people,
policy

■ Mature or existing projects
■ Large teams
■ Complex, multi-platform applications
  Distributed teams
■ Need for scalability, reproducibility, and
  traceability

■ Mature projects
■ Multi-platform
■ Growing in complexity
■ Remote or offshore work
■ Greater need for coordination and
  handoffs

■ Small team
■ New projects
■ Simple application
■ Co-located
■ Minimal need for documentation

Technical and Regulatory Drivers
Compliance
Governance
Application complexity

FIG 11.2 / The context for agile delivery in two dimensions

In the middle of the diagram, increasing complexity forces teams to address additional concerns, including:

• Larger team sizes requiring more co-ordination and transparency into planning and progress.

• Distributed teams supported by remote access, outsourced partnerships and varied access to artefacts and system knowledge.

• Complex or mission-critical applications requiring more attention to analysis, architecture and testing procedures.

• Multi-platform deployment environments often requiring more extensive and rigorous testing, management of multiple variants and enhanced support mechanisms.

As shown in the top right of the diagram, in the most complex situations we see teams that face an increasing number of issues, including:

• Very large team sizes, teams of teams and more complex management structures forcing additional attention to co-ordination and management. At this level there is an increasing need to standardize best practices to avoid reinvention and miscommunication across artefacts and processes.

‣ Distributed and global development, requiring attention to many technical, organizational and cultural issues as the teams interact to co-operatively deliver the solution.

‣ Compliance needs for domains in which regulatory controls require audits based on process conformance and regular collection of development information from multiple data sources.

‣ Very complex applications that may include safety-critical or mission-critical components, and hence require complex test environments, dedicated test teams and careful attention to analysis and architecture properties (e.g. recovery, fault tolerance, security monitoring,).

In short, complexity issues in software delivery can have significant impact on the adoption of agile approaches. Agile strategies must be evaluated, tailored and perhaps combined with traditional approaches to suit the particular context.

Agile scaling factors

Examining in more detail this need for adaptation, we discuss eight key factors that have major impact on the scaling of agile approaches, illustrated in Figure 11.3.

‣ **Geographic distribution**. For teams that are distributed across several locations, a primary challenge is the need for close, frequent interaction and collaboration. Short delivery cycles typical of agile projects force close co-operation across the team. Clearly, complexity surrounds the technical aspects required to connect the team in meaningful ways. Additional complexity includes the challenge of managing a common team approach in light of the various distances, time zones, work hours and labour laws, holiday schedules and so on.

‣ **Compliance requirements**. The agile principle of focusing attention on working software rather than documentation is challenged when that software will be controlling a power distribution network or be embedded in a medical device. In such situations (and many others)

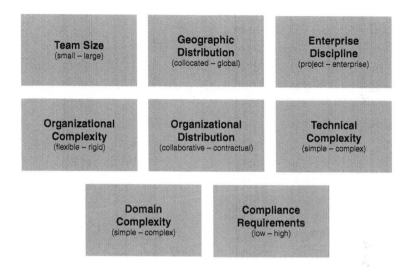

Team Size (small – large)	**Geographic Distribution** (collocated – global)	**Enterprise Discipline** (project – enterprise)
Organizational Complexity (flexible – rigid)	**Organizational Distribution** (collaborative – contractual)	**Technical Complexity** (simple – complex)
	Domain Complexity (simple – complex)	**Compliance Requirements** (low – high)

FIG 11.3 Key factors in agile scaling

there are explicit, mandatory compliance issues that require various documents to be produced and maintained, periodic audits of practices used, and clear traceability between a specified feature, its implementation and its executed tests. Agile delivery methods cannot ignore or subvert this documentation. Finding the right balance of effort is, of course, critical.

- **Technical complexity**. Systems that are very complex in scope can be difficult to understand and manage in practice. They require a great deal of upfront analysis to define their correct behaviour, and sophisticated analysis and verification to ensure they function correctly. Agile approaches seek to create working code early, involve stakeholders frequently and keep non-coding activities to the bare minimum. Such objectives must be balanced against the reality of the application system being produced.

- **Team size**. The classic approach to agility uses small, co-located teams. However, larger enterprise software systems require larger teams. One approach is to break those systems into smaller segments and divide the teams into 'teams of teams'. This approach increases the flexibility within agile teams, but increases the co-ordination challenges across those teams. Choosing and implementing an appropriate organization structure for enterprise software delivery is a critical early decision that can have profound consequences for the rest of the project.[2]

- **Enterprise complexity**. Different organizations will assume different approaches towards control, management and reporting in their enterprise software delivery organizations. Some aspects of the approach are a result of the operating domain (e.g. industry and government regulations, laws and guidelines). However, equally important is the culture and history of the organization. Management teams introducing and scaling agile approaches must take such elements into account as they come up against common perceptions and norms, and even the local political structures.

- **Organizational distribution**. As organizations engage in more complex supply-chain arrangements with partners, it's likely that projects will be delivered with resources from different organizations. They may be partners in one area of the business while competing head-to-head in other areas. Agile approaches encourage close, frequent, open co-operation among the teams, with high levels of transparency. Organizational distribution can severely limit what is feasible or what is advisable in this regard.

- **Organizational complexity**. We know that the biggest factor in the success of most projects is the people involved. Their specific experience, skills and attitudes bring a lot to the character and approach of the project. The need to recognize individuals and team dynamics is a major principle of agile approaches. This is very positive when a team is motivated, flexible and highly skilled. But individuals and team dynamics can also be a major roadblock when scaling agile practices to teams that have a 20-year heritage of skills, feel overwhelmed by the new techniques, and are suspicious of increased transparency and personal responsibility. Successful adoption of agile approaches requires that they adjust to these situations and take such personal factors into account.

---

[2] One of the common sayings in enterprise software is that 'you ship your organization' – the way you organize individuals and teams will undoubtedly have significant impact on the structure and effectiveness of the system delivered.

- **Domain complexity**. There are several implications for selecting the appropriate agile approach that depend on characteristics of the domain in which the enterprise software is being created and delivered. There may be less emphasis on managing technical and delivery risks in domains that are relatively stable and well understood than in domains where experimentation and innovation is needed to encourage a stable set of requirements to emerge. Highly complex domains (e.g. industrial device control, satellite image analysis) may also require specific attention to modelling, analysis and verification techniques to comprehend, analyse and manage domain knowledge.

These factors force adjustments in important areas to the practical realization of agility at scale. They encourage a disciplined approach to the scaling of agile techniques.

Cornerstones of Success

Our experience in introducing and assessing the viability of agile practices across several large programmes and projects leads us to focus on several important areas as the cornerstones of success. This is the set of underlying practices that supports communication and integration of people and processes in distributed teams, automation of key practices to facilitate standardization and productivity, and visualization across the life cycle to improve accountability and decision making. We refer to these as the 'foundation for agility at enterprise scale'. Here we summarize the key practices for organizations working on large-scale delivery programmes.

Real-time planning to improve time to delivery

We plan because we want to know what needs to be done and when it will be complete. The only way to know when the work is done is to ensure the plans are fully integrated with project execution and are always up to date.

Real-time planning improves time to delivery by providing a single plan that spans requirements, development and test; integrating planning with execution (ensuring the entire team understands the project status); allowing full participation in accurate planning; and providing teams with the real-time data to respond to the unexpected.

Life-cycle traceability to improve quality

A solution that allows for life-cycle traceability helps teams to answer the more interesting and harder questions: teams don't do traceability for traceability's sake. By linking related artefacts, teams are better equipped to answer questions such as 'which requirements have defects?' or 'which work-items are ready for test?'

Another way to think about traceability is that it helps make clear what everyone else on the team is doing. For example, a requirements analyst knows what requirements they have written. What they need to know, however, is whether the requirement is planned for a specific development iteration and, if so, which one? Or they want to know if the implementation of a requirement has been tested and with what result. Work can be triaged with insight to impact on others. For example, test cases that are linked to high-priority requirements should be run first. Defects affecting high-priority requirements, or blocking testing, should be triaged and fixed as they are found. Life-cycle traceability helps in understanding what the rest of the team is doing and how it impacts on each other's work. It improves quality by establishing relationships between software arte-facts, identifying and closing artefact gaps across disciplines, providing practitioners access to related artefacts so they can make fully informed decisions, and providing a clear view of completeness from requirement through release.

In-context collaboration to improve delivery value

Collaboration is not only about instant messaging and conference calls with each other. Improved collaboration makes a team faster to respond to changing events and contributes to better predictability on a project. Collaboration contributes to higher quality and improved value to the stakeholders: it's the key to innovation. It helps make information immediately accessible to all team members in the context of their work, and facilitates team reviews so that feedback is incorporated early and often.

Development intelligence for increased predictability

According to software engineering specialist Capers Jones, projects with strong measurement practices have much better success rates than those that don't. Yet even many Fortune 500 firms do not have measurement practices in place: less than half have defined quality measures and less than one-third have productivity measures. This is where development intelligence has a key role, by improving predictability. It does so by applying business intelligence techniques for development, enabling fact-based decision making (to communicate status, monitor progress, diagnose problems, identify corrective actions), and by doing so helps to steer projects and programmes to deliver on time.

Continuous improvement to reduce cost

When we talk about 'process' we mean far more than just a documented set of procedures and the production of shelves of paperwork. We design processes because we seek a best practice for team behaviour. When a process is defined or changed, an entire team of people need to change the way they behave. Think how hard it is to change one habit in one person: processes require changing the habits of a multitude of people at the same time. That is why process improvements are so hard, and are often avoided – meaning that many poor or bad processes remain in place.

Moving instead to a culture of continuous improvement will reduce cost by:

- improving software delivery through the adoption of best practices and automation;
- promoting incremental improvement of a project;
- enabling breakthrough improvement through the use of automation to capture best practices and reuse across teams;
- allowing everyone to participate with easily adopted best practices at their fingertips.

Implications for Government

Agile thinking has galvanized several important ideas relevant to successful delivery and hence the success of software-enabled programmes in organizations, all of which are applicable in the public sector. Consequently, an agile approach views itself differently and takes an agile software *delivery* view to how software is designed, created and placed into production.

Based on our work with many organizations in both the private and public sectors we believe that success requires placing emphasis on the following elements:

- **Collaboration**. Agile approaches focus on less paperwork and more on conversations across the team and with actively involved stakeholders.
- **Quality**. Agile practices encourage inclusion of test activities as early as possible in projects and continuously execute tests to maintain quality.
- **Evolution**. Agile projects create loosely coupled, highly cohesive architectures, and frequently refactor to keep them that way.
- **Working software**. Agile projects monitor progress based on what they can show works more than on designs and descriptions of what should or could be produced.
- **Individual and team flexibility**. Agile team members are 'generalizing specialists' who will be experts in some areas, but may perform many tasks on a project and work for the good of the team.

chapter 12

API Economy, Ecosystems and Engagement Models

Since the beginning of the twenty-first century, technological advances have driven fundamental change in how applications are created and deployed. Technologies such as cloud computing, mobile and the broader realization of smart devices have brought a growing reality to the 'Internet of Things' (IoT) vision for a massively intelligent, instrumented and interconnected world.

There has also been a parallel evolution in the design and delivery of applications to exploit this IoT vision. By necessity there has been a widespread shift in thinking in terms of how applications are constructed, and the characteristics of the environments in which they operate. Unlike the public sector solutions of the past, many critical applications can no longer be monolithic and designed for running on a single technology platform. It must be possible to create public services that are accessible from many kinds of devices, which adapt to the different operating environments and that evolve for new operating contexts yet to be defined.

It is simply not feasible to imagine hand-crafting new applications line-by-line from scratch for each new requirement or service – the model that the big suppliers to the public sector have long used. Applications instead need to be rapidly assembled from in-house or acquired components that exist independently, running locally with an organization's own infrastructure, remotely in a cloud infrastructure, or both. In such a context, a design metaphor based on assembly and orchestration of services and interfaces is necessary. Delivering a required application or service takes place through a series of co-ordinated interactions.

With the arrival of cloud computing, these new, service-based design approaches have been moving to the fore driven by the diversification of user needs and platforms, and the increasing commoditization of many basic computing capabilities. As a result, IT teams have been assuming the role of application assemblers and brokers of business services. The growing popularity of cloud-hosted services has accelerated this move. With SaaS, PaaS and IaaS (see Chapter 11) offering turnkey access to computing capacity, there is a move away from the bespoke building and management of specialized applications and towards solution delivery through composite service assembly to achieve new levels of speed, innovation and performance, while controlling the cost and risk characteristics of managing a large IT portfolio.

If we want successful, agile public services, we need to embrace these new methodologies and new technology opportunities in tandem: they enable us to implement flexible, agile and 'elastic' government, built from composable services designed around the needs of citizens rather than the providing organizations. Government will be able to manage its entire service fulfilment ecosystem across services, processes, organizations, suppliers and technologies as a suite of reusable components – many of them provided as commodity elements – that can continue to be refined, configured and reconfigured on demand.

Not surprisingly, this transition has required organizations to increase their use of service-based architectures through more efficient use and better control of APIs (application programming interfaces). An API exposes a collection of services to communities of potential users of those services. Primarily, the API acts as a control point between the service providers and their consumers: through the API the service providers have a managed way that not only enables access to data sources, but also imposes rules that guide and constrain how those data are accessed. API service consumers can take advantage of those services when constructing a new solution, so that delivery of a new capability by combing services assembled from several APIs becomes a faster, more predictable way to realize that solution.

The value of an API-based approach becomes more relevant in the context of the move to increasing interconnection of smart devices as envisaged by the IoT. Here, the service consumers are not human end users, but more frequently other software programs and agents. The implementation of a solution is then not a single application running on one computer, but a network or mesh of software programs deployed across multiple internet-enabled devices.

However, this use of APIs is far more than merely a technical issue. A traditional manufacturing-based view of an organization is conceived as a pipeline that takes raw materials through several stages to become finished goods or services. Each company plays a role in the manufacturing process, and end users consume the finished goods emerging from the pipeline. An API-driven approach to solution delivery is based around a fundamentally different approach that creates shared platforms of services. The shift to a platform-based view of business disrupts the traditional delivery model.

Unlike pipelines, platforms are not optimized around the manufacturing processes of producing finished goods to sell to consumers. Instead they facilitate a variety of business-to-business and consumer-to-consumer relationships to encourage communities of stakeholders to create and consume value. From a technology perspective, a platform-based view offers an infrastructure for developers to assemble and augment services using APIs. From a business perspective, some user categories (producers) create value for other user categories (consumers) to enjoy. An individual, team or organization can be both a producer and consumer of services. This represents a fundamental change to organizations, and creates opportunities for different organizational models, relationships and value creation.

Understanding the value and need for these changes is critical to government in terms of whether it will likewise be able to take a benefit from these new models, and encourage better ways of working and delivering services. In fact, many analysts are heralding a new era of solution design and delivery referred to as the 'API economy'. This represents a move towards a new way of conceiving, constructing and commercializing solutions based on novel economic models. APIs are becoming the means by which a product or service is connected to its users and other communities, allowing partners, developers and end users to find innovative ways to incorporate the features and services offered through the API into new applications and services. These relationships open up several alternatives for organizations to take advantage of the exchange of goods and services enabled by the APIs, the relationships built between suppliers and consumers, the scaled market dynamics of the communities formed, and the opportunities for offering additional value-added services to individuals.

As this approach matures, we are seeing a remarkable change in behaviour as APIs become the primary consumer interface for services, and a key channel for driving engagement. By early 2014, for example, Salesforce. com generates more than half of its $2.3 billion in revenue through its APIs, not its direct user interfaces. Similar figures are quoted for Twitter (around 13 billion transactions per day through its APIs), Google (around 5 billion transactions per day through its APIs) and Amazon (rapidly closing in on 1 trillion transactions per day through its APIs).

These remarkable figures point to a substantial move towards rethinking the way that organizations can employ technology to realize a user need. Conversely, it also highlights how technologists are designing new capabilities as reusable building blocks to be readily combined by users when needing to offer a new capability to a variety of stakeholders. For example, new mobile applications can readily be formed from a substantial set of capabilities of an acquired solution accessed through an API, elements that are custom-built, and those purchased from partners of the solution vendor through their partner network.

To understand how this thinking leads to the API economy, three interdependent dimensions must clearly be distinguished:

- a technology approach to expose services from a software component through well-defined interfaces;

* a strategic design approach for organizing a solution as a platform of services around which an ecosystem of suppliers and consumers can gather;
* a business model approach in which the API-derived services are monetized, and the ecosystem of suppliers and consumers is incentivized to grow use, maintenance and evolution of the platform services.

We examine each of these dimensions and make a number of observations.

Defining and Using APIs

The starting point for defining an API is not the technology but the philosophy underlying a service or system. The focus is typically centred on delivering the best user experience by providing a valued service without the need to install complicated software, or manage expensive hardware. To achieve this goal, many service providers began to leverage cloud-based services to deliver enterprise applications via a web browser – such as the way the UK government's web presence, at GOV.UK, is hosted in a commodity IaaS cloud.

This emphasis on simplifying the user experience has led to interest in interface-based design approaches, where collections of services are orchestrated to realize a required user-focused capability. To support such an approach, the interfaces within a system are publicized and maintained to allow new capabilities to be defined by a variety of different users. Over time, use of these interfaces grows as more consumers take advantage of the available services. This is particularly important as many users of services are other applications and devices rather than end users.

The interface-base design approach can be used within an organization as a convenient way to structure systems, and to support their managed evolution. However, it is more important when those interfaces are exposed externally to allow partners and customers to embed one organization's capabilities within those of another. For example, this could be the use of a shipping company's logistics services within the storefront of a retail organization. This is also applicable to government services. In the case of GOV.UK, for example, the same APIs that the site uses internally are also publicly available: for most of its content-rich pages the API enables anyone to obtain the full content of the page and some supporting information (such as which categories it lives in and whether it's designed for businesses) with a simple change of URL. Thus, a site page such as https://www.gov.uk/passport-fees is available via an API to potential consumers of that data. The majority of such content is published under the liberal Open Government Licence.

Building and delivering these kinds of collaborative services is especially important for fast-paced interactions when users require short, managed transactions across several service providers. The widespread adoption of mobile devices across all aspects of our lives has changed everything: instead of focusing on browser-based solutions accessed through a PC or laptop, users spend more time on mobile phones and tablets than ever before. They perform frequent, often short, interactions with many solutions through a vast collection of small device-specific services. Enabled by a range of personal awareness characteristics embedded in today's smart devices (such as location, purchase history and recent online activities) new opportunities exist for personalizing services delivered to individuals. This facilitates a fundamental reimagining of what services can be offered to support how citizens work and live. Consequently, and mirroring what has happened in the private sector, public service providers require a transformation in how their services are delivered. The culmination of this transformation, and the philosophy of delivering connected mobile solutions, is an API-driven design approach.

The concept of APIs and system construction through APIs is not new. What *is* new, however, is a set of web-centric design patterns that make new APIs lightweight, portable and easier to work with than previous interface-focused approaches. By leveraging the new API solutions, organizations can now deliver new services to customers, partners, employees and vendors more quickly via multiple mobile and web channels. Organizations such as the Government Digital Service (GDS) see APIs as a way to gain wider reach and more relevant channels for content access in a mobile and cloud-enabled world.

Underlying this move is a changing set of expectations from service consumers about the ease with which they interact with the services offered by a service provider, the flexibility of ways to consume those services, and the role that users play in shaping the evolution of those services to improve the way in which the services meet their changing needs. Service consumers no longer see themselves as passive users of the capabilities the services providers offer.

API Philosophy

The philosophy of transparency and open access that lies behind an API-based approach is at least as important as the technology. The lessons from successful internet-based organizations point to the ease with which they have allowed their products and services to be used, accessed and combined with other external capabilities to create new solutions. To enable this, organizations have needed to adopt a much more flexible, open philosophy based on co-operation within and outside the traditional organizational boundaries, and creating trust across the supply chain by enabling users and partners to feel encouraged to experiment, interact and provide feedback to developers. This is a very different, and significant, organizational and cultural model for government to embrace.

Elements of the API philosophy include:

- **Outside-in design.** Adoption of open innovation practices has led many organizations to look outside their own organizational boundaries when looking for the next great ideas to expend their products and services. The 'democratizing of innovation' has long been discussed. Now, with much easier direct access between producers and consumers, we see organizations encouraging early access to their products and services, and support for direct connection between those working within an organization and those outside. The resulting approach has led to an increased exchange of knowledge between producers and consumers of products and services, greater understanding of users' needs and more efficient prioritization of demand.

- **Meritocracies and priority-based decision making**. One of the most complex and polemic changes has been the move away from centrally controlled management and decision making of products and services towards a community-based meritocracy. The opening up of products and services to greater external collaboration blurs the lines between 'producer' and 'consumer'. Increased responsiveness to consumer demands can provide real benefits, but often with some costs. Longer-term strategic planning comes into conflict with short-term consumer priorities, and confuses typical product-planning practices. At one extreme of this spectrum of relationships is co-creation of solutions. Here, the user can take a first-class active role in solution delivery.
- **Diversity in delivery**. The traditional view of online services delivery is through a web browser running on a PC or laptop. However, more frequently the delivery channels for products and services will be smartphones, tablets and an increasing variety of web-enabled devices. Today, a key question is not which channel to use, but how to support all channels equally well. An API-based approach recognizes this diversity and ensures that products and service delivery is possible across a very diverse set of delivery needs.
- **Mash-ups and new solution combinations**. Organizations are used to being in control of the total scope of the product or service they deliver to their users. Development and delivery schedules are often focused around periodic product releases in which all the elements of a solution can be managed and co-ordinated. However, this situation has changed. Specialization in product and service delivery has meant that more frequently a user service is an assembly of capabilities from a variety of sources. Various mash-up and assembly approaches have changed how individuals and organizations want to consume a product or service. Whether it is integrating services as part of a supply chain, or combining capabilities to offer new insights, the flexibility to become part of larger processes is essential.
- **Community-focused**. Learning from open source projects, the most successful APIs have very active user communities either inside the organization or more widely outside the organization. They are actively using the API to create new solutions, advocating and supporting use of

the API, offering guidance and encouragement to those requiring help with the API, testing and providing feedback on changes to the API and so on. Such communities must be encouraged, nurtured and supported. Frequently it is the strength of activity and vibrancy of the supporting community that determines the success of an API-based approach.

Designing an API

The main challenge for the success of an API is designing the services exposed through the interface, and deciding on the critical capabilities that the users of that interface will require: in general, five key aspects of the API must be addressed.

First, the primary goal should be to offer services that are **valuable** to one or more communities. Hence, the services that are exposed through the API must provide capabilities that the community finds useful and unique. Much like any software design, the API design requires clear understanding of the user community needs, and will likely involve a great deal of iteration and rework to get right.

Second, an API must be **planned** to meet a well-defined need. From a technical perspective this means that a number of important technological choices must be made to decide on the appropriate ways to maximize the appeal of the API to potential users. However, more fundamentally the API must have a clear reason for its existence. It is not simply an ad hoc collection of capabilities that externalize a set of internal functions in an existing system. As a result, exposing existing capabilities as services may require redesign and implementation of those services, and new service implementation must be considered from the perspective of potential service users.

Third, to consume an API it must be simple to use, yet it also must be **flexible** to meet different user needs and styles of consumption. To achieve this, API providers typically offer several choices to users in terms of data formats, protocols and versions of the API supported. This way, they can be more readily consumed by a variety of devices and users employing different technology platforms. In addition, various developer controls and options will be provided to allow data to be accessed via batch or real-time streams, to adapt to different performance needs using caching, and to query information at different granularities.

Fourth, relying on API access means that the API must be **managed** by the API provider to ensure it operates consistently as defined, and encourages further use through its vitality. This requires access to measurement data about the API and its ecosystem concerning its performance, availability, change profile, developer community activities, adaptation, versions and so on. Versioning of an API is a particular concern, and may require backward compatibility of interfaces for significant periods of time.

And finally, the continued use of an API requires that it is **supported and extended** throughout its lifetime. The availability of a well-specified API is necessary but not sufficient for it to be successful. It must also be well documented, supported by enthusiastic developers and users, and cost-effective as part of a broader solution. For many of the most successful API-based solutions (e.g. Google, Twitter and eBay) it has been the supporting ecosystem that has significantly influenced the adoption and use of the API. The API provider must dedicate a great deal of initial effort to creating that ecosystem, and subsequently to encourage a self-sustaining ecosystem to support existing users, advise new users and evangelize the API to encourage further adoption

The API converts a system into a hub for connected devices and users. An API-first approach to exposing capabilities provides not just delivery of underlying data, but also access to granular services that enable developers to take advantage of the capabilities as they create new solutions for any connected device. Today there are many examples of APIs aimed at connecting devices with the service vendors and other communities, taking advantage of emerging technology properties such as wearable devices like Google Glass and smart watches. The core idea is that the API opens up to developers and other stakeholders the ability to take advantage of whatever underlying capability they need to create a richer user experience as part of their application, service or solution.

Implementing an API

One of the aspects of an API-based approach that distinguishes it from earlier service-oriented styles is the simple set of web technologies that are typically used to implement APIs. The SOA approaches that were encouraged from the late 1990s (and used for example in the UK Government Gateway's transaction orchestration, payments and identity services) were largely realized through complex middleware technologies and standards controlled by slow-moving standards bodies, and dominated by a handful of commercial technology providers such as IBM, Oracle, Microsoft and Sun Microsystems.

In contrast, a lighter weight set of web technologies began to emerge from internet-based solution providers such as Google, Amazon and eBay, and popularized by a plethora of small companies and individuals attracted to build additional services interfacing to those solutions. They largely bypassed these complex middleware technologies, instead focusing on opening up their systems to be:

- Operating system platform-independent (whether Windows, Unix, Mac or anything else).
- Language-independent (e.g. C#, Java, python, multiple languages and interoperable between components).
- Web standards-based (relies only on simple web technologies such as HTTP).
- Flexible for common distributed hardware topologies (desktops, laptops, devices; easily used in the presence of firewalls).
- Configurable to multiple architectural patterns (readily adapted to diverse usage scenarios and contexts).

While many variants exist, a small set of technologies has emerged for implementing APIs based on these principles. Most APIs today are based on a combination of three technologies:

- **REST** (Representational State Transfer) is an architecture style for designing networked applications. Rather than using complex technical mechanisms (such as CORBA, RPC or SOAP) to connect between machines, the web's simple HTTP protocol is used to make calls between machines. RESTful applications use HTTP requests to post data (create and/or update), read data (e.g. make queries) and delete data.

‣ **JSON** (JavaScript Object Notation) is a lightweight data-interchange format. Primarily it is a way to store information in an organized, easy-to-access manner. It is a text format that is completely language independent but uses conventions that are familiar to programmers. These properties make JSON an ideal data-interchange language.

‣ **OAuth** is an open protocol that aims to standardize the way desktop and web applications access a user's private data. It provides a mechanism for users to grant access to private data without sharing their private credentials (username/password). Many sites have started enabling APIs to use OAuth because of its security and standard set of libraries.

Summary – Implementing Digital Government

In Part 3 we aimed to navigate through some of the maze of core building blocks essential for the move to truly digital government. We looked at the foundations of digital transformation and the enduring principles of successful, agile digital organizations. We considered how profiling must be applied in practice to distinguish between those requirements that can be met by utility services, and those genuinely niche that need to be kept closer to home and built locally. In the context of an overall architectural framework, we explored some of the main elements that underpin these developments – the successful application of cloud computing, the use of agile processes and practices, and the API economy and the wider ecosystem it supports and creates. In so doing, we have laid out the core set of tools and techniques that can help to overcome the gap between aspiration and reality discussed in Part 1, and to realize the big idea and ambition of Part 2.

chapter 13

Conclusion and Recommendations

Conclusion

Our purpose in this book has been to examine the long-standing gap between political aspiration and the desire to use technology to improve public services, and – most importantly – to identify and recommend ways to close this gap. If the move to 'digital' is not merely to become a lazy rebadge of earlier online and e-government initiatives, government and its wider service provider and supplier ecosystem needs to learn and apply the lessons of successful digital organizations rather than merely continue to throw technology at existing services, processes and organizational structures.

The political intent since the 1990s and earlier to use modern technology as a lever of change has belied an insufficient underlying attention to redesigning and improving the essential infrastructure of twenty-first-century public services. Technology has all too often been used at arm's length – pushed outside the leadership and management circles, and often handed entirely to an outside commercial supplier. The result is that the inherited and increasingly creaking and ineffective organizational infrastructures, processes and systems that underpin public services remain everywhere around us.

In place of strategic change, there is often instead a tyranny of merely getting things done, rather than knowing why they are being done or doing the right thing well. The 'why' is very often vague, done merely because others are doing it – 'private sector companies are outsourcing' or '63% of successful companies are adopting social media such as Facebook and Twitter' for example – and, therefore, copying everyone else merely because they are all doing something seems like a good idea. As Simon Wardley has pointed out, the military equivalent would be as absurd as a general bombarding a hill merely because a report had discovered that '67% of successful generals bombard hills'.

If government is to move beyond merely being seen to 'do something' and hence being endlessly blown about by short-term issues and supplier-dictated agendas, it must identify where meaningful improvements need to be made, the options available to implement such changes and why one option might be chosen in preference to another. We have shown how properly analysing and mapping the current environment in an objective way – through digital profiling – is an essential step in this process: it gives us the ability to properly understand the public services landscape, to see where we might change and to determine why: why should we change *this* over *that*? At what pace should we make these changes? How do we evaluate the impact of those changes to accelerate future progress?

Governments seem unlikely to make meaningful progress on deciding what changes they need to make – and why – until they also resolve the highly emotive issue of what 'rightfully' belongs in public versus private and voluntary sectors. Yet it would be regarded as odd, if not a little eccentric, if we became similarly emotional about our public services needing special 'government electricity' – since electricity is a utility, with no need of a separate and 'unique' electricity service built exclusively for government's needs. So why do we become so emotional about other utility functions within our public service organizations, behaving as if they must be lavishly and extravagantly provided with the equivalent of special 'government electricity'? The dull reality is that much of what our public services do on a daily basis can draw upon standard functions that should be treated as simply and dispassionately as electricity – as utilities.

It's time we learnt to distinguish properly between these utility, common-place elements and those genuinely unique elements that are distinctive and specific to public services: those things that really matter to us.

One reason that proper debate about improving our public services has been stifled is the painful memory of the failure of earlier models of reform. Since the 1980s, the dominant public sector approach has attempted to shoe-horn private sector market models into public services, such as the widespread use of big-bang, wholesale outsourcing to the private sector. The results have been mixed and often of dubious quality and cost, failing to live up to the promise of better public services, and further illustrating the tyranny of 'what' we do over 'why'. The result is that alternative options for modernizing and operating our public services more efficiently have become tarnished by these previous poor experiences, and conflate public sector *ownership* of public services with public ownership of their *operation*.

Whilst the public sector struggles to organize and maintain its services, in the commercial world new organizational and economic models have emerged. These models are fundamentally changing the way organizations are designed and operated: if they are not now adapted to public sector needs, then our public services are in danger of being left even further behind and citizens increasingly disillusioned. This digital divide is dangerous for the future viability and social acceptance of public services and the essential role they play in our society: government needs to act swiftly and appropriately to correct this damaging gap.

Whilst at first glance it may seem counter-intuitive that lessons can be learned by the public sector from new economic titans such as Amazon, Google and Facebook, technology is enabling companies such as these to evolve new organizational models based on the economics of digital technology. They have broken down into small building blocks those elements of their operations that can or should be outsourced – the commodity or utility components – whilst ensuring that their more specialist requirements are maintained in-house. As a result, they have developed open, dynamic ecosystems of innovation, enabling their services to benefit from a cycle of continuous improvement.

The contrast with the state of our public services could not be more profound. The public sector has generally used technology to automate old, fragmented ways of doing things, rather than to improve them. The result has been expensive and dysfunctional as the public sector has increasingly standardized on a handful of technologies, suppliers and delivery vehicles with monopoly ownership of expensive, long-term contracts: merely replacing a state monopoly with a private sector one that has proved itself to be often both more costly and less efficient. Changes such as those currently being made by the UK government to disaggregate capabilities, remove tightly coupled and propriety systems, identify open standards to be used and to encourage the restoration and maintenance of a genuinely open and competitive marketplace will enable all suppliers – from SMEs to the large corporates – to play to their respective strengths, enabling government in turn to drive down costs whilst simultaneously re-engineering and improving the design of public services around the needs of citizens rather than administrators.

Whilst some of the public sector's needs are rightly specialist and therefore best kept in-house, others are generic and mature, and available as utility services. At the simple administrative level, such services span everything from payroll to e-mail facilities. Hand-crafting these commodity services in multiple departments and agencies in separate pockets across the public sector time after time is as absurd and wastefully extravagant as government building its own 'special' power stations generating electricity for its own services, rather than making use of the utilities that already exist. Government must consolidate and standardize its utility, non-specialist requirements to take advantage of much less expensive core services, enabling public sector organizations to procure commodity services in the open marketplace.

Such a change requires governments to adopt a more effective and agile approach to innovation and public service reform. Google's innovation ecosystem, for example, illustrates the difference between traditional outsourcing mechanisms and utility, platform-based ecosystems. By providing a cheap, commodity platform, Google has encouraged a broad range of content providers, consumers, innovators and advertisers to build applications, share data and purchase services in a way that allows it to crowdsource ideas and then cherry-pick and invest in the best of these. The resulting dynamic is very different from a fixed supply contract owned by one, or a small handful, of over-dominant suppliers.

Imagine if taxpayers were able to benefit from their own thriving, diverse service community competing to provide ever more innovative, better-value offerings. An open platform model aims to bring about just this way of doing things, making public services available to citizens when and where they need them: as internet guru Tim O'Reilly has noted, on such a model 'government *[becomes] a convener and an enabler rather than the first mover of civic action'*, and moves away from its outdated model of 'vending machine government'.

The role of government becomes that of an intelligent and account-able enabling function that sets strategy, architecture, procurement and governance in ensuring rigorous public service values. The question as to whether services themselves are best delivered by public sector, private sector, third sector, mutual, co-operatives, hybrids of these, or by citizens and communities themselves, is determined increasingly by the environ-ment established by government at the centre, and the ability – and willingness – of service providers to engage with these incentives.

Achieving this outcome can be seen, in simple terms, as the end of the era of public services organized around the needs of either state or private sector corporate monopolies and the emergence of an era where services are built around the needs of citizens. Government's ability to specify, procure and regulate public service delivery within this digital-era model is increasingly contingent upon its understanding and management of its underlying dynamic, its expertise in separating niche services from util-ity needs, a commitment to openness and transparency, and its ability to mobilize this understanding in its relations with service providers.

Many of the most successful organizations to develop ecosystems around core platforms and standards monitor new innovations and their recep-tion by users. They incorporate the best of these in their core offerings – the form of crowdsourcing practised by Google, as well as others who encourage innovation around their platform. Facebook, for example, which provides an open platform around which an entire ecosystem of third-party companies develops. Or SalesForce.com, which encourages direct customer engagement and innovation through its IdeaExchange.

Implementing digital public management will enable new innovations to be developed into core public services and made available to other users – which in turn will often lead to wholesale integration and development of the underlying platform. Government needs to build capability in the skills and approaches required to leverage successful innovations, and standardize these so that they can be delivered cheaply and efficiently at volume.

Such a change in the operation of public services will require a resolute focus on the use of open platforms and services as utilities. In turn, this will require a separation of high-risk, bespoke activities (those genuinely unique to the public sector) from low-risk, commodity activities, ensuring that volume procurements such as outsourcing are used only for known commodities and not, as in the past, thrown expensively at everything. As a matter of policy, there should no longer be any outsourcing permitted of undifferentiated services that have not been separated out beforehand, since innovations involving low certainty and ubiquity are likely to be more bespoke and therefore expensive. In turn, ensuring that services and parts of services that can use standardized and commoditized elements are identified, before being purchased in volume, both creates a platform for innovation, as well as providing funding for innovation. Such changes constitute a major shift from the current mode of public service design, delivery and operation.

So what is preventing governments from adopting these models in order to modernize and improve public services? With some notable exceptions, policymakers and those who operate our public services have remained unaware of how open platforms can revolutionize the business model of government. They are, in effect, too busy bombarding nearby hills, with no real idea why. There remains a widespread lack of understanding – both of technology and the new economic models that have come to dominate the post-internet organization – amongst our political classes and those who advise them, ably demonstrating Marshall McLuhan's 1967 observation that *'We look at the present through a rear-view mirror'*.

It is precisely this lack of understanding that we hope we have started to address in this book. Government needs to apply some of the lessons already learned in the best of the private sector, particularly in the areas of contracting, governance and accountability. The private sector has learned several things that governments should seek to adapt, including the need to buy capabilities little and often; to open up design to wider participation; to focus on outcomes not outputs; to govern through leadership not through contracts and penalties; to view solutions as continually changing capabilities that adapt to their environment; and to find ways to reward early intervention and flexibility, not long-term fixed plans based on resource management.

What is presently missing in particular is any clarity of purpose – a vision, a clear political map – one that sets out where we are and where we need to head and why, and to share and co-develop that vision with citizens, businesses and public sector workers in an open and inclusive way. The very real prize that is out there and within our grasp – cost-effective, locally tailored public services that are simpler to design and maintain, with a talent pool of cost-effective providers vying with one another to think of ever better, more innovative ideas to improve our public services – remains unclaimed.

Globalization, digitization and commoditization are challenging traditional, corporatist ways of designing and organizing services. Whether you are an international bank or a government tax revenue department, old, expensive and unresponsive business models are being challenged on all sides, and public services continue on lines that would look familiar to a 1940s civil servant stepping out of Dr Who's Tardis into our twenty-first century.

Many of the most envied, successful and most discussed businesses in the world are founded on open platforms – their accessibility encourages smaller businesses to innovate around them, dreaming up new, popular services that no one had thought of before. The same outcome applied to our public services could provide both the improvement they need and the spur to economic growth that is much needed. Adopting the platform model will be genuinely ambitious and disruptive. It amounts to nothing less than the 'de-corporatization' of the state and its major suppliers, exploiting recent seismic shifts in technology-enabled global capitalism to re-empower citizens.

We are not naive enough to overlook the political challenges involved in this reinvention of government: the proper use of technology will be as disruptive and threatening to many existing structures, processes, organizations and roles as earlier technology initiatives were in other industries. There will be many painful political choices to be made about personnel and organizations and whether they are needed any longer at all, and, if they are, where their functions best reside. But these contentious issues cannot be ignored just because they will be painful to resolve: to do so would be to fail our public services and risk fracturing the social contract and political settlement between the citizen and government. Rising to meet the challenge of meaningful reform of public sector infrastructure will require clear and sustained political and administrative leadership.

In 1998, the UK Parliamentary Office of Science and Technology included in a report a diagram (see Figure 13.1) showing staff reductions in banking and government in the years 1989–95 – in part as a result of the use of technology to transform and replace previously manual processes.

The potential for truly digital government could well have a similar dramatic impact now on government staffing as both earlier and current changes have had on the resourcing and configuration of retail banking: successful redesign of public services will undoubtedly remove many of the manual, duplicate and ultimately redundant administrative posts currently in the public sector and its many overlapping functions across departments and agencies. Such potential impacts are no reason not to face up to the reality of what digital transformation means: public services deserve to be optimally designed and run for the benefit of citizens. The separate issue, of how best to handle the inevitable impacts, is a political, economic, human and societal one that needs to be properly managed as

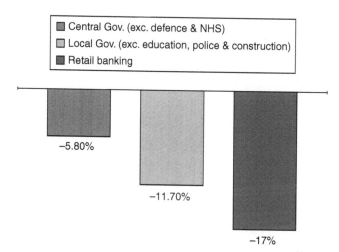

■ Central Gov. (exc. defence & NHS)
□ Local Gov. (exc. education, police & construction)
■ Retail banking

−5.80%

−11.70%

−17%

FIG 13.1 / Staff reductions in banking and government, 1989–95

part of this process – but it should not negate making the changes necessary to ensure our public services thrive and survive.

As political parties continue to consider their policies, they need to better understand what citizens and businesses need from twenty-first-century public services; what 'lean' government thinking might mean in terms of achieving better outcomes and better quality services; on the definition of what an open, platform-based business model for public services actually looks like in order to meet those needs; on championing vigorous and open debate about its limitations and boundaries; and the development of – we hope – a degree of cross-party consensus together with a collective mandate for rapid and effective implementation of a map to ensure both economic revival and the reinvention of our public services.

It is time to wake up, to redesign public services, to make the transition to truly digital public management. Time to start re-engineering our public services from inception to delivery. The outcome will be both radical and truly important, as O'Reilly describes it, becoming *'a system in which all of the outcomes aren't specified beforehand, but instead evolve through interactions between government and its citizens, as a service provider enabling its user community'*.

It is time to start properly mapping, planning and implanting these necessary strategic changes – and to stop bombarding the hills.

Summary of Recommendations

In the three parts of this book we have examined the gap between long-standing political aspirations to use technology to modernize and improve public services; explored the 'big idea' of how technology enables a fundamentally new approach to the design, development and operation of public services as part of a platform-based open architecture; and detailed some of the key tools, techniques and organizational improvements necessary to deliver on the promise. In each of these parts we have highlighted some of the key lessons that government needs to learn and apply if it is not to remain stuck in a sort of 'Groundhog Day' replay of the same dream. These recommendations need to be understood and acted upon as a whole, not in a partial or half-hearted way. Below, we bring together for convenience the recommendations of each part – together, they provide the basis for the creation of a truly digitized government.

Part 1

In Part 1 we explored why government needs to move away from the failed approaches of the past: it needs to break the cycle of endless publication of strategies without clear mechanisms for delivery; to stop using technology merely to automate existing manual procedures and processes based on the movement of paper and because it's the 'way it's always been done'; avoid the tendency for indiscriminate, undifferentiated outsourcing – and in particular the risks and problems of outsourcing elements that need to be part of government's own core operation; and challenge the lazy assumption that current organizational structures and processes are here to stay.

To see what might be possible, we also examined what has happened in the best of the private sector: their focus on outcomes and how best they can be achieved rather than the maintenance of the status quo; the use of technology as part of a cultural shift to move away from functional business units and to restructure organizations around the processes that support public services; the increased engagement of users, including enabling them to input, manage and control their own data; the need to recruit and maintain expert leadership, knowledge and oversight in-house; and the development of an open and competitive marketplace from which to choose suppliers, services and products.

Part 2

In Part 2, we made the case for a wholesale commitment to radical digital transformation across our public services. We developed the long-standing political aspirations and recent digital developments of Part 1 into a frame-work that can successfully deliver the long-awaited era of better public services, reimagined and reinvented through what technology now makes possible – but only as part of a wider cultural and organizational shift.

We also made the case for an urgent national discussion about the need to adopt a 'lean' mindset that asks necessarily frank and sometimes awk-ward questions about our current assumptions regarding the outcomes required of public services and how best they might be optimally delivered. Following from this, we have highlighted the necessity of *profiling* public services, using the innovate–leverage–commoditize framework and the power of open standards. By explaining the linkages between open stand-ards, platforms and innovation, we have shown that open architecture is ultimately not a matter of minor tweaks to processes here and there, whilst leaving the fundamental service organization unchanged in its bricks-and-mortar form, cushioned in its comforting public/private sector blocs.

Achievement of digital public services will require nothing less than a lean-thinking mindset that helps underpin a wholesale dis-integration of these organizations, and the reaggregation of their various functions in the form of digital profiles, in the way we have explained. The reaggregation is around information and data, the lifeblood of all modern service organ-izations, clustered around the citizen, not the corporate. Digital is thus an organization-wide undertaking, not a niche activity for technologists. It is for the minister, the chief executive, the permanent secretary – the citizen.

We also illustrated how the public sector is large enough to be able to reap many of the benefits of digital organizations such as Google, if its myriad organizations could only start to expose all that hidden commonality across government and de-duplicate standard ways of doing things. This calls for individual public organizations to develop enterprise-wide digital profiles, as well as maintaining continuous dialogue with the evolving profiles of others – perhaps initially within their sector, then nationwide. The taxpayer could sit at the centre of a powerful ecosystem of platforms and innovators, and our public services could better utilize these resources. There would be fewer managerial and bureaucratic opportunities within government, and more technical expertise.

Of course, we recognize that the state is not like Google in many ways: it is both provider and consumer of services, it can never outsource risk to suppliers, and it undertakes many activities that are either too sensitive or commercially incompatible to place outside the public domain. That said, it is not so different from the likes of Google in terms of the way it can become more efficient at designing and running its services and internal processes and operations. We have provided a clear framework for enabling this vision of government as a platform (or, more accurately, government as platforms) to become reality, based on lean-thinking digital profiling and open architecture.

Part 3

In Part 3 we navigated through some of the maze of core building blocks essential for the move to truly digital government. We looked at the foundations of digital transformation and the enduring principles of successful, agile digital organizations. We considered how profiling must be applied in practice to distinguish between those requirements that can be met by utility services, and those that are genuinely niche and need to be kept closer to home and potentially built.

In the context of an overall architectural framework, we explored some of the main elements that underpin these developments – the successful application of cloud computing, the use of agile processes and practices, and the API economy and the wider ecosystem it supports and creates.

In so doing, we laid out the core set of tools and techniques that can overcome the gap between aspiration and reality discussed in Part 1, and to realize the big idea and ambition of Part 2.

How, and Where, to Start – to Become a Digital Organization

It's difficult to provide a succinct digest of the many interlinked and nuanced topics we have discussed in this book – but that doesn't mean we shouldn't try. As a starting point, in Table 13.1 we have therefore aimed to summarize some of the key elements that we believe governments need to understand and adopt if they are to become successful digital organizations. We do so with a note of caution – and would encourage readers to read the sections in our book that deal with

TABLE 13.1   Selected recommendations to move towards a digital organization

Recommendation	Commentary
1. Developi ntegrated strategies, not 'IT strategies'	Too many attempts to modernize government have been based on the idea of separate 'IT strategies'. Don't develop 'digital' or 'IT' strategies late in the day after other public policies have already been decided: technology applied to the existing ways of doing things, or as an afterthought, has repeatedly failed to deliver the desired outcomes. Truly digital reform requires integrated, user-based models that redevelop and redesign services around users' needs and use technology as an integral part of that process.
2. Use lean thinking	The challenge is not technology: it is about finding the best way to design and deliver services. Focus on user needs and outcomes, not current processes and organizational structures. Question the way things are currently done compared to what actually needs to be achieved: using technology to automate current ways of doing things starts in the wrong place, will often be a waste of money and prevents an organization becoming truly digital. Think about the many different ways in which a policy outcome might be achieved – and identify the most effective means of meeting that outcome in a way that involves the minimum complexity, duplication and cost whilst delivering successfully in a user-focused, high-quality way.

(continued)

TABLE 13.1 Continued

Recommendation	Commentary
3. Bring in and cultivate the right skills	These changes will require new ways of thinking and new skills – bring the right change management experience and entrepreneurial skills in-house to identify and encourage the organizational and cultural changes: they will be seriously disruptive. Some current organizational structures will be radically modified – or even cease to exist – when the focus moves to front-line users and citizens: it's about a fundamental change to an outside-in mindset, rather than existing inside-out.
4. Establishe xemplary practices and lead by example in essential areas such as social inclusion, privacy, identity and security	Design services with inclusion and trust in mind from inception to delivery. This is not a matter of technology in isolation, but about the way all public service channels operate, whether the end delivery of a service is face-to-face in the home or a government office, or delivered on to a mobile device or PC screen. Government has the opportunity, and obligation, to lead by example in these important areas – and to build exemplars of trust. However, recent revelations by Snowden about habitual government intrusion into the daily lives of many citizens, and suspicions about governments' use of citizens' personal data, are likely to complicate the move to digital organizations, unless government can become more transparent.
5. Move to horizontal rather than vertical organizations	There is an obvious horizontal, not vertical, orientation to developing a truly digital organization, involving reuse, sharing and commonality across historical silos. These are the characteristics that government must develop and foster. Use technology as part of a cultural shift away from functional business units and to restructure organizations around the processes that support public services: the increased engagement of users, including enabling them to input, manage and control their own data; the need to recruit and maintain expert leadership, knowledge and oversight in-house; and the development of an open and competitive marketplace from which to choose suppliers, services and products.
6. Developd igital profiles	Once a potential optimal means of achieving an outcome (such as a redesigned and improved public service) has been identified, apply innovate–leverage–commoditize (ILC) and use tools such as Wardley Maps to break down the needs. It's essential to identify those elements that can use commodity elements versus those that genuinely need to be bespoke, and to ensure each is acquired or developed in the most appropriate way.

(continued)

TABLE 13.1 Continued

Recommendation	Commentary
7. Use an open architecture	Delivering meaningful improvements in public services requires exploiting the move towards becoming open – by which we mean the movement that spans everything from open standards to open source software to open architecture. Adopting an open approach means that government will be able to smartly use and reuse commodity and utility components within an overall architectural framework instead of building them time after time – and will open up the traditional vertical silos of multiple similar functional needs to enable them to be turned into common, horizontal building blocks underpinned by a consistent use of open standards.
8. Use platforms	'Platforms' does not refer to some standard technology, such as an 'IT platform': it is the demand created by standardizing things openly, and subsequent investment from the market, that forms the really important part. The platform is a dynamic – not a thing. Progressive convergence on open standards within an evolving open architecture will enable government to establish a sustainable and open platform for innovation – an open platform model that enables government services to become available to citizens when and where they need them.
9. Usefl exible architectures	Make use of the development of cloud computing as a new form of deployment platform. Take advantage of solutions and services on the cloud to adopt utility solutions to common needs and drive out costs while improving quality and performance.
10. Implementa gile processes and practices	Apply agile approaches in all aspects of service design and delivery. Encourage styles of service delivery that move away from early and artificial lockdown of decisions towards controlled discovery, experimentation and innovation: this transition is important if government is to avoid repeating the project delivery failures and costly overruns of the past.
11. Implement an API economy	APIs (application programming interfaces) provide a way for systems to share processes and data – enabling the smart reuse of components in building services, rather than point solutions with many duplicated components as in the past. Government should use a mixed model of government and commercial API service providers to enable the more flexible and effective design and delivery of services.
12. Remain an elastic organization	This is not a one-time change: it's a dynamic. The resulting services, processes, structures and organizations should constantly be reviewed and improved. The real-time flow of data, including user feedback, typical of digital organizations enables services constantly to be refined, improved, replaced and retired. Organizations need to be built to change to meet changing needs.

these aspects of digital reform: there are some important details that lie behind them if they are to be applied successfully.

We recognize that the challenge to rethink, redesign and improve public services represents both a significant opportunity and challenge for governments around the world. We hope that the background and framework we have set out in this book will prove useful to those interested in helping to redesign and reimagine public services for the digital age – of helping us to take at least one more step towards making people *'feel good about government again'*.

References, Sources
and Further Reading

Ambler, S. The Agile Scaling Model (ASM): Adapting Agile Methods for Complex Environments, IBM Whitepaper (December, 2009).

American Political Science Association Conference, Washington DC, USA, 4 September 2010.

Andreeva, G., Ansell, J., and Harrison, T. Civil Servants and Public Risk. Risk & Regulation Advisory Council, October 2009. http://www.bis.gov.uk/files/file53395.doc.

Australian National Audit Office. Measuring the Efficiency and Effectiveness of E-Government, Audit Report Number 26 (2005). http://www.anao.gov.au/uploads/documents/2004-05_audit_report_26.pdf.

Babar, M.A., Brown, A.W. and Mistrik, I. (eds.). *Agile Software Architecture: Aligning Agile Processes and Software Architectures* (Morgan Kaufman, 2013).

Broadbent, J. and Laughlin, R. 'Public Sector Professionals and New Public Management: Control of the Professions in the Public Services'. In *The New Public Management: Current Trends and Future Prospects*, ed. Kathleen McLaughlin, Stephen Osborne and Ewan Ferlie (Routledge, 2002), pp. 95–108.

Brown, A.W. 'Experiences with Cloud Technology to Realize Software Testing Factories'. In *Software Testing in the Cloud*, ed. S. Tilley and T. Parveen (IGI, 2013), pp. 1–27.

Brown, A.W., Ambler, S. and Royce, W. (2013). 'Agile at Scale: Economic Governance, Measured Improvement, and Disciplined Delivery', *Proceedings of the 35th International Conference on Software Engineering*, IEEE, May 2013.

Brown, A.W. *Enterprise Software Delivery: Bringing Efficiency and Agility to the Global Software Supply Chain* (Addison-Wesley, 2012).

Building the Change-Ready IT Organization. Corporate Executive Board, 2012. http://www.executiveboard.com/communications-blog/3-ways-to-build-a-change-ready-organization/.

Burton, A. *Comments on government use of cloud computing.* http://www.bm magazine.co.uk/news/1098/francis-maude-government-says-we-will-make-it-easier-for-uk-sme-business-to-sell-to-us/, 2011.

Cabinet Office. Government ICT Strategy, 11 March 2011. http://www.cabinetoffice. gov.uk/content/government-ict-strategy.

Carr, N. *Does It Matter? Information Technology and the Corrosion of Competitive Advantage* (Harvard Business Review Press, 2004).

Chopra, A. *Innovative State: How New Technologies can Transform Government* (Grove Press/Atlantic Monthly Press, 2014).

Cockburn, A. *Agile Software Development* (Addison-Wesley, 2001).

Cohn, M. *Succeeding with Agile* (Addison-Wesley, 2006).

Curtis, B., Hefley, W. and Miller, S. *The People Capability Maturity Model: A Framework for Human Capital Management*, 2nd edn (Addison-Wesley, 2009).

Denning, S. *The Leader's Guide to Radical Management* (Jossey-Bass, 2010).

Digital Economy. Report of the 2012 RCUK Digital Economy impact review panel, RCUK, 2013.

'Digital Transformation: Getting in Shape for a Digital World', 2014. www. apigee.com.

Downes, L. and Nunes, P. *Big Bang Disruption: Business Survival in the Age of Constant Innovation* (Penguin Books, 2014).

Drucker, P. 'The New Society of Organizations'. *Harvard Business Review*, September/October 1992, 95–104.

Dunleavy, P. and Margetts, H. 'Government IT Performance and the Power of the IT Industry: A Cross-National Analysis'. American Political Science Association, 2004.

Dunleavy, P. and Margetts, H. 'The Second Wave of Digital-era Governance: A Quasi-paradigm for Government on the Web'. *Philosophical Transactions of the Royal Society* 371/1987 (2013).

Dunleavy, P., Margetts, H., Bastow, S. and Tinkler, J. 'New Public Management is Dead – Long Live Digital-Era Governance'. *Journal of Public Administration Research and Theory* 16 (2005), 467–94.

Dunleavy, P., Margetts, H., Bastow, S. and Tinkler, J. *Digital Era Governance* (Oxford University Press, 2006).

e-commerce@its.best.uk. Performance and Innovation Unit (PIU), 1999. http://ctpr.org/wp-content/uploads/2011/03/ecommerce-at-its-best-1999-body.pdf.

e-Government Authentication Framework. Cabinet Office, 2000. http://ctpr.org/wp-content/uploads/2011/03/Authentication-Framework.pdf.

e-Government Strategy Framework Policy and Guidelines: Registration and Authentication. Cabinet Office, 2001. http://ctpr.org/wp-content/uploads/2011/03/e-govt-strategy-on-registration-and-authentication-2001.pdf.

'e-Government strategy: A Strategic Framework for Public Services in the Information Age'. CITU, 2000. http://ctpr.org/wp-content/uploads/2011/03/e-Government-Strategy-2000.pdf.

Eisenmann, T.R., Parker, G. and Van Alstyne, M.W. 'Platform Envelopment', Harvard Business School Working Paper No. 07-104, 2010. http://ssrn.com/abstract=1496336.

'Electronic Government: The View from the Queue'. http://ctpr.org/wp-content/uploads/2011/03/Electronic-Government-the-View-from-the-Queue-1998t.pdf.

Farrell, C. and Morris, J. 'The 'Post Bureaucratic' Public Sector Organization? New Organizational Forms and HRM in Ten UK Public Sector Organizations'. *International Journal of Human Resource Management* 18 (2007), 1578–88.

Fenwick. N. 'The State of Digital Business 2014', Forrester Research Report, May 2014.

Fishenden, J. and Thompson, M. 'Digital Government, Open Architecture, and Innovation: Why Public Sector IT Will Never be the Same Again, *Journal of Public Administration Research and Theory* 23/4 (2012), 977–1004.

Fitzgerald, M., Kruschwitz, N., Bonnet, D. and Welch, M. 'Embracing Digital Technology: A New Strategic Imperative'. MIT Sloan Management Review Research Report, 2013.

Gawer, A. and Cussamano, M. 'Platform Leadership', Harvard Business School Press, 2002.

Geist, M. (2013). 'Ottawa's Complete e-Government Failure', *The Star*, 29 November 2013. http://www.thestar.com/business/tech_news/2013/11/29/ottawas_complete_egovernment_failure_geist.html.

GDS (Government Digital Service) Identity Assurance Programme (IDAP). On-going blog posts at http://digital.cabinetoffice.gov.uk/category/id-assurance/.

Government Direct. 'A Prospectus for the Electronic Delivery of Government Services', 1996. http://ctpr.org/wp-content/uploads/2011/03/Government-Direct.pdf.

Government ICT Strategy. Cabinet Office, 2011. https://www.gov.uk/government/uploads/system/uploads/attachment_data/file/85968/uk-government-government-ict-strategy_0.pdf.

Hamel, G. *What Matters Now: How to Win in a World of Relentless Change, Ferocious Competition, and Unstoppable Innovation* (Jossey-Bass, 2012).

Hammer, M. and Champy, J. *Reengineering the Corporation* (Harper Business, 1993).

Handy, C. *The Empty Raincoat: Making Sense of the Future* (Arrow Business, 1995).

Heckscher, C. and Applegate, L. 'Introduction'. In *The Post Bureaucratic Organization: New Perspectives on Organizational Change*, ed. Charles Heckscher and Anne Donnelon (Sage, 1994), pp. 1–13.

Hennessy, P. *Whitehall* (Pimlico, 1989).

Herbert, James (2014) 'Change Ready Business Architecture for Local Government: an Opportunity for Platform Technology', 2014. http://www.methods digital.co.uk.

Highsmith, A. *Agile Project Management: Creating Innovative Products* (Addison-Wesley, 2009).

Hood, C. and Peters, G. 'The Middle Aging of New Public Management: Into the Age of Paradox?' *Journal of Public Administration Research and Theory* 14/3 (2004), 267–82.

House of Commons Public Accounts Committee. Twenty-Seventh Report, Session 2004–05, 6 April 2005.

Ibbs Report. *Improving Management in Government: The Next Steps: Report to the Prime Minister.* (HMSO, 1988).

'Improving IT Procurement: The Impact of the Office of Government Commerce's Initiatives on Departments and Suppliers in the Delivery of Major IT-enabled Projects'. National Audit Office, 2004. http://ctpr.org/wp-content/uploads/2011/03/NAO-report-on-improving-IT-procurement.pdf.

Iyer, B. and Davenport, T. H. 'Reverse Engineering Google's Innovation Machine'. Harvard Business Review, April 2008.

JISC. 'The Advantages of APIs: How to Jump the Information Gap', 2014. www.jisc.ac.uk/reports/the-advantage-of-apis.

Jones, C. *Software Engineering Best Practices* (McGraw-Hill, 2010).

Kable. 'Underlying Data 2009', cited in Maxwell, L. (2009) *It's Ours: Why we, not government, must own our data*, UK: Centre for Policy Studies.

Kamensy, J. 'National Partnership for Reinventing Government (formerly the National Performance Review): A Brief History', 1999. http://govinfo.library.unt.edu/npr/whoweare/history2.html.

Kernaghan, K. 'The Post-Bureaucratic Organization and Public Service Values'. *International Review of Administrative Sciences* 66/91 (2000), 91–104.

Kidson, M. 'Civil Service Capabilities. A Discussion Paper'. Institute for Government, 2013. http://www.instituteforgovernment.org.uk/sites/default/files/publications/20130621%20-%20Capabilities%20Discussion%20Paper%20-%20final.pdf.

Kruchten, P. 'Contextualizing Agile Software Development', EuroSPI 2010 Conference, Grenoble, France, EuroSPI.net, pp. 6.1–12, 9/2010. http://www.ece.ubc.ca/pubs/kruchten2010contextualizing.

Leonelli, N., Marshall, A. and Berman, S.J. 'Digital Disruption: Reinventing a Very Different Tomorrow', IBM Institute for Business Value, 2013.

Liker, J. *The Toyota Way: 14 Management Principles from the World's Greatest Manufacturer* (McGraw-Hill, 2004).

Martin, R. *Agile Software Development* (Prentice Hall, 2002).

Maude, F. 'Launch of GOV.UK a key milestone in making public service delivery digital by default', 2012. https://www.gov.uk/government/news/launch-of-gov-uk-a-key-milestone-in-making-public-service-delivery-digital-by-default.

Maxwell, L., Fishenden, J., Heath, W., Sowler, S., Rowlins, R., Thompson, M., and Wardley, S. 'Better for Less: How to Make Government IT Deliver Savings', 2010. http://markthompson1.files.wordpress.com/2012/02/better-for-less-final1.pdf.

Maxwell, L., Fishenden, J., Thompson, M., Heath, W., Rowlins, P., Sowler, J., and Wardley, S. 'Better for Less: How to Make Government IT Deliver Savings'. London, Network for the Post-Bureaucratic Age, September 2010.

Mazzucato, M. *The Entrepreneurial State: Debunking Public vs. Private Sector Myths* (Anthem Press, 2014).

'Measuring the Expected Benefits of e-Government'. HMT, 2003. http://ctpr.org/wp-content/uploads/2011/03/HMTGuidelinesVersion1_4.pdf.

'Modernising Government First Annual Report'. Cabinet Office, 2000. http://ctpr.org/wp-content/uploads/2011/03/modernising-government-1st-annual-report-2000.pdf.

'Modernising Government', March 1999. http://ctpr.org/wp-content/uploads/2011/03/modgov.pdf.

Moran, M. *The British Regulatory State High Modernism and Hyper-Innovation* (Oxford, Oxford University Press, 2003).

NAO (National Audit Office). 'Landscape Review. Information and Communications Technology in Government', 2011. http://www.nao.org.uk/publications/1011/ict_in_government.aspx.

NAO (National Audit Office). 'Improving IT Procurement: The impact of the Office of Government Commerce's initiatives on departments and suppliers in the delivery of major IT-enabled projects', 2004. http://www.nao.org.uk/wp-content/uploads/2004/11/0304877.pdf.

New Zealand Government. 'New Zealand e-Government Progress towards Transformation', 2007. http://ndhadeliver.natlib.govt.nz/delivery/DeliveryManagerServlet?dps_pid=IE775396&dps_custom_att_1=ilsdb.

New Zealand State Services Commission. 'E-government – a vision for New Zealanders', 2003. http://www.ssc.govt.nz/egovt-vision-for-nzers.

'Next-Generation API Delivery Platform', November 2013. Vordel White Paper.

Ng, I. *Creating New Markets in the Digital Economy: Value and Worth* (Cambridge University Press, 2014).

O'Reilly, T. 'Government 2.0', Chapter 2 in *Open Government*, ed. D. Lathrop and L. Ruma (O'Reilly Press, 2010). https://github.com/oreillymedia/open_government.

Obama '08. 'Barack Obama: Connecting and Empowering all Americans through Technology and Innovation', a paper produced by 'Obama for America', 2008. http://obama.3cdn.net/780e0e91ccb6cdbf6e_6udymvin7.pdf.

OECD Economic Outlook Tables. http://www.oecd.org/eco/outlook/economic outlookannextables.htm.

OECD Government at a Glance 2011. Country Note: UNITED KINGDOM. http://www.oecd.org/gov/47876677.pdf.

'Open Source Software use within UK Government'. Cabinet Office, 2002. http:///www.ctpr.org/wp-content/uploads/2011/03/Open-Source-Softward-Policy-2002.pdf.

'Open Source, Open Standards and Re-Use: Government Action Plan'. Cabinet Office, 2009. http://ctpr.org/wp-content/uploads/2011/03/Open-Source-Open-Standards-and-Re-Use-Govermnent-Action-Plan.pdf.

Osborne, G. 'Recasting the Political Settlement for the Digital Age'. Speech to the RSA, 2007. http://www.conservatives.com/News/Speeches/2007/03/George_Osborne_Recasting_the_political_settlement_for_the_digital_age.aspx.

Osborne, G. 'Policymaking after the Crash'. Speech to the RSA, 2009. http://www.conservatives.com/News/Speeches/2009/04/George_Osborne_Policy_making_after_the_crash.aspx.

Parliamentary Office of Science and Technology. Government IT Projects. Report number 200, 2003. http://www.parliament.uk/documents/post/pn200.pdf.

Peters, T. Liberation Management (Fawcett Columbine, 1992).

Pollitt, C. 'Bureaucracies Remember, Post-Bureaucratic Organizations Forget?' Public Administration 87/2 (2009), 198–218.

Poppendieck, M. and Poppendieck, T. Lean Software Development: An Agile Toolkit (Addison-Wesley, 1997).

Poppendieck, M. and Poppendieck, T. Leading Lean Software Development: Results are Not the Point (Addison-Wesley, 2009).

Portal Feasibility Study. CITU, 1999. http://ctpr.org/wp-content/uploads/2011/03/Portal-Feasibility-Study-19991.pdf.

Public Administration Committee–Twelfth Report. 'Government and IT-'A Recipe for Rip-Offs': Time for a New Approach', 18 July 2012. Volume I. http://www.publications.parliament.uk/pa/cm201012/cmselect/cmpubadm/715/715i.pdf.

Public Administration Committee – Twelfth Report. (2011). 'Government and IT – 'A Recipe for Rip-Offs': Time for a New Approach', HC751-I, 18 July 2011. http://www.publications.parliament.uk/pa/cm201012/cmselect/cmpubadm/715/715i.pdf.

Ramaswamy, V. and Gouillart, F. The Power of Co-Creation (Free Press, 2010).

Read, M. 'Back Office Operations and IT'. In 'Operational Efficiency Programme: Final Report' (HM Treasury, 2009), pp. 13–27. http://www.bis.gov.uk/assets/biscore/shex/files/oep_final_report›210409_pu728.pdf.

Rogers, E. The Diffusion of Innovation, 5th edn (Free Press, 2003).

Reed, M. and Anthony, P. 'Between an Ideological Rock and an Organizational Hard Place'. In The Political Economy of Privatization, ed. Thomas Clarke and Christos Pitelis (Routledge, 2003), pp. 185–204.

Ries, E. *The Lean Startup: How Constant Innovation Creates Radically Successful Business* (Penguin Business, 2011).

Rochet, J. and Tirole, J. 'Platform Competition in Two-Sided Markets', *Journal of the European Economics Association* (2003), 23–4.

Savage, M. 'Labour's Computer Blunders Cost £26bn'. *The Independent*, 19 January 2010. http://www.independent.co.uk/news/uk/politics/labours-computer-blunders-cost-16326bn-1871967.html.

Sawhney, M., Walcott, R.C. and Arroniz, I. 'The 12 Different Ways for Companies to Innovate', *MIT Sloan Management Review* 47/3 (2006).

Solis, B., Li, C. and Syzmanski, J. (2014). 'Digital Transformation: Why and How Companies are Investing in New Business Models to Lead Digital Customer Experiences', Altimeter, 2014. www.altimetergroup.com.

Stone, B. Creating 'Reinvention University'. The Public Manager (Potomac, MD) (1061–7639), 27/1 (1998), p. 47.

'Successful IT: Modernising Government in Action'. Cabinet Office, 2000. http://ctpr.org/wp-content/uploads/2011/03/Successful-IT-Modernising-Government-in-Action-2000.pdf.

Szelnyi, F. 'Dell exec questions UK.gov's value proposition', Channel Register, 9 July 2010. http://www.channelregister.co.uk/2010/07/09/dell_francis_maude_it_spending_cuts.

Tapscott, D. *Grown Up Digital: How the Net Generation is Changing the World* (McGraw-Hill, 2010).

Teece, D.J. 'Business Models, Business Strategy and Innovation'. In *Long Range Planning* 43 (Elsevier, 2010), pp. 172–94.

'The Agile Manifesto', 2001. http://agilemanifesto.org/.

'The Coalition: Our Programme for Government', HMG, 2010. https://www.gov.uk/government/uploads/system/uploads/attachment_data/file/78977/coalition_programme_for_government.pdf.

Thompson, M. 'Open Source, Open Standards: Reforming IT Procurement in Government, an Independent Report Commissioned by George Osborne for the Conservative Party', 2008. http://markthompson1.com/research/.

Thompson, M. 'Open Source, Open Standards: Reforming IT Procurement in Government', 2009. http://markthompson1.files.wordpress.com/2012/02/open-source-and-open-standards-osborne-report1.pdf.

'Transformational Government Annual Report'. Cabinet Office, 2006. http://ctpr.org/wp-content/uploads/2011/03/trans_gov2006.pdf.

'Transformational Government Annual Report'. Cabinet Office, 2007. http://ctpr.org/wp-content/uploads/2011/03/tg_annual_report07.pdf.

'Transformational Government Annual Report'. Cabinet Office, 2008. http://ctpr.org/wp-content/uploads/2011/03/tg08_part1.pdf. Supplementary parts also at http://ctpr.org/wp-content/uploads/2011/03/tg08_part2.pdf and http://ctpr.org/wp-content/uploads/2011/03/tg08_part3.pdf.

'Transformational Government Annual Report'. Cabinet Office, 2008. http://webarchive.nationalarchives.gov.uk/+/http://www.cabinetoffice.gov.uk/cio/transformational_government/annual_report2008.aspx.

'Transformational Government Annual Report'. Cabinet Office, 2008. Retrieved from http://webarchive.nationalarchives.gov.uk/+/http://www.cabinetoffice.gov.uk/cio/transformational_government/annual_report2008.aspx.

'Transformational Government: Enabled by Technology'. Cabinet Office, 2005. http://ctpr.org/wp-content/uploads/2011/03/transgov-strategy.pdf.

'Trust Framework Provider Adoption Process (TFPAP)'. ICAM, 2009. http://www.idmanagement.gov/sites/default/files/documents/TrustFrameworkProviderAdoptionProcess.pdf.

Vitalari, N. and Shaughnessy, H. *The Elastic Enterprise: The New Manifesto for Business Revolution* (Telemachus Press, 2013).

Walden, B. 'The White Heat of Wilson', 2006. http://news.bbc.co.uk/1/hi/magazine/4865498.stm.

Walsh, K. *Public Service and Market Mechanisms: Competition, Contracting and the New Public Management* (Macmillan, 1995).

Watmore, I. 'The three E's: Efficient, Effective and Electronic', 2004. http://ctpr.org/wp-content/uploads/2011/03/Ian-Watmore-commitments-on-arrival.doc.

Weill, P. and Woerner, S.L. 'Optimizing Your Digital Business Model', *MIT Sloan Management Review* 54/3 (2013), pp. 71–8.

Womack, J.P. and Jones, D.T. *Lean Thinking: Banish Waste and Create Wealth in Your Corporation* (Free Press, 2003).

'Working Together – Public Services on Your Side'. HM Government, 2009. http://webarchive.nationalarchives.go.uk/20100803100454/hmg.go.uk/media/15556/workingtogether.pdf.

Index